Silenced Victims of Wartime Sexual Violence

The condemnation of wartime sexual violence as a gross violation of human rights has received widespread support. While rape and other forms of sexual violence have attracted considerable local and international attention, this often excludes wartime sexual violence among women belonging to so-called 'perpetrator' war-torn nations. This book explores the silence surrounding women's experiences of wartime sexual violence within academic, legal and public discourses. Olivera Simić argues that the international criminal law and feminist legal discourse on wartime sexual violence can construct a problematic victim hierarchy that excludes and misrecognises certain women's experiences of sexual violence during and after armed conflict.

The book focuses on the experiences of Bosnian Serb women, where the collapse of the former Yugoslavia led to brutal war and gross human rights violations throughout the 1990s. Two decades after the war, women in Bosnia and Herzegovina are still facing the legacies of the violence in the 1990s. Through this case Simić argues that while all women survivors of rape face problems of stigma, shame and lack of political visibility, their legal and symbolic status differ according to their ethno-national identity.

Drawing on interviews with Bosnian Serb women survivors of rape in Bosnia and Herzegovina, feminist activists, local media, documentary and archival sources, the book examines 'post-conflict justice' as it is seen, lived and interpreted by women who belong to 'perpetrator' nations and will be of great interest and use to researchers, students and practitioners within post-conflict law and justice, international criminal law, security studies and gender studies.

Olivera Simić is a Senior Lecturer at the Griffith University Law School, Brisbane, Australia.

Post-Conflict Law and Justice

International law has great relevance in post-conflict contexts, but the complexity of its role, both as a supporting and restraining factor, can be underestimated. This series explores the role of law, and in particular international law, in securing 'justice' in post-conflict contexts. The remit of the series extends to matters of law connected to, for example: post-conflict legal reforms and the development of constitutions; the establishment of the rule of law; the place of international organizations in post-conflict; peace-keeping; transitional justice mechanisms (including criminal justice); and discussion of jus post bellum. It also seeks self-reflexive works on notions of post-conflict justice, transitional justice, and similar.

Series Editors: James A. Sweeney, Lancaster University, and Matthew Saul, University of Oslo

Available titles in this series include:

International Law and Post-Conflict Reconstruction Policy
Matthew Saul and James A. Sweeney

Silenced Victims of Wartime Sexual Violence
Olivera Simić

Forthcoming:

UN Territorial Administration and Human Rights
The Mission in Kosovo
Gjylbehare Bella Murati

Silenced Victims of Wartime Sexual Violence

Olivera Simić

Routledge
Taylor & Francis Group
LONDON AND NEW YORK

First published 2018
by Routledge

2 Park Square, Milton Park, Abingdon, Oxfordshire OX14 4RN
52 Vanderbilt Avenue, New York, NY 10017

Routledge is an imprint of the Taylor & Francis Group, an informa business

First issued in paperback 2019

British Library Cataloguing-in-Publication Data
A catalogue record for this book is available from the British Library

Library of Congress Cataloging-in-Publication Data
Names: Simic, Olivera, author.
Title: Silenced victims of wartime sexual violence / Olivera Simic.
Description: Abingdon, Oxon [UK\ ; New York, NY : Routledge, 2018. | Series: Post-conflict law and justice | Includes bibliographical references and index.
Identifiers: LCCN 2017053447| ISBN 9781138918627 (hardback) | ISBN 9781317421016 (wed pdf) | ISBN 9781317421009 (epub) | ISBN 9781317420996 (mobipocket)
Subjects: LCSH: Rape as a weapon of war. | Rape as a weapon of war—Bosnia and Herzegovina. | Women—violence against—Bosnia and Herzegovina. | Women—Crimes against—Law and legislation—Bosnia and Herzegovina. | Yugoslav War, 1991-1995—Women—Bosnia and Herzegovina. | Women (International law) | War crimes. | Women and war.
Classification: LCC KZ7162 .S56 2018 | DDC 341.6/9—dc23
LC record available at https://lccn.loc.gov/2017053447

ISBN: 978-1-138-91862-7 (hbk)
ISBN: 978-0-367-89367-5 (pbk)

Typeset in ITC Galliard Std
by Swales & Willis Ltd, Exeter, Devon, UK

'What does that mean, this *silence* (*dieses Schweigen*)?'
'*Das Schweigen* actually amounts to making it not have happened.'[1]

1 German woman survivor of rape by the Red Army in 1945, in Helke Sander and Barbara Johr (eds), *BeFreier und BeFreite: Krieg, Vergewaltigung, Kinder* [Trans: *Liberator and Liberated: War, Rape, Children*] (Taschenbuch, 1995) 166–167.

Contents

Preface

Drinking coffee in Bosnia: listening to stories of wartime violence and rape[1]

'This young man, our waiter, graduated from the Faculty of Business and Economics with a high distinction and has now worked as a waiter for the past – how many years, Jovan?' A young man with deep dark eyes, timidly responded, 'Four, five years or so.' 'You see, Olivera, this is our Bosnia; the country which employs its best students to work as tradespersons, waitresses, salespersons, carpenters,' half-jokingly, half-sarcastically a well-known long-term feminist activist, Dragana, told me while gently tapping Jovan on his shoulder. Although sarcasm is not unusual for Bosnians but rather represents 'some kind of "Bosnian way" of dealing with or reacting to the war',[2] the two had obviously known each other for a long time. Their brief exchange was the first thing I would hear upon my arrival to Tarnovo.[3]

Dragana picked me up from the bus station and took me straight to the *kafana* (pub) for a coffee to be made by Jovan, a graduate economist turned waiter. Going to the *kafana* is the most expected and natural thing to do in Bosnia and Herzegovina (Bosnia), since drinking coffee with friends and guests is an important ritual to obey; a part of the country's cultural tradition. Coffee in Bosnia is not about drinking. Rather, it is about socialising and taking time to be together, going on a journey of listening and talking to your friends and family. Bosnians do not have coffee in a rush; they take time to *ćeif* it[4] by gradually drinking small sips of coffee, the breaks serving to allow opportunity to converse and enjoy its aroma.[5] Born into this tradition, I was prepared to take time and listen to Dragana's stories.

1 The version of this chapter was previously published as: Olivera Simić, 'Drinking Coffee in Bosnia: Listening to Stories of Wartime Violence and Rape' (2017) 18(4) *Journal of International Women Studies* 321.

2 Nedin Mutić, 'Self and Other in Balkan (Post-) War Cinema' in Pal Kolsto (ed.), *Media Discourse and the Yugoslav Conflicts: Representations of Self and Other* (Routledge, 2016) 219.

3 I have changed the original names of the people, the places where conversations had been conducted and of the women's association to protect people's identities for security reasons. Women who I spoke to still feel afraid to speak up publically about the war crimes. All interlocutors knew that I am a researcher and consented to me using their stories to write publications as long as I conceal their identity.

4 The word ćeif or *ćef* is of Turkish origin and means: joy, enjoyment, happiness, good will and good mood.

5 On the importance of coffee drinking in Bosnia, see, for example: Tone Bringa, *Being Muslim the Bosnian Way: Identity and Community in a Central Bosnian Village* (Princeton University Press, 1995);

The 'welcoming' story about Jovan, that portrays the country's complete socio-economic fiasco, was not news to me, but it set the scene for all the other stories to come that afternoon. For those who follow post-war life in Bosnia, a life of poverty and corruption – of highly educated young people, intellectuals, working for a minimum wage for often half-illiterate owners of private businesses – is all too common. While we were waiting for our coffee, Dragana went on to tell me about Jovan's parents, originally from Tarčin, near Konjic, who are now trying to survive by buying some cheap clothes in Turkey and Italy and selling them in the city's market place. Jovan's parents, like the majority of people in Bosnia, are making ends meet by clinging to the informal, underground, black-market economy, which has been the main mode of survival for the past two decades.[6]

His mother, Anka – a Croat – was once a chief inspector in a factory that manufactured ammunition in Konjic and his father, Milan – a Serb – also worked in the same factory as a production-line worker. Both of them could probably never have imagined that the ammunition they made would one day turn against them. Milan was detained in the infamous *Čelebići* concentration camp[7] during the war and survived severe beatings and torture. After he was released from the camp, he and Anka, together with their young son, escaped to Tarnovo. 'He [Milan] grows a beard,' Dragana raised her right hand and covered her cheeks and chin, 'to hide the deep scars imprinted on his flesh left after the torture'. She muttered these words, looking quickly around her making sure people couldn't hear us. Then she put her left hand behind her back, 'He has a huge scar across his back too.' This is how Dragana and I started our feminist-activist 'dealing with the past' chat over coffee.

Telling the stories

Dragana, a long-term and well-known feminist activist, knows and is known by everyone in this small town. *Duga* was one of the very first women's organisation founded in Tarnovo, in 1996. Together with other women's organisations in the region, it makes a significant impact on the local community. Since its

Tone Bringa, 'Reconciliation in Bosnia-Herzegovina' in Elin Skaar, Siri Gloppen and Astri Suhrke (eds), *Roads to Reconciliation* (Lexington Books, 2005) 194; Elissa Helms, *Innocence and Victimhood: Gender, Nation and Women's Activism in Postwar Bosnia-Herzegovina* (University of Wisconsin Press, 2013); Elisa Helms, 'The Gender of Coffee: Women, Refugee Return, and Reconciliation Initiatives after the Bosnian War' (2007) 7(57) *Focaal – European Journal of Anthropology* 17–32.

6 For more on the black market economy and high rates of unemployment in Bosnia, see, for example: Peter Andreas, *Blue Helmets and Black Markets: The Business of Survival in the Siege of Sarajevo* (Cornell University Press, 2008); Ana E. Juncos, *EU Foreign and Security Policy in Bosnia: The Politics of Coherence and Effectiveness* (Manchester University Press, 2013) 105.

7 The Čelebići prison camp was a prison camp run by Croat and Bosnian Muslim forces in Čelebići, a village in the central Bosnian municipality of Konjic, during the Bosnian War. The camp was used to detain Serb civilians and prisoners of war, rounded up in and around Konjic in May 1992. Prisoners at the camp were subjected to killings, torture, sexual assaults, beatings and otherwise cruel and inhuman treatment. See the ICTY Judgment, *Prosecutor v. Zdravko Mucic et al.* ('Celebici case') (IT-96-21-A), 20 February 2001.

inception, *Duga* has been working on gender equality and the empowerment and political education of young girls and women. Their most significant work has been on implementing projects related to women's return to their pre-war homes and their reintegration with the local population. *Duga* has organised a series of workshops, round tables, seminars and lectures with an aim to transcend ethnic animosities and build sustainable peace, democracy and pre-war multiculturalism in the eastern Bosnian region. Tarnovo, although only a small town, has one of the highest numbers of returnees in the country. Dragana spent the wartime in her hometown and witnessed the war first hand. Together with *Duga*, she has helped many women return to their pre-war homes, start small businesses, gain some psychological support, and cross ethnic borders and divisions.

Dragana keeps in her mind and heart many stories women have told her about their ordeals during the war. To me, she truly represents, as do many other feminist activists in the region, a living library of women's stories of pain and suffering, and of their courage and resilience too. While we were sitting and talking about the difficult situation in which women survivors of wartime rape and torture live today, one such woman passed by the *kafana* where we were sitting. Dragana pointed with her head in the woman's direction. It was Milka, Dragana informed me, a woman displaced from Zenica, who is only in her late forties but looks like she is in her sixties. Milka is mentally ill; she wanders through the town and talks to herself. People know of her, but not the story hidden in her bodily appearance.

Dragana knows what is behind Milka's strange look and behaviour. She and her two daughters were beaten and kicked out of their home by her violent husband because of her ethnic identity. Her daughters then decided to change their identities and names to those of Orthodox Christians. They do not want to remember their father and have no contact with him. They both are now married with their own families. Their husbands do not know about their past. Dragana lifted up her coffee cup, took a sip and told me another story.

'There is another woman living in this building; a young woman, who is not well either. She was raped during the war.' Dragana pointed towards one of the communist-style grey and yellow pre-war buildings behind her back. Many of these women never talked about their experiences with anyone apart from Dragana and *Duga*. Some are seriously mentally ill, yet receive neither psychological assistance nor state welfare. Some, as young girls, either witnessed their mothers being gang-raped or were raped themselves. A woman, Tanja, who was only 10 when she was raped, is now married with two children. Dragana said she could not talk and walk for two years after the rape. 'She never returned to school after that. She has only four grades of primary school.' She is in her thirties now, without the status of civilian victim of war. She has no health care or social welfare secured by the state. *Duga* is assisting Tanja to enrol in a course for hairdressers and start her own small business.

Some women have never returned to their pre-war homes. To them, it is too painful to go back to what has become a 'crime scene', since many of them survived rape in their homes, in front of their children. They also do not want to meet their rapists who have frequently stayed in the communities and have either never been prosecuted for what they did, or if so, have often returned back home after serving only two-thirds of their sentences.[8] What came out in some of the stories that Dragana told me, was that some female children were not only witnesses but also victims of wartime sexual abuse themselves. None of these women, according to Dragana, are interested in seeking justice from the criminal justice system. They, in fact, do not want to tell anyone about their experiences. These women are now adults; all have children and families. Why would they come out to tell their stories when all they may face is ostracism and possible divorce?

Dragana slowly shifted in her chair while lighting her cigarette and took another sip of coffee. I could see that she was preparing to tell me more stories. Although she sat next to me, she seemed far away, immersed in her own thoughts, oblivious to the people around us. Her eyes were red but there were no tears in them. She took a deep breath and murmured:

> There was one young woman who told us that her father had been taken to a concentration camp during the war and she, her younger sister and mother were detained in their house. Many soldiers, belonging to different military and paramilitary groups, would come in and out of their home and her mother was forced to make pies and other food for them. She and her sister would hide under the table when soldiers came into the house and she would often cover her sister's eyes so she could not watch when they became violent. She never used the word 'rape' to describe their behaviour.

Dragana said that she wanted to take this young woman, Branka, to her pre-war home to see it; to start the process of property return. However, Branka and her family were not even interested in exchanging the property; they simply did not want to go back there, not even for a quick visit. After many months of talks and negotiations, the young woman finally agreed to go with Dragana to visit her pre-war home.

They sat in Dragana's car and set off. Dragana was driving and everything was fine until they came very close to the house and the young woman suddenly started screaming and shouting. In this state of acute rage, she smashed a car window with her right elbow. Branka was screaming, 'I don't want to see your big cock, I hate you!' The moment of realisation about what had really happened in that house 20 years ago and why Branka never wanted to return, hit Dragana with full force. Dragana was shocked and struggled to calm Branka down. For Dragana, even with many years of experience working with women with trauma: 'This was the first time,' as she told me, 'I saw what it really means to live with trauma.'

8 On the early release of war criminals see Barbora Holá and Joris van Wijk, 'Life After Conviction at International Criminal Tribunals' (2014) 12(1) *Journal of International Criminal Justice* 109–132.

Listening to the stories

While I was listening to one story after another, I started to think what should we, as feminist academics and activists, do with the stories that we would never have heard if it were not for local feminist activists who had gained the trust of women survivors and became the recipients of their shared stories? I asked Dragana if she had ever written down these women's stories. She replied:

> We don't have the time and resources. We don't have the skills. We don't speak or write English, but most of all – we don't know how to do it. That is why I am telling you them. I hope you can document some.

Duga has listened to hundreds of such stories over the past 20 years but has never documented even a single one.

What is our responsibility when local activists themselves do not document stories? Dragana and her colleagues, who are activists and practitioners working in the field, have – by their own report – insufficient time to document them. Also, many women who tell their stories over coffee may not necessarily want their histories to be repeated publically, or at least not with their names attached. Yet, feminists know how important it is to document women's lives and experiences. Women do not want their identities to be revealed; they are afraid of stigmatisation and ostracism; of their husbands' and families' reactions. However, for many it is important that their voices are transmitted and translated into the public domain. Elisabeth Porter notes that while storytelling is crucial, the quality of listening is too. Articulating truth-narratives is important for women who have been traumatised in order to promote the search for justice and healing.[9] Women's testimonies are important for feminist theory of all kinds, which is grounded in the variety of real-life stories that women tell about themselves.[10] Feminist scholars have written extensively about the power of women's life stories to create theory and to establish woman as the subject.[11]

The listening to of truth-narratives also implies bearing 'witness to the testimony' by which 'the responsibility for finding justice is shared'.[12] The documenting and preserving of women's stories are important segments of a larger feminist project, which aims to capture women's experiences of war and violence

9 Elisabeth Porter, 'Women's Truth Narratives: The Power of Compassionate Listening' (2007) 5(2) *Critical Half: Bi-Annual Journal of Women for Women International* 21.

10 Maria C. Lugones and Elizabeth V. Spelman, 'Have We Got a Theory For You! Feminist Theory, Cultural Imperialism and the Demand for "The Women's Voice"' in Susan Archer Mann and Ashly Suzanne Patterson (eds), *Reading Feminist Theory: From Modernity to Postmodernity* (Oxford University Press, 2016) 25.

11 Mimi Arnstein, 'Consciousness Raising: Self-Defining Feminism and the Problem of Postmodern Politics' in Gail Currie and Celia Rothenberg (eds), *Feminist (Re)visions of the Subject: Landscapes, Ethnoscapes, and Theoryscapes* (Lexington Books, 2001) 160.

12 Susan McKay, 'Gender Justice and Reconciliation' (2000) 23(5) *Women's Studies International Forum* 564.

that have been denied, ignored and silenced. Documentation is, if not finding, then seeking justice for women's suffering.

Building connections

A few days before I arrived in Tarnovo, I travelled through north-east Bosnia and visited a community that had been displaced and then resettled in a village called Veliki Han, near Kluj. There I met Marija, a woman who had been detained in a camp with her three children. The youngest was her daughter Radmila, only 9 months old at the time. Her 5-year-old son, Milorad, suffers from a permanent speech impediment caused by the shock of witnessing her mother being repeatedly gang-raped. I have known Marija for some years now and closely followed her struggle to obtain some form of justice for the rape she survived during the war. Although I have known her for the past few years, it is only recently that I started to gather the pieces together and gain the full story of what had happened to her and why she has failed to receive any form of justice. I have built my relationship with Marija carefully. Over the years, I told Marija about myself and replied to all her questions about my education, job and life during and after the war. This process of building rapport with Marija is important feminist methodology that allowed me to gain access to information that she has hardly shared with anyone so far. Traditional feminist theory suggests the benefits of using engagement, closeness and empathy to build rapport.[13]

I have never used an audio recorder in our meetings and always let Marija guide our conversations. I was never in a hurry to find out 'all of it', and did not lead any structured interview with her. I purposely did not want to do so, since I strived to create, as much as possible, a non-hierarchical research relationship between the two of us. I utilised a 'participatory model' that would allow me to overcome the separation between the researcher (me) and the researched (Marija).[14] To Marija, and in Bosnia, I am at once both an insider and outsider, and I constantly had to negotiate these positions. I grew up in an urban, middle-class and well-educated family and did not share experiences of life in rural communities before, during or after the war. From this perspective, I had feelings of being an 'outsider' regardless that I was born and grew up in Bosnia. As Nancy Naples and Radhika Parameswaran argue, insider and outsider concepts are not binary but rather shifting, fluid and subject to negotiation within the research setting.[15]

13 Shulamit Reinharz and Lynn Davidman, *Feminst Methods in Social Research* (Oxford University Press, 1992).

14 Pamela Cotterill, 'Interviewing Women: Issues of Friendship, Vulnerability, and Power' (1992) 15 *Women Studies International Forum* 593–606.

15 Nancy Naples, *Feminism and Method: Ethnography, Discourse Analysis, and Activist Research* (Routledge, 2003); Nancy Naples, 'The Outsider Phenomenon' in Carolyn D. Smith and William Kornblum (eds), *In the Field: Reading of the Field Research Experience* (Praeger, 1996) 139–159; Radhika Parameswaran, 'Feminist Media Ethnography in India: Exploring Power, Gender, and Culture in the Field' (2001) 7(1) *Qualitative Inquiry* 69–103.

Marija and many other women survivors that I met are rural women with little or no education, severely traumatised and yet have been provided with little or no psychological – or any other form of – assistance so far. It is often difficult for these women to articulate their experiences of deeply traumatic crimes, such as rape, in a fully comprehensive narrative. Although I was listening attentively, I needed a few years to connect the dots and understand the whole story that was woven slowly during our sporadic conversations over coffee. In June 2016, when Marija and I met in her home for coffee, Marija handed me her 'case file' with neatly stacked documents about the time she had spent in a rape camp with her children, including their medical and legal documents. These were confidential files that she wanted me to take, read through and see if there was anything more she could do to achieve some justice. 'You know the law. I don't know where to go anymore, what to do. Maybe you can find something in there that I can use, some facts, something so I can get some justice.'

She wanted me to read them all carefully and tell her if she still had a chance to receive some form of legal justice. She trusts me. But, we had had to travel a long way to get to this point – to me being invited for coffee in Marija's house. I had never been invited previously nor met any of her children. I was privileged and honoured since I knew what a long time it had taken Marija to gain that confidence in me. She knew I would not share her confidential files with anyone. But, it had taken four years of knowing each other to reach that place.

Over a few late nights, I read Marija's documents carefully and I realised I needed to find a way to tell her that unfortunately she should not waste her time, funds and health battling an already lost battle with the state. Her sister Jovana, who had also been detained and raped in a camp with her two children, died of a heart attack two years ago. She died just when the first court proceedings for the wartime rapes of Serb women in the Posavina region started before the State Court in Sarajevo. Jovana was to become one of its key witnesses.

Marija's sister was in poor health already, but her heart betrayed her once the case was opened and proceedings started. 'She was happy when she learned that the proceedings against rapists would start. We had been waiting for this moment for 20 years, but her heart could not cope with it all,' Marija told me. Jovana was excited, but also afraid for her children's well-being and future once the trial took off. She told Marija that she often felt fear of riding her bike alone through the nearby woods, as she expected that someone may attack her for bringing the rapists to trial. Her husband had left her a long time ago, once she went public with her story of gang rape in 1992. At that time, they were both young women in their late twenties and with young children when they were detained and gang-raped.

Marija had also had a heart attack last year, but luckily survived it. She thinks her daughter, who was with her when she had the attack, was the one who saved her life. 'She called an ambulance and took me to emergency,' Marija told me. Her heart, as with her general health, was already weak. But once she finally lost the battle with the administrative system and laws in Republika Srpska (RS), which did not want to recognise Marija's other two children as civilian victims of war – even though they had also been detained in the camp with her – her heart betrayed her. After several years of battling with the system, appealing its decisions, appearing in front of various commissions that determine the status of victims, and telling her story numerous times in front of her children, Marija lost her administrative battle for good. Two of her children, although with her in the camp, will not be recognised as civilian victims of war.

To gain the status of civilian victim is important since it provides access to a monthly pension, which although very low would provide at least some means for survival. Both of her children (now adults in their thirties) have no employment and have each two children of their own. The reason why they did not gain the status is that they did not reach the extremely high threshold level of 60 per cent bodily damage, according to the law.[16] Her children could not prove 60 per cent but only 40 per cent of bodily damage. There is no logic or justice behind these numbers.

(No) justice for women

I read all Marija's documents, all the administrative decisions and legal judgments that had freed her rapists because there was not sufficient evidence that *these men, the men that Marija accused*, were the rapists. All four defended themselves by claiming that they were not in Bosnia at the time of the alleged rape. And while not negating that women, including Marija, were raped, the judges concluded that there was not enough evidence that these four particular men were the rapists. Marija was shattered by this decision. 'I need to see some justice. I invested all my life into this. If they could at least get one year in prison, only one year, I would be satisfied. But to release them, I cannot accept that,' said Marija to me. I was speechless. What was I supposed to tell her? That there is justice but she just needs to be a little bit more patient and wait? For how long? She has already waited 20 years to hear that the highest institutions of justice do not trust her and that her rapists were family men with children, who were *allegedly* in Germany and Switzerland with their wives when the rapes occurred. This was what the rapists told the court, what their wives confirmed, and what the court decided to believe in.

The rapists had been released and were back in their community; a community that is only half an hour's drive from Marija's house. Marija wholeheartedly believed in the Bosnian justice system and declined the offered witness protection. 'I have nothing to be ashamed of. They are the ones who should be ashamed. I did not have protection in 1992 and I don't need protection now.' She went public with her story; her children and community know it. She exposed herself

16 'Law on the Protection of Civilian Victims of War in the Republika Srpska', *Official Gazette*, no. 25/93 of 30 December 1993, with amendments published in the *Official Gazette* no. 1/94 – Special edition, 32/94, 37/07 and 60/07.

and her children to the great risk of not only being ostracised, but being threatened by those on the rapists' side. In March 2016, three months after the rapists had been released, a car pulled up in front of Marija while she was walking home from the market. A man, who was sitting next to the driver, tried to pull her in. She fought with him and managed to run away while he sped off. She called the police but she could not remember the car registration number, and the driver was never identified.

Marija has been living in fear for the past 20 years. After her heart attack, her heart now beats at only 38 per cent capacity and she is on daily medication. Marija, a petite woman with bright blue eyes, is only 53. She lost the battle with the institutions, with a corrupted system that does not take care of women. The criminal system is rough and merciless. It raised the hopes of women such as Marija that it would provide justice, but then left female witnesses and victims on their own. It offers little or no support to those, such as Marija, who decide to pursue justice. Marija had to cover her own travel expenses to the Court and received little to no legal aid.

The prosecutor did not prove the identity of the rapists, so they walked free and returned to their community – the community in Marija's vicinity. I agonised over the necessity to tell her that she would be better off investing her fragile strength, energy and life elsewhere, away from the state and its institutions. Where should Marija seek justice 20 years after her hopes for justice had been raised? After she had repeated her story of torture and rape countless times before various state organs, hoping that it was worthwhile re-traumatising herself over and over again since someone may finally listen to her, take her story seriously and trust her – where? She feels betrayed, untrusted, her story misused and reinterpreted as a false accusation with even the possible motivation of revenge – as it was argued by the defence – since her husband was killed two weeks before she was raped.

Writing women's stories

Stories of Milka, Tanja, Branka, Jovana and Marija are exemplary stories that represent so many untold, buried accounts that risk never being documented in feminist archives; yet they stay part of a living feminist-activist and experience-based practice knowledge – of a theory that 'walks'. After many years of listening to women's stories, I find it more and more difficult to employ traditional, empirical, qualitative-research methods and think it is more ethically responsible to listen to women stories, as narrated by feminist activists who listened and vividly remember what women survivors have told them. I could not bear to sit down with women survivors for an interview and ask them a set of questions. I had planned to do this, but in my time travelling through Bosnia, I could not bring myself to do so.

I simply could not stop the natural flow of women talking over coffee and turn it into formalities. I felt it would be disrespectful; it would be invasive and unethical. I spent lots of time thinking about research methodologies and concluded that my traditional methods of non-structured interviewing no longer made sense. I wanted women to tell me what they think is important for them to share. I did not want to give them false hope that, with my research, I could change their lives for the better. They had been betrayed by their government so many times and had had their hopes raised high, only to have them fall again and again, with no support apart from what they occasionally receive from each other. I decided my work is to listen attentively, to write carefully, and to bring these stories to the public eye.

Acknowledgements

The making of this book took more than five years and spanned two continents. My fieldwork was based in Bosnia and Herzegovina (BiH), my writing in Brisbane and Belfast, and the presentation of my ideas and work across Europe and Australia. None of this, however, would have been possible without the generous time and trust of women survivors of conflict-related sexual violence who decided to share their stories with me. They graciously allowed me to be a witness to their struggle to receive some justice for the harms inflicted on them. I cannot thank you enough for letting me accompany you on parts of your difficult journey. I feel extremely privileged for having had the opportunity to be introduced to some of the bravest women I have ever met. I would also like to thank women activists from the former Yugoslavia for sharing their experiences and perspectives on women survivors in BiH. Your insights were extremely valuable and I learned a lot from you about how it is still difficult, sensitive and often risky to talk about and do research into the topic of wartime rapes that occurred in BiH over two decades ago. There is no doubt that your insights informed and enriched my study. The women and their stories all challenge and inspire me to continue to work for justice for women victims of wartime violence.

As author, I received invaluable feedback, comments and support from scholars and practitioners in a variety of settings as this project took shape. Thanks to those who took the time to engage with the ideas in this book and assist me in pushing them further than I had initially thought of doing. I've had the opportunity to discuss my research with outstanding colleagues and participants at talks I gave at the Griffith Law School (Brisbane), Melbourne Law School, Transitional Justice Institute (Belfast), Women, Peace and Security Centre (London School of Economics), SOAS (University of London), Kent University (Canterbury) and King's College (London). Many thanks to the following organisers: Associate Professor Marsha Henry, Professor Fionnuala Ni'Aolain, Professor Dianne Otto, Dr Rachel Kerr, Dr Sara Kendall and Dr Gina *Heathcote.* Invaluable feedback was provided during these exchanges. My friends and community in the former Yugoslavia are always supportive and welcoming and I imagine my intellectual, professional and personal commitment to them and to the Balkans region will continue.

I would also like to thank employees in several BiH government organisations for sharing sensitive data and information with me. They know who they are – thank you. In the course of my writing, I have been generously supported by the Griffith Law School and Griffith University, through the provision of a stimulating intellectual environment in which to write and think. I thank, particularly, the Dean, Professor Penelope Mathew and the Deputy Dean of Research Professor Mary Keys for securing my leave of absence and providing material and emotional support so necessary for this project. I would also like to thank to my colleague, Associate Professor Afshin Akhtarkhavari for the numerous intellectual exchanges we have had over the years. The Griffith Law School Feminist Reading Group has listened to me and provided advice on some of the content I struggled with in my chapters. I want to express my appreciation to Ms Zoe Rathus, Dr Karen Crawley, Associate Professor Sue Harris Rimmer, Professor Mary Keys, Ms Kate Van Doore and Ms Joanne Stagg-Taylor. My thanks go to Laura Muir and Routledge for their patience and belief that this book is important work and worthwhile taking on board, and also to the two anonymous reviewers for their thoughtful and reflective comments. I am grateful to my editor, Larah Seivl Keevers, who has done impeccable editing work with my manuscript and Jessica Ritchie who has provided much needed research assistance.

I owe my thanks to Associate Professor Dubravka Zarkov for her academic and emotional support and for her time spent engaging with my ideas and critically assessing them. My thanks also go to Professor Dianne Otto, Associate Professor Sue Harris Rimmer, and Dr Karen Crawley who read and commented on different chapters of the book. Your generosity and comments improved my thinking. Feminist scholars, such as Dianne Otto, Dubravka Zarkov, Fionnuala Ni'Aolain, Heather Douglas, Cynthia Enloe and Kimberly Theidon have served as role models of committed scholarship and have greatly influenced my work. I feel immensely privileged and fortunate that I had an opportunity to engage in discussions with them and many other bright feminist minds during my writing, researching and academic engagement. My friends, Milica Smiljanić, Danijel Kiš, Gorana Šaula, Edin Jusufović, Joan Nestle, Dianne Otto and Maricarly Escalona provided much needed friendship and support, moments of laughter and relaxation at times when I needed them the most. Last, but not least, without the love and patience of Andrej and Stojan, all this work would not have been possible. Thank you for being who you are, for enduring my frequent absences and travelling light heartedly with me on this journey.

Olivera Simić
Brisbane, February 2018

Abbreviations

BAM	Bosnian Convertible Mark (currency)
BiH	Bosnia and Herzegovina
CRSV	conflict-related sexual violence
ECHR	European Court of Human Rights
EUR	official currency of the European Union's member states
FBiH	Federation of Bosnia and Herzegovina
ICC	International Criminal Court
ICTR	International Criminal Tribunal for Rwanda
ICTY	International Criminal Tribunal for the former Yugoslavia
IDPs	internally displaced persons
NGO	non-government organisation
OSCE	Organization for Security and Cooperation in Europe
PPT	Permanent People's Tribunal
RECOM	Regional Commission for the Establishment of Facts about War Crimes and Other Serious Violations of Human Rights Committed in the Former Yugoslavia from 1 January 1991 until 31 December 2001
RPF	Rwandan Patriotic Front
RS	Republika Srpska
SFRY	Socialist Federal Republic of Yugoslavia
UN	United Nations
UNFPA	United Nations Population Fund
UNGA	United Nations General Assembly
UNSCR	United Nations Security Council Resolutions
WCC	War Crimes Chamber
WiB	Women in Black, Belgrade
WWII	World War II

Introduction

Disrupting the legacy of mass rape in Bosnia and Herzegovina

The condemnation of conflict-related sexual violence (CRSV)[1] as a gross violation of human rights has received widespread support in academia and international law, as well as in celebrity activism, mass media reporting, and non-governmental and governmental initiatives. Yet, while rape and other forms of CRSV have attracted considerable local and international attention, this recognition is predicated on an 'ideal' victim[2] subject. This book examines the excluded or silenced narratives of CRSV among women belonging to so-called 'perpetrator' war-torn nations. In the book, although these denials and silences are contextualised more generally, I specifically focus on the silence surrounding Bosnian Serb women survivors and their (lack of) treatment within academic, legal and public discourses. I argue that the Bosnian Serb women survivors of CRSV were silenced not because they did not want to tell their stories, but because their stories were not really sought after; their experiences not readily fitting into the constructed identity of a 'Bosnian woman rape victim'.

I contend that international criminal law and feminist legal discourse on CRSV have created problematic victim hierarchies and binaries that exclude and misread certain women's experiences. While there has been much written and published over the past two decades about CRSV, to the extent that some feminist legal scholars rightly raised concerns over the privileging this crime over the other war crimes experienced by women,[3] this book aims to shed new light and enlarge our understanding of mass rapes in Bosnia and Herzegovina (BiH) by (re)claiming

1 In this book I use the term 'conflict-related sexual violence' as adopted by the UN Secretary-General. The term 'conflict-related sexual violence' refers to rape, sexual slavery, forced prostitution, forced pregnancy, forced abortion, enforced sterilisation, forced marriage and any other form of sexual violence of comparable gravity perpetrated against women, men, girls or boys that is directly or indirectly linked (temporally, geographically or causally) to a conflict. See UNSC, *Report of the Secretary-General on Conflict-Related Sexual Violence* (S/2016/361), 20 April 2016, para. 2.

2 Throughout this book, I use interchangeably the terms 'victim' and 'survivor'. I prefer to use the term 'survivor', but I acknowledge that some Bosnian women would rather identify themselves as victims (*žrtve*) than survivors (*preživjele*). The term survivor is hardly ever used in local languages and is not part of the local legalese.

3 See, e.g. Nicola Henry, 'The Fixation on Wartime Rape: Feminist Critique and International Criminal Law' (2014) 23(1) *Social and Legal Studies* 93–111.

the hidden experiences of Bosnian Serb women. Although women in BiH suffered CRSV en masse, I will show how and why not all Bosnian women received equal attention from the law, media and academia.

The needs of Bosnian Serb women survivors have been invisible to women's networks, overlooked by government, non-government organisations, and largely neglected by researchers, journalists and academics in ways not conducive to securing needed attention to their experiences, needs and rights. This book explores why Bosnian Serb women survivors have received so little attention from the local and international actors charged with protecting and promoting women's rights to truth, justice and reparation. The experiences of these women remain unpopular not only internationally, but also among the Serb politicians, government and civil society. I also explore the consequences of such neglect on their lives. My overall argument is that the casting of blame on Serbs as a nation for atrocities they committed has deflected attention away from the harms the Serb women experienced. As Charlie Carpenter argues: 'blaming in one context affects framing in other . . . in conflict zones the social construction of rights claim is contingent partly on the social construction of the wrongs'.[4]

This book grew out of the country report that I completed for the Gender Center, the governmental body of Republika Srpska (RS), which is the majority Serb entity in BiH.[5] The report discusses some aspects of the silencing of Bosnian Serb women and the effects this had on their lives in post-war BiH. Intended as the first document to be produced in the last two decades that attempts to provide some overview of services available to women who live in the RS, and to offer insights into the experiences of Serb women survivors of CRSV, it is exploratory in its nature and tackles only some issues that I explore in greater depth in this book. The country report was finalised in May 2015 and its official launch scheduled at Parliament House in RS, Banjaluka, but just 24 hours prior, the launch was cancelled by the director of the Gender Center. The occasion was to be attended by the highest representatives of the RS, over 100 representatives of international and local agencies and most importantly, by women survivors themselves.

At the time, I was in BiH in the eastern part of the country driving with my family to Banjaluka, the administrative, business and governmental centre of RS, to give a speech and launch the report. I was informed that representatives of the government, the UN (United Nations) agencies, local media and women survivors themselves were ready to depart for Banjaluka and be present at the launch. However, on my way to Banjaluka, I received a phone call from a woman survivor telling me that the launch had just been cancelled. I was perplexed and shocked.

After so many months of preparations and anxiety about how the report would be received, along with my hopes that Bosnian Serb women survivors would finally receive at least public acknowledgement from the RS government that they

4 Charlie Carpenter, *Forgetting Children Born of War: Setting the Human Rights Agenda in Bosnia and Beyond* (Columbia University Press, 2010) 2.

5 Bosnia and Herzegovina is one state comprised from two entities: Republika Srpska and Federation of Bosnia and Herzegovina, and Brčko district.

too were victims of CRSV, it all came to a halt. Bosnian Serb women were once again reduced to silence. I didn't receive an explanation for the launch's cancelation apart from a brief generic email sent to all invitees, which stated that 'due to a lack of interest by the governmental representatives of RS, the launching of the report will be cancelled'.

My disappointment was great and I was angry and sad about this sudden change of plans about which no one had consulted or informed me directly. From my point of view, the Gender Center rationale for cancellation was meaningless. I thought of the launch as a symbolic reparation to women; as a long-awaited, two decades late, acknowledgement by the RS government that Bosnian Serb women were also victims of CRSV. It was also meant to provide a platform for women to gather, network and share their stories. The fact that the report had not been printed for distribution at the launch also came as surprise. Two days before the launch I was told that there were no funds for printing and that in BiH it is the 'usual business to organise a book launch without hard copies ready to be distributed to the audience present'.[6]

Now looking back, I realise that something like a cancellation at the last moment should not have been so surprising. The public acknowledgement that Bosnian Serb women were also victims has been delayed, ignored and simply avoided for more than two decades. At the moment of this book going into production, the report has still not yet been officially launched and it is uncertain whether it will ever see the light of day, or under what circumstances it ever would. This unfortunate event can be seen as yet another in a series of betrayals of the Bosnian Serb women survivors and this time publically; not only by one of the governmental institutions, but by the one whose specific mandate, among other gender-related issues, is to work for the improvement of the status of women survivors of war. Luckily, there are other avenues that allow disruption of silenced legacies of wartime rape and this book is one of them.

Aims of the book

The book, based on primary data collected in BiH, intends to contribute to the growing body of critical studies on women and war by providing insight into how transitional justice mechanisms are established on the premise of an 'ideal' victim. It also aims to contribute to the scarce research that has been done on the long-term consequences of war, in particular CRSV, and its 'silenced' victims. My book builds on literature on sexual hierarchies and the notions of the 'authentic victim subject',[7] and an 'ideal victim'[8] – that is, one that generates

6 Email from Gender Center Banjaluka, May 2015, on file with author.

7 Ratna Kapur, 'The Tragedy of Victimization Rhetoric: Resurrecting the "Native" Subject in International/Post-Colonial Feminist Legal Politics' (2002) 15 *Harvard Human Rights Law Journal* 1.

8 Nils Christie, 'Ideal Victim' in Ezzat A. Fattah (ed.), *From Crime Policy to Victim Policy: Reorienting Justice system* (Palgrave, 1986) 17.

the most sympathy from society. It aims to fill in a gap in literature on mass rape in BiH by critically analysing 'other' missing narratives on rape that are highly contested – politically and socially. Bosnian Serb women victims of CRSV are a group of women who are socially and politically excluded from representations of victimhood. This book is about how the politics of victimhood has been played out in the local context of BiH and what its impact on the transitional justice agenda has been. Such analysis has so far been largely ignored in the field and limited to constructed victim–perpetrator dichotomy.

With the collapse of the former Yugoslavia, BiH was embroiled in brutal war and gross human rights violations throughout the 1990s. Political constituencies were formed around so-called 'ethnic' definitions, resulting in a struggle for territories and for political representation, power and recognition. New ethno-political identities were formed, which led to policies of exclusion in areas with multi-ethnic populations. Two decades after the war, women in BiH are still facing the legacies of the 1990s violence on a daily basis.

Many Bosnian women, regardless of their ethnicities, who lost their relatives, health, homes or property during the war, still wait for acknowledgement, reparation and justice. Women survivors need to be presented with an opportunity to be heard, to be valued, to be supported and respected in their loss and grief. It is only then, as Elizabeth Odio Benito has written: 'we will be finding paths towards justice'.[9] Yasmin Sooka has also noted that

> the most important components of transitional justice must be the rights of victims, which include the right to the truth, the right to acknowledgment, the right to reparations, and the obligation to take steps to ensure that violations will not occur again.[10]

Although all women survivors of rape in BiH face problems of stigma,[11] shame and lack of political visibility, their legal and symbolic status differ according to their ethno-national identity. Likewise, the gestures of symbolic and material recognition, reparations for victims of CRSV and healing processes are not equally accessible to all women survivors. Many Bosnian women have barely received any reparations and many perpetrators of war crimes remain unpunished due to lack of cooperation between national authorities to engage meaningfully in dealing with the past.[12] Still, the Bosnian Serb women survivors have not received even

9 Sara Sharratt, 'Interview with Elizabeth Odio Benito, Justice of the International Criminal Tribunal for the Former Yugoslavia' in Sara Sharratt and Ellyn Kaschak (eds), *Assault on the Soul: Women in the Former Yugoslavia* (Haworth Press, 1999) 39, 47.

10 Yasmin Sooka, 'Foreword to the Book' in S. Peté and M. du Plessis (eds), *Repairing the past: International Perspectives on Reparations for Gross Human Rights Abuses* (Intersentia, 2007) vii.

11 For more on stigma from CRSV, see UNFPA, *Stigma Against Survivors of Conflict-Related Sexual Violence in Bosnia and Herzegovina: Research Summary* (2016), http://unfpa.ba/upload/documents/UNFPA%20Stigma%20Short%20ENG%20FIN1.pdf.

12 Gentian Zyberi and Jernej Letnar Černič, 'Transitional Justice Processes and Reconciliation in the Former Yugoslavia: Challenges and Prospects' (2015) 33(2) *Nordic Journal of Human Rights* 132.

symbolic justice and only a handful of them, material reparation. This book aims to reveal why this has been the case and what the consequences of lack of recognition of their experiences are.

Methodology

To my knowledge, there have been no systematic and scholarly empirical studies into experiences of Bosnian Serb women victims of CRSV. In my study, I used primary and secondary sources including authentic and archival women's testimonies, participant observation, unstructured interviews and informal conversations with survivors and activists conducted over the past five years, documentary films and local and international media reports. As someone who was born in the region, I speak local languages and have long-term relationships with many women and non-governmental organisations (NGOs) that work with women survivors of CRSV. I conducted phone, skype, email and face-to-face non-structured interviews with women activists (14), survivors (16) and governmental representatives (7) with an aim: to map out what type of available assistance is on offer to women survivors of rape and torture in RS, if any. In November 2013, I also sent an email questionnaire to 18 women's NGOs in RS consisting of three questions:

1. Does your organisation offer any form of assistance to women survivors of rape and/or torture? If yes, could you please tell me what type of assistance do you offer (systematic and long term/have developed programs and projects or ad hoc/within other projects you have)?
2. Do you have contact with women survivors from all ethnic groups?
3. Which are the most common problems, in your opinion, that these women survivors face in BiH?

Of the 18 NGOs that were sent the initial email questionnaire, 6 replied to the questionnaire to inform that none has any specifically developed and fully funded program of assistance to women survivors of CRSV. Only two offered ad hoc assistance to women survivors (legal and psychological).[13] In this book, the identities of all interviewees have been protected and concealed due to the sensitivity of the topic.

13 On 1 January 2015, a two-year project to support development of a network of women's NGOs that will support women witnesses was funded by the EU. Two NGOs from Federation BiH – Medica Zenica, Vive Žene Tuzla – and two from RS – Udružene žene Banjaluka and ACED Banjaluka – are running the project. The main aim of the project is strengthening capacities of government and non-government organisations and establishing multidisciplinary teams in psychosocial support to survivors/witnesses, women and men. It is still too early to evaluate the results of this project. For more about this project, see Vive Žene, *Osiguranje pristupa pravdi za svjedoke/žrtve kroz jačanje postojećih i uspostavljanje novih mreža podrške svjedocima diljem Bosne i Hercegovine* [Trans: *Securing Access to Justice for Witnesses/Victims Through Strengthening Existing and Establishing New Networks of Support for Witnesses in Bosnia and Herzegovina*] (2016), www.vivezene.ba/download/Finalna%20verzija%20Rezime%20projekta%20bos.pdf>.

This book is about post-conflict justice as it is seen, lived and interpreted by women who belong to the 'perpetrator' nation. It is a probing investigation into the victimisation of women whose experiences are excluded from dominant narratives on mass rape in BiH and beyond. I argue that for those silenced victims, contributing to their country's national narrative and raising awareness of past violence, experiencing a sense of relief from sharing their stories with others, and receiving reparation as well as empathetic support are important for facilitating a sense of healing, and, in turn, restoring their dignity. Such a contribution is an important milestone in rebuilding a post-conflict society and providing justice for all.

Scope and limitations of the book

It is as necessary to specify what this book does not deal with, as it is to say what it does. This book has no intention of offering another estimation of the number of Bosnian women victims of CRSV. I believe that one woman raped is one too many. Misusing the numbers is dangerous and may prioritise certain women victims' experiences over others and consequently, may impose (ethnic/race/national) hierarchies among women victims and victimhood. The continuous and ongoing efforts to calculate how many women (of particular ethnic groups) were raped during the BiH war[14] and by whom, has become an endless exercise, and one that does not bring any relief to women survivors. On the contrary, these efforts further contribute to divisions across ethnic lines, as some women may feel they have exclusive rights to victimhood while others feel ignored and muted. As I will elucidate, such appropriation of victimhood presents a significant challenge to not only bringing women survivors together but also to moving ahead with comprehensive legislative and policy measures.

As Linda Grant asserts: 'arguing how many women have been raped and why it was done has overshadowed another issue: What has happened to the women since the ordeal ended?'[15] Instead of a comparative counting of women victims, feminist collective energy should be invested into developing programs of assistance that will benefit all women survivors. Victims should never be turned one against the other, but rather 'added' onto the existing list of victims.[16] We must

14 According to some of the latest local press releases, the numbers cited are around 50,000. See RTV SLON and AdRev, 'Skoro 50,000 žena u BiH silovano u ratu' [Trans: 'Nearly 50,000 Women Raped in Bosnia During the War'], 25 November 2014, www.youtube.com/watch?v=Z1j6fwy8l2c; Dženana Karabegović, 'Silovane žene i muškarci žrtve i stigmi u društvu' [Trans: 'Raped Women and Men Victims and Stigma in Society'], *Radio Slobodna Evropa* (online), 19 April 2016, www.slobodnaevropa.org/a/silovane-zene-i-muskarci-zrtve-i-stigmi-u-drustvu/27683892.html.

15 Vesna Nikolić-Ristanović, *Women, Violence and War: Wartime Victimization of Refugees in the Balkans* (Central European University Press, 2000) 44.

16 Arundhati Roy, 'Brutality Smeared in a Peanut Butter: Why America Must Stop War Now', *Guardian* (online), 23 October 2001, www.theguardian.com/world/2001/oct/23/afghanistan.terrorism8.

never take away from any group of women their historical sufferings, however, being more inclusive lays the groundwork for another kind of future.

Although I acknowledge that other groups may also be classified as silenced victims such as males who were also victims of CRSV, the analysis of such experiences is beyond the scope of this study. I have also excluded experiences of Roma,[17] Jewish and women of other ethnic (and sexual[18]) minorities who lived in BiH during the war. This is not to suggest that such research is not long overdue, but due to the limitations of this study, I have not included experiences of these groups in my analysis.

The unfinished business of listening to women's stories

Drawing on literature in the fields of feminist legal theory, international criminal justice and transitional justice, this study is guided by a feminist curiosity[19] about why some victims of CRSV in post-conflict settings have received attention and were endorsed as 'authentic' or 'ideal', while others were ignored, downplayed and shunned. Existing studies have identified a range of positive benefits of being recognised and acknowledged as a victim. However, the socio-legal consequences of victims' lack of recognition in post-conflict processes remain under-researched. This book seeks to begin clarifying why it is important to overcome the disempowerment and marginalisation of victimisation of some groups of women in post-conflict societies. Intended to be exploratory and theory-building, this book investigates the potential negative impact of the exclusion of victims who are members of the 'perpetrator' nations from transitional justice processes.

This book analyses the (lack of) feminist academic and activist efforts in naming and addressing harm of certain victims of CRSV. It provides a wider understanding of the complexity of victims' experiences; those who do not fit the notion of 'ideal' victim. The marginalisation and lack of engagement with 'less popular' victims of CRSV has turned them into the 'others', while continuous support and reference to 'ideal' victims has brought those classified as such recognition, and material and symbolic support. Due to such complex political reality, Bosnian

17 While Roma people were not a warring party, at least one case of mass killing and rape is known today – the *Skočić* case. At least three women and a 13-year-old girl were repeatedly gang raped by a member of the Serb paramilitary army *Sima Chetniks*. The 13-year-old girl, Zlatija Ribić, was later killed.

18 There has been a dearth of research into victimisation of gay people in wartime. See, for example, Henri Myrttinen, Lana Khattab and Charbel Maydaa, '"Trust No One: Be Aware of Everyone": Vulnerabilities of LGBTI Refugees in Lebanon' in Jane Freedman, Zeynep Kivilcim and Nurcan Özgür Baklacıoğlu (eds), *A Gendered Approach to the Syrian Refugee Crisis* (Routledge, 2017); Henri Myrttinen and Megan Daigle, *When Merely Existing Is a Risk: Sexual and Gender Minorities in Conflict, Displacement and Peacebuilding*, Report, International Alert (2017). There are also other groups of victims that so far have received very little attention, such as women with disabilities, who still need to be recognised as victims of gender-based violence, including sexual violence.

19 'A feminist curiosity', as Cynthia Enloe claims, 'finds all women worth thinking about, paying close attention to . . .' See Cynthia Enloe, *The Curious Feminist: Searching for Women in a New Age of Empire* (University of California Press, 2004) 4.

Serb women victims were not perceived as women who had also suffered from CRSV, but as an abstract concept, a 'collateral damage' and somehow 'deserving' of their misfortune.

Perhaps one of the saddest consequences of such ill treatment is that it divided many women survivors along ethnic lines and prevented them from recognising themselves as victims of the same male crime. This complex reality has been analysed by revisiting a scholarship produced on CRSV in BiH in the past two decades, and by analysing its legacy on post-conflict judicial and non-judicial mechanisms developed in relation to these crimes. By unpacking the stories of mass rape, what becomes more crystallised is that the CRSV narratives in BiH are too complex to fit neatly into generic and homogenous narratives of 'Bosnian women' survivors. Rather, these narratives remain deeply national and ethnic and, as such, perpetuate almost cemented ethnic divisions in the country.

I argue that women survivors who belong to 'perpetrator' states fall *in between* the victim–perpetrator dichotomy, are regarded as 'guilty by association' and are consequently being silenced; their experiences muted and of no interest to transitional justice projects. They have been shunned and ignored by local and international communities and their experiences largely given no voice and often portrayed as incidental, unintentional, opportunistic and exaggerated by the 'perpetrator' state nationalist propaganda.

As such, the victimisation of Bosnian Serb women has never been adequately expressed, recognised or listened to, but rather suppressed by the continuous demand and insistence on recognition of the collective guilt for crimes committed by Serbs. Bosnian Serb women have been perceived as an 'extension' of Serb men who have often been collectively portrayed as aggressors and genociders.[20] The consequence of such treatment and perceptions is a lack of any substantial and long-term governmental and non-governmental support, which has left them feeling, as one woman survivor told me, like 'victims of peace'.

Many local feminist activists who were once outspoken about Bosnian Serb women's experiences now shy away from speaking about these women. There is an assumption that talking about these women means minimising or denying the experiences of Bosnian Muslim and Croat women, or even worse, supporting the Serb ultranationalist rhetoric that portrays Serbs as the 'ultimate' victims.[21] Due to such circumstances, many Serb women activists have decided to not speak publically about Serb women survivors out of fear, and are unwilling to risk their

20 The Serb army, under the command of General Ratko Mladić, committed genocide in Srebrenica on 10 July 1995 killing approximately 8,000 men. The governments of Serbia and Republika Srpska are still in denial of this crime.

21 The framing of the Serb people as 'victims' dates back from the thirteenth century when the Serbian army lost the epic battle in Kosovo against the invading army of the Ottoman Empire. The Serbs lost this battle and were subjugated to five centuries of Ottoman rule. In legend, the battle was also a Serbian sacrifice, which elevated them to the status of a 'heavenly and a chosen people'. See, for example, Sabrina Ramet, *The Dissolution of Yugoslavia: Competing Narratives of Resentment and Blame* (De Gruyter Oldenbourg, 2007); Milica Bakić-Hayden, 'National Memory as Narrative Memory: The Case of Kosovo' in Maria Todorova (ed.), *Balkan Identities: Nation and Memory* (Hurst & Company, 2004).

rhetoric being misinterpreted and portrayed as nationalist. Similarly, women survivors have self-censored their stories as they feel their testimonies are not welcomed and of no interest to anyone.

Speaking up about Bosnian Serb women victims comes with a price. Some Serb feminists and women's groups have been denounced as traitors for adopting a position that treats *all* women as victims of wartime rape; for treating Bosnian Serb women in the same way as Muslim and Croat women survivors. Those feminists who have tried to speak about rape as a crime committed against all women, rather than as a crime against *ethnicity* and *ethnic–nationalist identity*, have been denounced as Serb nationalists and apologists.

Caught up in this complex web of (mis)interpretations, they have spoken out less and less and now a large majority of them remain silent for fear of losing painstakingly bridged inter-ethnic relationships with their feminist activist friends and colleagues from other ethnic groups, in particular Croats and Bosniaks.

In the course of writing this book there were attempts to silence me too, sometimes directly sometimes more discretely. In the first case, I was told that I should not write the book at all, and in the latter some long-term feminists and friends told me that my study is under great risk of being used and misused by the Serb nationalists, who only recognise Serbs as victims. This is after all the reason why many activists, and also perhaps feminist scholars, do not want to write or talk about Bosnian Serb women. They simply do not want to give *topovsko meso* [armour][22] to the right-wing nationalists who will then use the stories of women's suffering to advance their nationalist propaganda. I understand and respect their choice. I am well aware of such risks, but between the option of continuing to be silent and the high risk of this research being misinterpreted for nationalist goals, I have chosen with my writing to disrupt the silence. This book is written with an aim to reoccupy these silenced spaces and unpack their multilayered difficulties. I admit that I have already stirred nationalist sentiments and that my work has already been interpreted as a nationalist story to advance the Serb position.

Terminology

This book adopts a definition of 'perpetrator population' as the one that encompasses those groups who, in a greater majority, committed the crimes.[23]

22 One long-term activist from Serbia told me that any writing about Serb women is giving 'armour to nationalists'.

23 See Elzar Barkan, *The Guilt of Nations: Restitution and Negotiating of Historical Injustices* (W. W. Norton & Company, 2000) who discusses the nations that have committed gross human rights violations in the past. According to Barkan, the guilt of these nations 'is not limited to wrong-doing' but 'includes inaction and at times even lack of empathy toward fellow humans' 301. Serbs have largely been perceived as such a nation during and after the 1990s' war. See also, Susanne Karstedt work in which she refers to 'the nation of the perpetrators' when speaking about German people. For example, Susanne Karstedt, 'From Absence to Presence, from Silence to Voice: Victims in International and Transitional Justice since the Nuremberg Trials' (2010) 17(1) *International Review of Victimology* 9–30; Susanne Karstedt, 'The Life Course of Collective Memories: Persistency and Change in West Germany between 1950 and 1970' (2009) 1(165) *Polish Sociological Review* 27–38.

Among those who are seen to belong to the 'perpetrator nation', often are included bystanders who may not have been involved in dehumanisation directly, yet still may benefit socially, if not economically and politically, due to their population membership.[24] The book, however, goes beyond the scope of this definition to encompass women survivors of CRSV who are seen as belonging to the 'perpetrator population' such as wives, daughters, sisters and mothers. It is important to note that the construction of Serbs as the 'chief villain'[25] has not been adopted by the large majority of members of this group, and many of them are still in denial about the crimes committed in their name.

As Woodward argues, all Serb actors are accused of aggression and lumped up under one category – 'Serbs'.[26] Such a view is reinforced by the fact that the largest proportion of defendants in the completed International Criminal Tribunal for the Former Yugoslavia [ICTY] cases are Serbs.[27] Here, however, I am not interested in disputing the claims that speak of one nation as almost exclusively guilty for the crimes committed, but instead show how such discourses affected women who are seen as belonging to the Serb ethnic group. I am also interested how and why those women survivors' experiences fell on deaf ears because of their perceived 'guilt by association' and of their belonging to the group that has been, by and large, accused of gross human rights violations.

While I use throughout the book 'Serb women' victims and activists, my intent was not to generalise all victims and activists who have a Serb name. I acknowledge that identities do not afford us homogeneous experiences and that it is important to understand that Serb women do not have one essentialised voice or experience. Not all victims and activists think or act the same. Still, rather than using 'some Bosnian Serb' women, I found it easier to simply use 'Serb women' throughout the book.

I also acknowledge that many women activists explicitly reject their ethnic or national identity as their primary identity, so not all women of Serb ethnic origin would agree that I should call them 'Serb'. The ethnic identity is much more complex and reducing the identities of women who I talked with to their ethnicity does not reflect these nuanced post-war identities. However, I decided to use ethnic denominators for the sake of an easier understanding of my analysis, although I am aware that by adopting such a process I may perpetuate some ethnic and nationalist group stereotypes and assumptions.

24 Norman K. Denzin and Michael D. Giardina (eds), *Qualitative Inquiry and the Politics of Advocacy* (Left Coast Press, 2012) 108.

25 Victor Peskin, 'Beyond Victor's Justice? The Challenge of Prosecuting the Winners at the International Criminal Tribunals for the Former Yugoslavia and Rwanda' (2014) 4 *Journal of Human Rights* 216.

26 Susan L. Woodward, 'Violence-Prone Area or International Transition? Adding the Role of Outsiders in Balkan Violence' in Veena Das, Arthur Kleinman, Mamphela Ramphele and Pamela Reynolds (eds), *Violence and Subjectivity* (University of California Press, 2000) 19, 35.

27 According to some estimates 67 per cent of defendants were Serbs. See Sanja Kutnjak Ivkovich and John Hagan, *Reclaiming Justice: The International Tribunal for the Former Yugoslavia and Local Courts* (Oxford University Press, 2011) 22.

Structure of the book

Chapter 1 is concerned with demonstrating that although CRSV has been recognised as a crime against women, it is often hierarchised and not *all* women survivors will necessarily be recognised as its victims. Often only those women survivors who fit within socially constructed narratives of victimhood will have an opportunity to claim the status of victim. Chapter 2 provides an overview of the literature that has been produced over the past two decades on mass rapes in BiH. Here, I show how scholars, in particular feminist scholars, have engaged with and reinforced the notion of popular and less-popular women victims. The politics surrounding the 'numbers' of women victims of CRSV has been instrumental in the creation of an 'ideal' victim, which in large has determined the status of women victims. Chapter 3 discusses the feminist debates around defining and linking CRSV with ethnicity and gender. The legacy of early disagreements among feminists as to how a woman survivor of CRSV should be recognised – by her sex or ethnicity – reverberates till today. I show that these 'edges' between feminist activists and survivors have not dissolved much over the past two decades. Chapter 4 provides an overview and analysis of the complex legal framework in BiH and different treatment of women victims in the country's various jurisdictions. Here, I first overview the judicial systems in BiH and then discuss the laws and treatments of women victims of CRSV in each entity. I then look at the issues of redress and compensation. This chapter aims to emphasise that women victims of CRSV in RS have far fewer opportunities to 'become a victim' in a legal sense, which precludes them from exercising their rights.

Chapter 5 offers an analysis of the Women's Court, held in Sarajevo in 2015. I discuss the challenges that this Court faced during the process of its establishment, preparation and realisation, which, as I will show, may impact its legacy. Here, I draw on feminist activists' reflections on the Court two years after it finished its work. I argue that while the Court should be applauded for its originality and creativity it did not, however, use its potential to bring Bosnian women victims from different ethnic groups together. I conclude that, unfortunately, the Court did not manage to overcome entrenched and cemented ethnic divisions that penetrate all levels of Bosnian life: political, social, economic and civic. Chapter 6 gives an overview of the services available to women survivors of CRSV in BiH, in particular in the RS entity. In the second part of this chapter I seek to unearth the impact that lack of services in RS has had on the daily lives of women survivors. The chapter interrogates women's lives two decades since the end of the armed conflict and seeks to elucidate the challenges they face due to an absence of long-term and sustainable governmental and non-governmental support.

Finally, in Chapter 7 I reflect on the challenges and difficulties that I have encountered in the process of researching and writing this book. As a feminist scholar, I believe it is important to situate myself within the context of my research. In this chapter, I first draw on a reflexive practice and self-critical introspection, which is a valuable methodology and essential when conducting fieldwork. I then turn my attention to the lack of intersectionality in feminist theory and the practice of transitional justice, which has resulted in silencing specific experiences of CRSV. This book is a testament of what it takes to do sensitive feminist research with a group of women who are considered an out-group – of unpopular, non-authentic and non-ideal victims – by a researcher (me) who is at the same time insider and outsider and who seeks to disrupt the popular and mainstream discourse that recognises only one victim and one perpetrator in a fragile and ethnically divided country; a country in which divisions are still very strong and where no one who thinks outside the box is particularly welcomed. Even more, those who write and speak against the constructed narrative still risk being prosecuted, threatened and ostracised.

This book hopes to fill an important gap in the existing body of literature and bring to light silenced narratives largely missing from the feminist scholarship that interrupts the standard discourse of CRSV in BiH. From a practical standpoint, by enhancing our understanding of how inclusion can promote justice and reconciliation, the findings obtained from this research provide insight into how the design of transitional justice processes may be improved in the future to better respond to the needs of *all* victims of mass violence. The book seeks to provide space and allow discussion about CRSV of *all* women, including those perceived to belong to the 'perpetrator population'. I believe that further unpacking and understanding of the victim–perpetrator dichotomy is not only necessary in order to extrapolate the complexity of the problem, but also in order to identify possibilities for change.

1 Conflict-related sexual violence and its 'silences'

Prohibition of conflict-related sexual violence in armed conflicts

For centuries, CRSV was considered a natural by-product of war, and any 'collateral damage' suffered by women was often overshadowed by large-scale massacres or genocide. Rape and other forms of CRSV against women and girls have accompanied warfare in almost every historical era. These crimes have been systematically carried out, regardless of whether men have been fighting offensively or defensively.[1] However, in the last few decades, the nature of war has changed. In the so-called 'new wars' that have taken place after the end of the Cold War, civilians have become more exposed to war,[2] and CRSV against women and girls has become a weapon of warfare,[3] 'as deadly as any bullet and as destructive as any gun'.[4] These are the wars fought on and through women's bodies – wars in which rape often becomes a part of military strategy. Despite its harrowing prevalence, and the significant documenting and analysis of these crimes,[5] the former United Nations Special Rapporteur on Violence against Women, Radhika Coomaraswamy, has described rape as the 'least condemned war crime'.[6]

1 SOS Magazine, 'Žene za Žene' [Trans: 'Women for Women'] (Beograd, November 1993), 107.

2 Mary Kaldor, *New and Old Wars* (Polity Press, 2012).

3 UN Secretary-General, *Women, Peace and Security: Study Submitted by the Secretary-General Pursuant to Security Council Resolution 1325*, Report, United Nations (2002), www.un.org/ruleoflaw/files/womenpeaceandsecurity.pdf; Bülent Diken and Carsten Bagge Laustsen, 'Becoming Abject: Rape as a Weapon of War' (2005) 11(1) *Body & Society* 111.

4 Foreword by the United Nations (UN) Special Representative of the Secretary-General on Sexual Violence in UN Development Programme, *Sexual Violence in Conflict, in Team of Experts, Rule of Law/Sexual Violence in Conflict, Annual Report 2012* (2013), www.undp.org/content/undp/en/home/librarypage/crisis-prevention-and-recovery/un-team-of-experts--rule-of-law-and-sexual-violence-in-conflict-.html.

5 UNSC Report, S/2015/716, Report of the Secretary-General on Women and Peace and Security (16 September 2015), 28.

6 UN Human Rights Office of the High Commissioner, *Special Rapporteur on Violence Against Women, Including Its Causes and Consequences, Preliminary Report on Violence Against Women, Its Causes and Consequences*, 263, U.N. Doc. E/CN.4/1995/42 (22 November 1994), www.ohchr.org/EN/Issues/Women/SRWomen/Pages/SRWomenIndex.aspx (Ms Radhika Coomaraswamy).

Rape in war has served as a means of attacking a victim's identity, culture and dignity, with an aim of humiliating the female victims, the men in their families, and their entire communities.[7] The violence usually associated with CRSV leaves women traumatised – physically as well as psychologically – in their most intimate being. Many women suffer lifelong damage to their internal organs and experience miscarriages or chronic ovarian infections. Raped women are often forcibly impregnated and sometimes purposely infected with diseases such as syphilis and HIV/AIDS. Those who manage to survive are quite often rejected by their own families for having given birth to a child 'of the enemy', or simply for being raped.

CRSV began to be prohibited in national military codes as early as the fourteenth and fifteenth centuries. The *Ordinances of War* promulgated by Richard II (1385) outlawed women's rape and subjected convicted persons to capital punishment by hanging. Similarly, Henry V drew on the laws of Richard II, particularly the provisions denouncing women's rape; his *Ordinances of War* also declared the crime a capital offence.[8] Rape was, for example, prohibited for US armed forces under the 1863 *Lieber Code.*[9] Articles 44 and 47 of this code prohibited rape under the penalty of death.[10]

Still, perpetrators of rape and other acts of CRSV go largely unpunished and for the most part enjoy impunity. After World War II (WWII), no rape charges were brought at any of the Nuremberg military tribunals (1945–1946), although rape was included in *Control Council Law No. 10* as a crime against humanity. The International Military Tribunal of the Far East (The Tokyo trials) (1946–1948) and a US military tribunal convicted Generals Toyoda[11] and Matsui[12] of command responsibility for the violations of the laws or customs of war committed by their soldiers in Nanking. These charges included sexual

7 Susan Brownmiller, *Against Our Will: Men, Women, and Rape* (Bantam Books, 1975).

8 Kelly D. Askin, 'Prosecuting Wartime Rape and Other Gender-Related Crimes Under International Law: Extraordinary Advances, Enduring Obstacles' (2003) 21(2) *Berkeley Journal of International Law* 288, 299; Rhonda Copelon, 'Gender Crimes as War Crimes: Integrating Crimes against Women into International Criminal Law' (2000) 46 *McGill Law Journal* 217, 220; Sharon A. Healey, 'Prosecuting Rape under the Statute of the War Crimes Tribunals for the Former Yugoslavia' (1995) 21(2) *Brook Journal of International Law* 327, 330.

9 *The Lieber Code* of April 24, 1863, also known as Instructions for the Government of Armies of the United States in the Field, General Order No. 100. It set clear rules for engaging with enemy combatants. But the code also clarified how Union soldiers should treat civilians, and in particular women.

10 Two articles under Section II declared that 'all robbery, all pillage or sacking, even after taking place by main force, all rape, wounding, maiming, or killing of such inhabitants, are prohibited under the penalty of death' (Article 44); and that 'crimes punishable by all penal codes, such as . . . rape, if committed by an American soldier in a hostile country against its inhabitants, are not only punishable as at home, but in all cases in which death is not inflicted the severer punishment shall be preferred' (Article 47).

11 *Soemu Toyoda*, US Military Tribunal sitting in Tokyo, 6 September 1949, Official Transcript of Record of Trial, 4998–5007.

12 *Iwane Matsui*, International Military Tribunal for the Far East, 12 November 1948.

assaults and widespread rapes.[13] In the case of *Yamashita*,[14] the former general was convicted of war crimes committed by troops under his command, which included rape. The rape of Nanking women by the Japanese army is considered one of the largest mass rapes in history.

Over the course of just a few weeks in 1937, according to some estimations Japanese military men raped and killed between 20,000 and 80,000 women.[15] Iris Chang provides a detailed account of the rape, mutilation and killing of Chinese girls and women, which have never been officially acknowledged by the Japanese government.[16] According to Chang, the later establishment of an underground system of military brothels by the Japanese army during WWII was a result of the Nanking legacy. In the early years of WWII, the Japanese army rounded up and forced about 200,000 women from Korea, China, Taiwan, the Philippines and Japan to work as prostitutes in these brothels. It has taken 50 years for these atrocities to become a human rights issue. Jan Ruff-O'Herne, a survivor of Japanese military sex-slavery compounds asks:

> Why did it take so long? Perhaps the answer is that these violations were carried out against women. Women are always victims of war. We all heard it being said: they are only women, this is what happens to women during war . . . Rape in war is a power game. It is used as a reward for the soldiers.[17]

Although Japanese women were also among those recruited and trafficked to comfort stations, according to Caroline Norma there is 'pervasive denial' in the literature that the victimisation of Japanese women in comfort stations took place at all. Norma argues that historians either 'forget' to mention Japanese women when they list nationalities of women recruited, or they suggest that there were only 'insignificantly few' of them.[18] Other historians 'actively deny' that they were targeted for trafficking. Japanese women have been largely excluded from the 'justice' campaign for 'comfort' women.[19] Nishino Rumiko notes that such exclusion represents 'denial of harm inflicted on Japanese victims' and asks 'why this may be the question'.[20] The answer may lie in the hypothesis that Japanese women were seen as belonging to the 'perpetrator nation' and as such denied of their victimhood.

13 For detail account of rape and massacre in Nanking see Iris Chang, *The Rape of Nanking: The Forgotten Holocaust of World War II* (BasicBooks, 1997).

14 *In re Yamashita* (1945) 327 U.S. 1. Yamashita was formerly Commanding General of the Fourteenth Army Group of the Imperial Japanese Army in the Philippine Islands.

15 Chang, above n 13, 89.

16 Ibid.

17 Jan Ruff-O'Herne, 'Fifty Years of Silence: Cry of Raped' in Helen Durham and Tracey Gurd (eds), *Listening to the Silences: Women and War* (Brill Academic Press, 2005) 3.

18 Caroline Norma, *Japanese Comfort Women and Sexual Slavery During the China and Pacific Wars* (Bloomsbury, 2016) 49.

19 Ibid., 36.

20 Ibid.

A closer look at the Nuremberg and Tokyo trials proceedings reveals that gender-based crimes were treated, at both tribunals, as less important offences and the victims considered as second-class casualties of war. Indeed, the marginalisation of gender-based crimes here, and elsewhere, may be attributed to the fact that rape has been accepted throughout the history of armed conflicts as a natural consequence of war and a form of collateral damage affecting women, rather than a condemnable war crime.[21]

After WWII the *Geneva Conventions* (1949) explicitly banned the humiliating and degrading treatment of civilians in wartime and required women to be protected against any attack on their personal dignity (Common Article 3). The *Fourth Geneva Convention* states in Article 27 (2) that 'Women shall be especially protected against any attack on their honour, in particular against rape, enforced prostitution, or any form of indecent assault.'[22] The Additional Protocols specifically mention rape and enforced prostitution: 'Women shall be the object of special respect and shall be protected in particular against rape, enforced prostitution and any other form of indecent assault.'[23]

Despite these explicit promulgations and the fact that CRSV has been considered the most widespread form of violence during wartime, this form of violence in war has generally not been a priority for prosecution.[24] According to some estimates, at least 250,000 women were raped during the genocide in Rwanda, yet the International Criminal Tribunal for Rwanda (ICTR) has prosecuted less than a dozen people for these crimes.[25] In Columbia, where sexual violence was a continuous feature of the war, the impunity rate runs at 98 per cent.[26]

21 Sherrie L. Russell-Brown, 'Rape as an Act of Genocide' (2003) 21 *Berkeley Journal of International Law* 350.

22 *Geneva Convention Relative to the Protection of Civilian Persons in Time of War* (75 U.N.T.S. 287) (entered into force 21 October 1950).

23 *Protocol Additional to the Geneva Conventions of 12 August 1949, and Relating to the Protection of Victims of International Armed Conflicts* (API), 8 June 1977, Article 75(2)(b) fundamentally guarantees prohibits 'outrages upon personal dignity, in particular humiliating and degrading treatment, rape, enforced prostitution and any form or indecent assault' and 76(1) Protection of Women; *Protocol Additional to the Geneva Conventions of 12 August 1949, and Relating to the Protection of Victims of Non-International Armed Conflicts* (APII), 8 June 1977, Article 4(2)(c) fundamental guarantees prohibits 'outrages upon personal dignity, in particular humiliating and degrading treatment, rape, enforced prostitution and any form or indecent assault'.

24 Margaret M. deGuzman, 'Giving Priority to Sex Crime Prosecutions at International Courts: The Philosophical Foundations of a Feminist Agenda' (2011) 11 *International Criminal Law Review* 515; Heidi Nichols Haddad, 'Mobilizing the Will to Prosecute: Crimes of Rape at the Yugoslav and Rwandan Tribunals' (2011) 12 *Human Rights Review* 109; Patricia Viseur Sellers, 'Gender Strategy Is Not a Luxury for International Courts' (2009) 17(2) *American University Journal of Gender, Social Policy & the Law* 327.

25 Alice Priddy, 'Tackling Impunity for Sexual Violence' in Annyssa Bellal (ed.), *The War Report: Armed Conflict in 2014* (Oxford University Press, 2015) 680.

26 Global Justice Center, 'Ending Impunity for Widespread and Systematic Use of Sexual Violence in Columbia's Ongoing Armed Conflict' on *Global Justice Center Blog* (9 December 2013), http://globaljusticecenter.net/blog/405-ending-impunity-for-widespread-and-systematic-use-of-sexual-violence-in-colombia-s-ongoing-armed-conflict. This may change with the recent peace deal with the Revolutionary Armed Forces of Columbia (FARC) in which prosecutions for rape were demanded.

It was not until the mid-1980s that the process of defining violence against women within a human rights context actively commenced, with important contributions from feminist scholars.[27] The feminist academics and activists demanded that the era of silence be replaced with international recognition, and that the shame should not reside within the victim but in the perpetrator. They also focused their attention to find causes of CRSV by analysing militarism, patriarchy, gender and structural inequality, all of which enable and encourage violence against women. However, it was only in 1993 during the Vienna Conference on Human Rights, when the world had become aware of the horror of mass rape in war in Bosnia and Herzegovina (BiH), that sexual violence against women was finally accepted within the mainstream human rights discourse as an issue of high priority.

Due to the wars in the former Yugoslavia and Rwanda, international norms and standards have evolved rapidly. These wars 'shocked the conscience of the world' with effective media coverage and international mobilisation to develop global capacity to prosecute war crimes and crimes against humanity.[28] The International Criminal Tribunal for the former Yugoslavia (ICTY) was established in 1993 due to persistent and well-organised local and international feminist efforts to break the silence on CRSV. The feminists lobbied that rapes should not be perceived as 'a natural by-product of war' or as male games and rewards for their military labour.[29] The first arrest warrants and indictments for crimes against humanity arose out of the mass rapes. In 2001, the ICTY declared three Bosnian Serb men guilty of rape, torture and sexual enslavement of Bosnian Muslim women and girls in special detention centres in 1992, and sentenced them to between 12 and 28 years in prison.[30] It was rape that, at last, caught the world's attention and 'thanks' to which, the serious and pervasive gender-based violence – in particular sexual and reproductive violence during war – finally gained recognition under international criminal law.

When the International Criminal Court (ICC) was created in 1998, the *Rome Statute* of the ICC promulgated wartime rape as a crime of war and a crime against humanity.[31] This development has been strengthened further by the unanimous

27 Brownmiller, above n 7; Nancy Farwell, 'War Rape: New Conceptualizations and Responses' (2004) 49(4) *Affilia* 389; Meredeth Turshen, 'The Political Economy of Violence against Women During Armed Conflict in Uganda' (2000) 67(3) *Social Research* 803; Nicola Henry, 'Theorizing Rape: Deconstructing Gender, Sexuality and Violence' (2016) 30(1) *Gender and Society* 44; Catharine A MacKinnon, 'War, Genocide and Women's Human Rights' (1994b) 17 *Harvard Women's Law Journal* 5.

28 Radhika Coomaraswamy, 'Sexual Violence during Wartime' in Helen Durham and Tracey Gurd (ed.), *Listening to the Silences: Women and War* (Leiden, 2005) 53, 59.

29 Tanja Djuric-Kuzmanovic, Rada Drezgic and Dubravka Zarkov, 'Gendered War, Gendered Peace: Violent Conflicts in the Balkans and its Consequences' in Donna Pankhurst (ed.) *Gendered Peace: Women's Struggles for Post-War Justice and Reconciliation* (Routledge, 2007) 265.

30 *Prosecutor v Kunarac (Trial Judgment)* (International Criminal Tribunal for the former Yugoslavia, Trial Chamber, Case No. IT-96-23-T and IT-96-23/1-T. T-96-23 and 23/1, 22 February 2001).

31 *Rome Statute of the International Criminal Court* (opened for signature 17 July 1998) (2187 UNTS 90) (entered into force 1 July 2002) pts 7–8.

adoption of the United Nations Security Council Resolutions (UNSCR), dealing with the situation of women in armed conflict. The most widely known is probably UNSCR 1325 from 2000,[32] followed by UNSCR 1820 from 2008, which specifically deal with CRSV.[33] In these resolutions, sexual violence in conflict and post-conflict situations was addressed and the view of the widespread and/or systematic use of CRSV as an instrument of terror was established.

The need to end CRSV and to hold perpetrators to account was asserted again in 2009 when the UNSCR 1888 reiterated the need to make global efforts to end violence against women and children in war.[34] Rape finally ceased to be perceived as the unrestrained sexual behaviour of individuals and was recognised as a powerful tool of war, used to intimidate, persecute and terrorise the enemy. Despite enormous and continuing efforts by feminists who are committed to ensuring that women's and girls' experiences of CRSV are taken seriously, that the harm they suffer is recognised, and that those who inflict that harm are held accountable, CRSV is still endemic and continues to happen with impunity even in societies that can prosecute, such as Bosnia and Herzegovina (BiH). Although it has been recognised as a crime against humanity, rather than a violation of family honour, CRSV is still treated as less significant in comparison to other war crimes and has yet to be fully recognised and taken seriously as a crime of gender.[35] In the aftermath of every war, many women continue to live with the effects of rape and other forms of torture, without proper access to the medical, psychological, legal and financial assistance they need to rebuild their shattered lives. Meanwhile, most of the perpetrators go unpunished.

Silenced rapes before the 1990s

During the Holocaust, Jewish women were particularly vulnerable to rape by German soldiers,[36] while German women were the target of mass rape by the Soviet Red Army and their allies after Germany surrendered. The rape of German women marked the final defeat of Nazi Germany. Yet these women were ignored and invisible as victims for decades – they were denied victimhood because the Germans were collectively seen as responsible for the horrors of WWII and, as such, its people could not be perceived as 'legitimate' victims of war. Marta Hillers' autobiography, *Eine Frau in Berlin* (*A Woman in Berlin*),[37] for the first time lifted the silence surrounding mass rapes committed in Berlin.

32 UNSC Res. 1325, 4213th mtg, UN Doc S/RES/1325 (31 October 2000).

33 UNSC Res 1820, 5916th mtg, UN Doc S/RES/1820 (19 June 2008).

34 UNSC Res. 1888, 6195th mtg, UN Doc S/RES/1888 (30 September 2009).

35 Catherine N. Niarchos, 'Women, War, and Rape: Challenges Facing The International Tribunal for the Former Yugoslavia' (1995) 17 *Human Rights Quarterly* 649, 676–679.

36 Helene Sinnreich, '"And It Was Something We Didn't Talk About": Rape of Jewish Women During the Holocaust' (2008) 14(2) *Holocaust Studies: A Journal of Culture and History* 1, 4; Rochelle G. Saidel, *The Jewish Women of Ravenbrück Concentration Camp* (The University of Wisconsin Press, 2006); see also Hans Fallada, *Alone in Berlin* (Penguin Books, 2010).

37 The book was first released anonymously in the United States in 1954.

It is a book that explores the idea that Germans were not only aggressors but also victims of terror and suffering during WWII. Although the book was published in 1954, research on this topic remains scant and has not been discussed publicly until recently.[38]

In their groundbreaking movie and book, *BeFreier und BeFreite: Krieg, Vergewaltigung, Kinder* (*Liberators take Liberties*),[39] Barbara Johr and Helke Sander tried to establish figures for mass rapes that occurred in Berlin using women's testimonies, stories, estimates and projections, and concluded that between April and September of 1945, after the invasion by the Red Army, nearly 110,000 of 1.4 million female residents of the city were raped. Many of the women and girls were repeatedly gang raped.[40] While the number of abortions cannot be estimated due to the high number of unreported cases, over 1,000 children were born as a result of the rapes.[41] A number of women died of torture, some committed suicide and those who survived were ostracised, stigmatised, and shunned by their husbands and children.[42] As in other cases of 'vindictive rape',[43] it can be alleged that many of these women were not targeted because of any specific reason other than their membership of 'a hated category'.[44]

BeFreier und BeFreite was only published in 1995 and, in response to journalists' questions as to how they came to the subject of their research, the authors

38 See, for example, Richard Bessel and Dirk Schumann (eds), *Life after Death: Approaches to a Cultural and Social History of Europe During the 1940s and 1950s* (Cambridge University Press, 2003); Miriam Gebhardt, *Crimes Unspoken: The Rape of German Women at the End of the Second World War* (Polity, 2016); R. M. Douglas, *Orderly and Humane: the Expulsion of the Germans after the Second World War* (Yale University Press, 2012).

39 Helke Sander and Barbara Johr (eds), *BeFreier und BeFreite: Krieg, Vergewaltigung, Kinder* [Trans: *Liberator and Liberated: War, Rape, Children*] (Taschenbuch, 1995). The documentary movie was first made and released in 1992. The transcription of the film later appeared in a book under the same title. The book also contains further interviews, essays and documentation. It is notable that the book has not been translated yet into English or any other language.

40 A German woman in her seventies confided to her female neighbour in 1990s that she was a victim of rape by Russian soldiers. She reportedly said: 'The only experience I had with men was being gang raped by Russians.' She said that the depth of her trauma could never be understood by her mother who although knew about her traumatic experience urged her to 'find a man' and 'get married'. Personal sources, on file with author. See also Ingo von Münch, *Frau, komm!: Die Massenvergewaltigungen deutscher Frauen und Mädchen 1944/45* [Trans: *Women, Come!: The Mass Rape of German Women and Girls 1944/45*] (ARES Verlag, 3rd ed., 2009); According to Beevor an estimated 2 million German women were raped by Soviet soldiers, see Antony Beevor, *The Fall of Berlin 1945* (Viking, 2002), 410.

41 Sander and Johr, above n 39, 54.

42 Ingeborg Jacobs, *Freiwild: Das Schicksal deutscher Frauen 1945* [Trans: *The Destiny of German Women in 1945*] (Taschenbuch, 2009).

43 Jon Elster, *Closing the Books: Transitional Justice in Historical Perspectives* (Cambridge, 2004), 97 On rapes by the Prussian troops in France after Napoleon's second abdication in 1815; see Henry Houssaye, *1815: La seconde abdication – la terreur blanche* [Trans: *1815: The Second Abdication – The White Terror*] (Perrin, 1906), 492–494; Elster, 97; see also David Markham, *The Road to St Helena: Napoleon after Waterloo* (Pen & Sword, 2008) 51.

44 Ibid., Elster, 97.

replied: 'Why for nearly fifty years *was it not* [original emphasis] a subject?'[45] Sander further notes that her aim, motivated by the silence surrounding this topic, was to establish these rapes as significant historical events.[46] A German woman survivor of rape raised a similar question:

> It's hard for me to understand why no one until today has dealt with this topic, as if absolutely nothing had happened to women . . . What I experienced personally injured my dignity as a woman deeply . . . But hasn't the silence for decades, the indifference and lack of interest in the fate of these women on the part of significant social and political groups taken away a piece of our dignity for the second time?[47]

Sarah Helm argues that there are three possible reasons why women victims of the Nazi Holocaust went unnoticed and their experiences were not of interest until recently. While Helm's research was about women camp survivors of the infamous Ravensbrück camp, Hitler's only concentration camp for women, she offers compelling reasons why women's stories stayed hidden for a long time. She argues that after the Holocaust began to emerge in its fullest in the 1960s and 1970s it took time to realise that while the Jewish Holocaust remained the biggest crime humanity had known, that should not be the reason to obscure other aspects of the Nazi horror. The second reason is that the mainstream historians are largely men not interested in women's experiences.[48] The third reason, according to Helm, is that the Russians and allies were 'victors' and the stories of crimes committed by them at the end of the war towards civilians were censored. The stories of glory, communist heroism and the anti-fascist fight were the ones to be cherished, while stories of the victor's terror and inflicted victimhood were to be swept under the carpet. Similarly, Elzar Barkan notes that the German victims 'could claim no part of public sympathy'. The sufferings of Germans were viewed as 'unexceptional when compared to those who had survived the camps under the Nazi regime'.[49]

Miriam Gebhardt in her book *Crimes Unspoken: The Rape of German Women at the End of the Second World War* presents a further insight into the question why the topic of German women raped by the Allied forces was neglected for so long.

45 Norman M. Naimark, 'The Russians and the Germans: Rape during the War and Post-Soviet Memories' in Raphaelle Branche and Fabrice Virgili (eds), *Rape in Wartime* (Palgrave Macmillan, 2012) 201, 206.

46 Marie-Luise Gättens, 'Helke Sander's *Liberators Take Liberties* and the Politics of History' in Ingeborg Majer O'Sickey and Ingeborg von Zadow (eds), *Triangulated Visions: Women in Recent German Cinema* (State University of New York Press, 1998) 261.

47 Ingeburg Menz, as cited in Richard W. McCormick, 'Rape and War, Gender and Nation, Victims and Victimizers: Helke Sander's *BeFreier und Befreite*' (2001) 16(1) *Camera Obscura* 99.

48 Sarah Helm, *Forced Abortions and Medical Experiments: Last Survivors of Nazi Women's Camp Tell Their Horror Stories*, www.dw.com/en/forced-abortions-and-medical-experiments-last-survivors-of-nazi-womens-camp-tell-their-horror-stories/a-18997838.

49 Elzar Barkan, *The Guilt of Nations: Restitution and Negotiating of Historical Injustices* (W. W. Norton & Company, 2000) 131.

She argues that German women were 'wrong victims' because they were not victims of the Nazi regime; because they were not men and did not belong to the ranks of those who had been killed, traumatised or crippled, but might have even been implicated in the Nazi crimes; because they were subjects of violence by the victorious powers and the unheroic victims of morally charged crime often accused on bringing a shame upon themselves. Gebhardt has also shifted almost exclusive attention to the mass rapes by Soviet soldiers to the members of American, French and British forces and estimates that around 190,000 German women were raped by victorious powers.[50]

Although mass rape of German women by the victor's army was established early on, a silence surrounding these rapes was entrenched for almost 40 years. Sheila Johnson describes Sander's movie and book as being directed against 'the physical rape of women by men' and 'the sociopolitical rape of women by history'.[51]

According to Ingrid Schmidt Harzbach, the socio-political meaning of mass rapes of German women at the end of WWII has not been the focus of research, but rather these rapes have been regarded as 'taboo' and 'untold' fact.[52] Some commentators believe that the sudden interest in German women's victimisation was due to the conflict in the former Yugoslavia, and a growing global awareness of rape as a war crime in civil and ethnic conflicts.[53]

Crimes against German women could be described as 'collateral damage', paying the high price of 'collective guilt' for the actions of their male fellows. While the whole of German society was to some degree collectively punished for the Nazis' crimes,[54] atrocities committed towards German women by Allied soldiers speak of the proportion of silence they had to endure for being part of that community. Probably, what Jon Elster calls 'the clearest case of collective guilt' in the post-1945 Nuremberg trials, was the loss of Dutch citizenship imposed on the wives of those Dutch men who had lost their citizenship because they collaborated with Nazis.[55]

Silenced rapes after the 1990s

In Rwanda, during the genocide that took the lives of an estimated 800,000 people, rape was widespread and thousands of women were individually or

50 Gebhardt, above n 38, 10.

51 Sheila K. Johnson, 'Helke Sander's *BeFreier und BeFreite: Krieg, Vergewaltigung, Kinder* and Postmodernism' (1993) 28(1) *Pacific Coast Philology* 81.

52 Ingrid Schmidt-Harzbach, 'Eine Woche im April' [Trans: 'One Week in April'] in Helke Sander and Barbara Johr (eds), *BeFreier und BeFreite: Krieg, Vergewaltigung, Kinder* [Trans: *Liberator and Liberated: War, Rape, Children*] (Taschenbuch, 1995) 21.

53 Atina Grossmann, *Jews, Germans, and Allies: Close Encounters in Occupied Germany* (Princeton University Press, 2007), 29.

54 US Senate Committee on the Judiciary, *The Morgenthau Diaries (Germany)*, US Government Printing Office (1967); Avizier Tucker, 'Paranoids May Be Prosecuted: Post-Totalitarian Transitional Justice' in Jon Elster (ed.) *Retribution and Reparation* (Cambridge, 2006) 181.

55 Elster, above n 43, 130.

gang-raped, held in sexual slavery, or sexually mutilated. The ICTR held that rape and sexual violence 'constitute genocide in the same way as any other act as long as they were committed with the specific intent to destroy, in whole or in part, a particular group, targeted as such'.[56] The court held that these acts constituted acts of genocide: 'Sexual violence was an integral part of the process of destruction, specifically targeting Tutsi women and specifically contributing to their destruction and the destruction of the Tutsi group as a whole.'[57] The large majority of women victims were Tutsis but some Hutu women were also targeted with rape, often because they were married to Tutsi men.[58] According to Judith Herrmann, to both Hutu women that she recently interviewed in Rwanda, husbands and children were killed because they had been married to a Tutsi and 'one of these two women is still being harassed by the Hutu wife and family of the perpetrator who was imprisoned for the killing her husband and children'.[59] Another Hutu woman that Herrmann met 'was abandoned by her Hutu family, since they held her responsible for having "produced" Tutsi children by marrying a Tutsi man . . . her family held her responsible for having caused the death of her children (by them being Tutsi)'.[60]

With the Tutsi being the principal victims, and the Hutu the perpetrators ('genociders'), a delineation of victim and offender along ethnic lines strongly informed not only the Tutsi-dominated government, but also the international-community approach to post-conflict reconstruction. Nuanced experiences of Hutu women raped by Hutu men during the genocide, such as the ostracism they face nowadays from both communities – Hutu from being once married to Tutsi and Tutsi for simply being a Hutu – have scarcely been captured and documented. As Johan Pottier argues, according to this approach 'Tutsi were cast as victims/survivors and Hutu as perpetrators, with anyone who deviated from this "rigid typology" at risk of being labelled a genocide denier.'[61] As a result of such strong delineation, Hutu women's experiences of rape have been entirely excluded from the jurisprudence of the ICTR and also largely absent

56 *The Prosecutor v Jean-Paul Akayesu* (International Criminal Tribunal for Rwanda) Case No. ICTR-96-4-T, 2 September 1998 [731].

57 Ibid.

58 Binaifer Nowrojee and Regan Ralph, 'Justice for Women Victims of Violence: Rwanda after the 1994 Genocide' in Ifi Amadiume and Abdullahi An-Na'im (eds), *The Politics of Memory: Truth, Healing and Social Justice* (Zed Books, 2000) 162, 167; Jennie Burnet, *Genocide Lives in Us: Women, Memory, and Silence in Rwanda* (The University of Wisconsin Press, 2012).

59 Judith Herrmann is a PhD candidate at the James cook University. She shared her research data at the Annual Conference of Genocide Scholars held in Brisbane from 10–14 July and via personal email communication (25 July 2017). The title of her presentation was 'Analysing the Experiences of Survivors of Genocidal Sexual-Violence with Transitional Justice Processes'.

60 Ibid.

61 Johan Pottier, 'Escape from Genocide: The Politics of Identity in Rwanda's 1994 Massacres' in Vigdis Broch-Due (ed.) *Violence and Belonging: The Quest for Identity in Post-Colonial Africa* (Routledge, 2005) 195.

from the feminist discourse on rapes in Rwanda. Hutu women survivors of rape during the war or genocide 'are erased by the public discourse'.[62] Such one-sided focus on Hutu crimes during the genocide had deepened, rather than smoothed, ethnic divisions.[63]

In the 1990s, rape was a common practice during the wars in the former Yugoslavia. Even though the *Fourth Geneva Convention* of 1949 prohibited war-time rape, it was not until Nusreta Sivac and Jadranka Cigelj, former judges from Prijedor, and victims of CRSV themselves, presented their overwhelming evidence to the ICTY, that women became legally recognised as victims of CRSV. Thanks to Sivac's and Cigelj's efforts to gather testimony from women across BiH, rape has been categorised as a war crime under international law. They collected evidence that exposed the magnitude of rape, which courts could no longer ignore and which has become a major turning point in recognising rape as a war crime. These violations ranged from dehumanisation to mutilation, rape, forced motherhood, forced prostitution, torture and sexual murder, and they were based on both sex and ethnicity. Rape of women was used as a weapon of war and as a tool for *ethnic cleansing*. In the *Kunarac* case, the ICTY found, for the first time in judicial history, that rape was 'used by members of the Bosnian Serb armed forces as an instrument of terror'.[64]

In the ICTY jurisprudence, the Čelebići case was the only case in which Bosnian Serb women were specifically recognised as victims of rape by Croat and Bosniak soldiers. Hazim Delić was charged that, while the deputy commander of the Bosnian Croat and Muslim run Čelebići camp, he repeatedly raped Gordana Ćećez and Milojka Antić who were prisoners at the camp. The Trial Chamber found that the rapes were acts causing severe physical and mental pain and the suffering was committed by an official to obtain information, coerce, intimidate, punish and discriminate, and as such constituted torture.[65] The representatives of the Bosnian Serb association of former combatants refer to this case as 'the only Serb judgement'[66]; meaning the only one in favour of Serb women. Looking back on the time she served as the international prosecutor at the ICTY, the then judge, Elizabeth Odio Benito, reflected on her work on this particular case and disappointment of being involved in it:

> I have been really sorry and angry at the irony of life that has made me one of the judges in the only case where the accused are Muslims. They suffered the highest number of casualties in what had been recognised as numerous

62 Burnet, Jennie E., 'Situation Sexual Violence in Rwanda (1990–2011): Sexual Agency, Sexual Consent, and the Political Economy of War' (2012) 4 *Anthropology Faculty Publications* 1.

63 Lars Waldorf, *Mass Justice for Mass Atrocity: Transitional Justice and Illiberal Peace Building in Rwanda* (PhD Thesis, National University of Ireland, Galway, 2013).

64 *Prosecutor v Kunarac (Trial Judgment)*, above n 30.

65 *Delalić et al v Prosecutor* (Trial Judgment) (International Criminal Tribunal for the former Yugoslavia), Trial Chamber, Case No. IT-96-21-T, 16 November 1998, [470, 493, 941, 963].

66 Interview with a representative of the Association of the Former Camp Inmates in Višegrad, 15 July 2015.

> crimes against humanity . . . So it is ironic that three out of four accused are Muslim . . . how people who know suffering can become victimisers of others . . . The four men are human beings.[67]

The statement made by Odio Benito in a rape case is, at least, perplexing. Why is it relevant that the males in question were Muslims if they committed a crime against humanity? Does it matter to which ethnic group they belong? What does Odio Benito's comment mean for feminist struggles for justice for women victims of CRSV?

Constructing sexual hierarchies in the Bosnian war: 'ideal' and 'silenced' victims

It has taken feminists decades to deconstruct problematic binaries and myths around rape in domestic contexts but the notion of the 'real' rape victim nonetheless continues to hold sway. Feminist scholars have used Christie's 'ideal victim'[68] to explain the apparent discrepancy in the treatment of victims of peacetime rape. Christie describes 'ideal victim' as 'a person or category of individuals who, when hit by crime, most readily are given the complete and legitimate status of being a victim'.[69] One of the characteristics of an 'ideal victim' is that the offender is unknown to the victim. Victims that are not regarded as 'ideal' are less likely to be recognised as victims and ascribed a special status. As Strobl argues, without such status, a victim 'will not be . . . a victim in the social world' and as such will be deprived from emotional support from their family but also financial support from compensation schemes.[70] Sara Kendall notes that, without efforts within the field of international criminal law to 'inscribe and transform the experience of suffering into legally recognisible categories', victimhood won't be eligible for recognition.[71] As Vincent Druliolle argues: 'victimhood is not given . . . it is historcally and socially constructed, which of course does not mean that victims' suffering is not "real"'.[72] Once recognised though, victimhood establishes a space for a specific kind of politics and poses itself as an 'indisputable starting point' from which debates, discussions and actions 'can and must proceed'.[73]

67 Sara Sharratt, 'Interview with Elizabeth Odio Benito, Justice of the International Tribunal for the Former Yugoslavia' in Sara Sharratt and Ellyn Kaschak (eds), *Assault on the Soul: Women in the Former Yugoslavia* (The Haworth Press, 1999) 39, 45.

68 Nils Christie, 'Ideal Victim' in Ezzat A Fattah (ed.), *From Crime Policy to Victim Policy: Reorienting the Justice System* (Macmillan, 1986) 17.

69 Ibid. 19.

70 Rainer Strobl, 'Becoming a Victim' in Shiomo Giora Shoham, Paul Knepper and Martin Kett (eds), *International Handbook on Victimology* (CRC Press, 2010) 5.

71 Sara Kendall, 'Archiving Victimhood: Practice of Inscription in International Criminal Law' in Stewart Motha and Honni van Rijswijk (eds), *Law, Memory, Violence: Uncovering the Counter-Archive* (Routledge, 2016) 1.

72 Vincent Druliolle, 'Recovering Historical Memory: A Struggle Against Silence and Forgetting? The Politics of Victimhood in Spain' (2015) 9(2) *International Journal of Transitional Justice* 319.

73 Laura Jeffery and Matei Candea, '"Introduction" in "The Politics of Victimhood"' (2006) 17(4) *History and Anthropology* 289.

Being a victim of CRSV encompasses a different kind of dichotomy. As during peacetime, in the aftermath of war, one of the obstacles in assigning victim status can result from the *relationship* from different groups in society: those who belong to 'an unaccepted' group are more likely to be seen as offenders rather then victims.[74] They are divided along the lines of ethnicity or national identity and as such not all of them will fit into an 'ideal' or 'authentic' victim subject.[75] According to Ratna Kapur, the nationalistic discourse becomes implicit in constructing the identity of a nation-state. While she welcomes the growth of the international women's rights movement and its emergence as a field of research and advocacy, Kapur also finds it culpable of creating the 'woman-as-victim' subject, 'geographically captive' in the 'barbaric' cultures of the 'Third World'.[76]

Although rape has been interpreted to fit within the 'grave breaches'[77] regime (since courts have decided that rape can constitute a form of torture, slavery and genocide), debate continues about whether or not rape should exist as a standalone crime that is subject to universal jurisdiction under customary international law.[78] Along with these ongoing debates, it is notable that sexual violence, in both peace and war contexts, has frequently been the subject of hierarchisation. It is well known that in domestic criminal jurisdictions, rape by a stranger is pursued and prosecuted far more vigorously and successfully than rape by an acquaintance.[79] Stranger rape, for instance, is far more likely to succeed at trial, and victims who suffer sexual violence at the hands of a stranger are less likely to receive biased treatment both inside and outside the criminal justice system. In comparing wartime and peacetime rape, some have commented on the contrastable gravity of war-related rapes. For example, at the recent Global Summit against Sexual Violence in Conflict it was noted that

> [s]exual violence is a problem found in every society in the world, and all countries have to do more to tackle it at home. *But* it is in the context of war and conflict that sexual violence is found to the most appalling degree, and on a scale most of us cannot imagine.[80]

74 Strobl, above n 70, 13.

75 See Ratna Kapur, 'The Tragedy of Victimization Rhetoric: Resurrecting the "Native" Subject in International/Postcolonial Feminist Legal Politics' (2002) 15(1) *Harvard Human Rights Law Journal* 1.

76 Ibid. 9.

77 The 1949 Geneva Conventions prohibit a set of 'peremptory' norms ('grave breaches'), such as genocide, slavery and torture, which are absolutely prohibited under international, local and customary law.

78 Hilary Charlesworth and Christine Chinkin, 'The Gender of Jus Cogens' (1993) 15(1) *Human Rights Quarterly* 63; David S. Mitchell, 'The Prohibition of Rape in International Humanitarian Law as a Norm of Jus Cogens: Clarifying the Doctrine' (2005) 15 *Duke Journal of Comparative & International Law* 219; Patricia Viseur Sellers, 'Sexual Violence and Peremptory Norms: The Legal Value of *Rape*' (2002) 34 *Case Western Reserve Journal of International Law* 287.

79 Susan Estrich, *Real Rape* (Harvard University Law Press, 1987).

80 Foreign and Commonwealth Office, 'Foreign Secretary Announces UK Initiative on Preventing Sexual Violence in Conflict' (Announcement, 29 May 2012), www.gov.uk/government/news/foreign-secretary-announces-uk-initiative-on-preventing-sexual-violence-in-conflict (emphasis added).

Similarly, Hollywood celebrity and UN Goodwill Ambassador, Angelina Jolie recently noted that the rapes in times of war are particularly vicious: '*This* rape is so brutal, with such extreme violence, that it is even hard to talk about it.'[81] The hierarchy that is constructed around wartime rape, as opposed to rape in peacetime, is a product of the separation of ordinary and exceptional crimes. What makes a crime exceptional in its gravity and a crime against humanity, as David Luban argues, are offences that violate a fundamental humanity of all 'humankind'.[82] The Council of Europe describes wartime rape as 'worse' than 'ordinary', peacetime rape, since it is accompanied by other war-related trauma and the loss or death of a husband, partner or child.[83] It also differs from ordinary rape since it is committed in 'a political context which often engenders organised violence'.[84] The substantial imagination captured by wartime rape resulted in categorising armed-conflict rape as 'extraordinary' violence of wartime atrocity, which facilitates easy dislocation of one category of harm (wartime rape) from the other (peacetime rape).[85]

Among CRSV crimes, wartime rape reserves a privileged position in the hierarchy of crimes against women.[86] A narrow focus on this crime has become of primary concern to feminist academics over other women-related experience of war violence that remain not fully addressed. Still, even with such attention, rapes of certain groups of women remain under-researched. Some women's stories are encouraged and reinforced, while others silenced. The reason for recognition of some women victims and not others is due to dominant understanding of what it meant to be a victim in war and that was to not be on the side of 'the recognised

81 Ninemsn, 'Jolie Moved to Tears After Meeting Rape Victims', *Nine News* (online) 29 March 2014, www.9news.com.au/entertainment/2014/03/29/09/27/jolie-moved-to-tears-after-meeting-rape-victims (emphasis added).

82 David Luban, 'A Theory of Crimes Against Humanity' (2004) 29 *Yale Journal of International Law* 85, 90.

83 The Council of Europe Parliamentary Assembly, 'Rape in Armed Conflict', para. II (A) 'A Necessary Distinction: Rape in Peacetime and in Wartime', 15 March 2000.

84 Ibid. Scholars, such as Chiseche Salome Mibenge, would disagree with clear-cut distinctions between the two. Mibenge argues that rape and other forms of gender-based violence in peacetime are also committed in a political context of hegemonic power, which has serious repercussions for gender equality and non-discrimination in women's enjoyment of fundamental human rights. See Chiseche Salome Mibenge, *Sex and International Tribunals: The Erasure of Gender from the War Narrative* (University of Pennsylvania Press, 2013), 13. On continuum of violence from peace to war and peace see also, Jelke Boesten, *Sexual Violence During War and Peace: Gender, Power and Post-Conflict Justice in Peru* (Palgrave Macmillan, 2014).

85 Fionnuala Ní Aoláin, 'Gendered Harms and their Interface with International Criminal Law: Norms, Challenges and Domestication' (2014) 16(4) *International Feminist Journal of Politics* 622, 626.

86 Beyond rape, there are other crimes of sexual violence committed during armed conflict, such as forced marriage, sexual slavery and enforced prostitution. On even slower development of international criminal law when it comes to these crimes, see Melanie O'Brien, '"Don't Kill Them, Let's Choose them as Wives": The Development of the Crimes of Forced Marriage, Sexual Slavery and Enforced Prostitution in International Criminal Law' (2015) 20(3) *The International Journal of Human Rights* 386. Also, on recent critique of exclusive focus on rapes, please see Nicola Henry, 'The Fixation on Wartime Rape: Feminist Critique and International Criminal Law' (2014) 23(1) *Social & Legal Studies* 93.

perpetrator'.[87] For example, as some commentators note, although rapes occur in all wars, the role of rape in BiH was 'unique' in its molestation and degradation of Bosniak women.[88] In reference to the distinct nature of mass rape against Bosniak women, feminist scholars, such as Catharine MacKinnon, exceptionalised the rape of Bosniak women by Serb men. She argues that

> [s]ex has also been used before to create, mobilize, and manipulate ethnic hatred, from the Third Reich to *Penthouse* . . . [but] the world has never seen sex used this consciously, this cynically, this elaborately, this openly, this systematically, with this degree of technological and psychological sophistication, as a means of destroying a whole people.[89]

After rape was explicitly included as a crime against humanity in the ICTY statute in 1993, feminist scholars, legal professionals and activists were prompted to turn their attention to consider whether all rapes or just the 'worst' ones should be subject to prosecution in international criminal courts. Advocates of prosecuting 'genocidal rape' have taken a one-sided approach to the war. The most prominent among them was MacKinnon, who argued that the problem is that the war in BiH was misinterpreted as a bilateral, civil war of ethnic dimensions:

> [R]apes in this war are not grasped as either a strategy in genocide or a practice of misogyny, far less both at once . . . What is happening here is first a genocide, in which ethnicity is a tool for political hegemony: the war is an instrument of the genocide; the rapes are an instrument of the war.[90]

MacKinnon further elaborates that the actions of Serb men were particularly heinous because they exemplified male aggression, and this particular ethnic aggression is 'beyond question'[91] and 'incontestable'.[92] Insistence on (Serb) genocidal rape has been met with resistance from some feminist scholars and activists in the former Yugoslavia, such as Vesna Kesić, who accused MacKinnon of the 'nationalistic creation of an enemy'.[93] Likewise, Zarkov argues that MacKinnon 'used war rapes in Bosnia to advance her anti-pornography struggle in the United States'.[94]

87 Karen Engle, 'Feminism and its (Dis)Contents: Criminalizing Wartime Rape in Bosnia and Herzegovina' (2005) 99 *The American Journal of International Law* 796.
88 Roy Gutman, 'Foreword' in Alexandra Stiglmayer (ed.), *Mass Rape: The War Against Women in Bosnia-Herzegovina* (University of Nebraska Press, 1994) ix, x.
89 Catharine A. MacKinnon, *Are Women Human?: And Other International Dialogues* (Belknap Press, 2007) 161–162.
90 Catharine MacKinnon, 'Rape, Genocide and Women's Human Rights' in Alexandra Stiglemayer (ed.), *Mass Rapes Against Women in Bosnia-Herzegovina* (University of Nebraska Press, 1994) 183, 186–187.
91 Ibid. 186.
92 MacKinnon, above n 89, 161.
93 Vesna Kesić, 'A Response to Catharine MacKinnon's Article "Turning Rape Into Pornography: Postmodern Genocide"' (1994) 5 *Hastings Women's Law Journal* 267, 275.
94 Djuric-Kuzmanovic et al., above n 29, 286.

Elissa Helms notes that the use of term 'genocidal rape' erases rapes perpetrated by those '*other than Serbs*' and implies that only Serbs were capable of rape.[95] These opposing feminists strongly disagreed and argued that genocide should not be the focus of attention since it reduces the dynamics of rape between Serb males and Bosniak and Croatian females,[96] and in turn portrays Serbs as the exclusive perpetrators of CRSV. Such single focus on Serb males distorts and deflects attention from the fact that Croatian and Muslim soldiers also raped in the war.[97] MacKinnon also accused Serb combatants of producing and selling rape videos as pornographic materials, which she described as a new contribution to the depravity of war.[98]

In 1993, already predicting a danger in collectively accusing one ethnic group of men – Serb – of rape, a message by feminists from Belgrade was sent to feminist networks across former Yugoslavia:

> Since [the] beginning of the war in Croatia and Bosnia testimonies show that rape is widely spread; that victims of rape are of all nationalities, including Roma, Albanian and other women that do not belong to any warring parties. All the same, perpetrators belong to all military and para military formations, as well as [the] civilian population.[99]

Some feminists in Croatia similarly reported: 'Women are potential victims of violence primarily because they are women, then because they are Croats, Muslims or Serbs, but each of them is firstly an individual human being who should get adequate support and help.'[100] The feminists from Serbia very early on tried to articulate their concern about dividing rape across ethnic divide. Lepa Mladjenović cautioned against establishing 'hierarchies of rape in war':

95 Elissa Helms, *Innocence and Victimhood: Gender, Nation, and Women's Activism in Postwar Bosnia-Herzegovina* (University of Wisconsin Press, 2013) 259. Already in 1995, the Human Rights Watch conducted interviews with Bosnian Serb women who were raped by Croatian forces in the municipalities of Bosanski Brod and Odzak. Human Rights Watch, *The Human Rights Watch Global Report on Women's Human Rights*, Report, Human Rights Watch (1995), www.hrw.org/sites/default/files/reports/general958.pdf 21–24 (emphasis in original).

96 Vesna Nikolić-Ristanović, 'Sexual Violence' in Vesna Nikolić-Ristanović (ed.), *Women, Violence and War: Wartime Victimization of Refugees in the Balkans* (Central European University Press, 1999) 41, 63.

97 Janine Natalya Clark, 'Working with Survivors of War Rape and Sexual Violence Fieldwork: Reflections from Bosnia-Herzegovina' (online) *Qualitative Research*.

98 Catharine MacKinnon suggested that Serbs were turning rape into pornography, see Catharine MacKinnon, 'Turning Rape into Pornography: Postmodern Genocide' (1993) IV(1) *Ms Magazine* 24. This argument has been widely accepted by many feminist scholars, see e.g. Sheila Jeffreys, *The Industrial Vagina: The Political Economy of the Global Sex Trade* (Routledge, 2009) 115, and has informed UN policies on the Bosnian war, see for example, Radhika Coomaraswamy, above n 28, 53, 57. Vesna Kesić feminist and activist from Croatia opposed to MacKinnon theory and allegations, see Kesić, above n 93, 267.

99 Lepa Mladjenovic, 'Nacrt projekta za centar za žene silovane u ratu' [Trans: 'The Draft of Project for the Centre for Women Raped During the War'] (*Žene za Žene*, Beograd 1993) 111.

100 From the Letter of Intention, Women's Lobby Zagreb, 21 December 1992.

> Although some feminists distinguish between 'ordinary' and 'genocidal' forms of wartime rape, there are others, myself included, who would argue that any such distinction is dangerous, since it posits a rape hierarchy that places the violation of nations ahead of that of women. Whether one sees such rapes as instruments of war or of genocide, they are all acts of torture, war atrocities, and crimes against humanities.[101]

MacKinnon, who was at the time heavily embroiled in these discussions, accused feminist activists who refused to consider the rape of Bosnian Muslim women as a form of genocide, of being involved in a nationalistic campaign that tried to cover up Serb crimes. She openly defied Serb feminists. In June 1993, at the UN Human Rights Conference in Vienna, Vesna Kesić, a prominent Croatian activist, noted how MacKinnon went public with her hostility to Serbian feminists. She claimed that MacKinnon made the following comment in response to a question raised by Belgrade feminist Nadežda Ćetković: 'If you are in opposition to the regime in Serbia, why aren't you already dead?'[102]

MacKinnon strictly restricted the label of 'genocidal rape' to the rape of Bosnian Muslim and Croatian women, and never called for prosecution of the rape of Serb women by Croatian and Bosnian Muslim forces.[103] Rhonda Copelon offers a broader concept of the Balkan mass rapes to include rapes on all sides, irrespective of ethnicity, race, and religion – to be recognised as a crime against humanity. She adds that accounting for the rape of women on the basis of their ethnic relationship to the enemy, constitutes another attack on the basis of gender by completely denying their subjectivity, and constitutes a failure to acknowledge the sexual persecution that these women endured.[104]

Still, not only Serb males are blamed for rapes – their wives, daughters and sisters have been portrayed as 'cheerleaders' for their husbands.[105] Helke Sander, for example, argued in 1993 that

101 Lepa Mladjenovic, 'Beyond War Hierarchies: Belgrade Feminists' Experience Working with Female Survivors of War' in Sara Sharratt and Ellyn Kaschak (eds), *Assault on the Soul: Women in the Former Yugoslavia* (Haworth Press, 1999) 83, 87.

102 Kesić, above n 93, 267; Jill Benderly, 'Rape, Feminism, and Nationalism in the War in Yugoslav Successor States' in Lois A West (ed.), *Feminist Nationalism* (Routledge, 1997) 59, 67. In 2007, 14 years after this event and the infamous question MacKinnon raised, I experienced a close encounter with MacKinnon at the international feminist conference in Townsville. Over a coffee break, my close Bosniak girlfriend and I introduced ourselves to MacKinnon. She asked me where I was from and I said that I was from BiH. She then asked from which city, and I said Banjaluka. 'Are you a Serb?' was MacKinnon's next question. I responded that my parents are Serbs. She then said: 'Do you know that Serbs are genocidal people?' Then she slowly turned to my Bosniak girlfriend and told her: 'I am surprised to see that the two of you are friends.' In the eyes of this acclaimed feminist scholar I was first a Serb and *then* a woman from BiH; a woman that belongs to a 'perpetrator' nation and as such I was simply dismissed.

103 Hilmi M. Zawati, *Fair Labeling and Dilemma of Prosecuting Gender-Based Crimes at the International Criminal Tribunals* (Oxford, 2014) 98.

104 Rhonda Copelon, 'Surfacing Gender: Re-Engraving Crimes against Women in Humanitarian Law' (1994) 5(2) *Hastings Women's Law Journal* 243. For more citations, see Zawati, above n 103.

105 Helke Sander, 'Prologue' in Alexandra Stiglmayer (ed.), *Mass Rapes Against Bosnian women* (University of Nebraska Press, 1994) xvii.

> even a nationalistic and uninformed Bosnian Serb woman can know that, if their husband belongs to the Chetniks, to Arkan's or Seselj's people, or to the volunteers from Serbia, he is almost with 100 per cent certainty a multiple rapist.[106]

Similarly, and more recently, a few Bosniak women survivors of rape have accused Serb women of nurturing their male children (later to become 'adult warriors') in a culture of violence, death and (Serb) nationalism: 'their women simply bring up their children this way [encouraging violence] and they find those kinds of husbands'.[107] Reinforcing the suggestions that Serbs, both men and women, are violent and barbaric is dangerous and leads to further ostracism and negation of any form of Serbian victimisation.

These views enabled complete denial of the possibility that Serb women could have also been raped, displaced or victimised during the war. Sander refers to them as the 'wives of the enemies'.[108] She goes further to suggest that it is to be expected that Bosniak and Croat women do not want to reach out to them as

> it seems to be asking too much to expect the Muslim and Croatian women who are being threatened, displaced, and raped in a war of aggression to simply sit down together at one table with the wives of their enemies.[109]

She also compares Nazi Germany with Serbia and suggests: 'just imagine if anyone had demanded the like of German and Polish women after the World War II'.[110] Sander suggests that no reconciliation is possible between the women from the 'perpetrator' and the 'victim' sides and reinforces a notion of collective guilt. Zarkov also emphasises animosity towards Serb women by citing a Croatian woman who said: 'I am not sorry for Serb women. Bosnian [meaning Muslim] and Croat mothers were crying when they had to send their sons into war, and Serb mothers were singing'.[111]

Kelly Dawn Askin also notes how isolated and ostracised Serb women survivors of rape were, and refers to these women as 'sexual assault survivors from the aggressor side'. She argues, that Serb women survivors suffer an additional layer of psychological harm because of the lack of empathy by society, whose attitude was that Serb women 'deserve' to be raped since Serb men raped 'so many' Bosniak and Croat women.[112] Some Serb women victims were told that they 'deserved' to be raped and tortured simply because they were Serbs:

106 Ibid., xix.
107 Helms, above n 95, 136.
108 Sander, above n 105.
109 Ibid., xxi.
110 Ibid.
111 Dubravka Zarkov, *The Body of War: Media, Ethnicity, and Gender in the Break-Up of Yugoslavia* (Duke University Press, 2007) 184.
112 Kelly Dawn Askin, *War Crimes Against Women: Prosecution in International War Crimes Tribunals* (Martinus Nijhoff, 1997) 287.

> On the day when I was about to be exchanged[113] I asked a captain who detained and tortured me for 322 days, 'so, it is now the end of this whole all ordeal. Can you now tell me what was I guilty of?' He told me, 'Why do you need to be guilty for anything? You are a Serb that is what you are guilty of.'[114]

Feminist scholars, such as Doris Buss, cautioned against ceasing the analysis of CRSV at the point of strategic or genocidal rape. In Rwanda, the widespread rape of Tutsi women was characterised by the ICTR as genocidal rape. By framing rape as a weapon that one side uses against another, we enact a 'rape script' that 'naturalise[s]' sexual violence and ignores rapes that contradict that rape script.[115] According to the ICTR, genocidal rape is defined as a crime against a particular group of women: Tutsi women. It thus renders some CRSV and abuse invisible, such as the rape of Hutu women, but also of Tutsi men and boys and Hutu boys who resisted violence. Buss argues that although the rape of Hutu women did not occur with the same magnitude as did the rapes of Tutsi, it is troubling that victims were ignored by the ICTR.[116] Hutu people were invisible as victims and denied of victim status, even when reports on the mass scale of the killings and human rights abuses by the Tutsi-led Rwandan Patriotic Front (RPF) army were documented.[117] Many Hutu women were raped and tortured before being killed. These crimes have been largely ignored, not only by the ICTR but also by the scholars and researchers.[118]

The reason that the ICTR did not investigate atrocities committed by the Tutsi-led RPF army, lies in the fact that the international tribunals have focused on the chief perpetrator's crimes – Hutu crimes. The ICTR in Arusha failed to initiate any judicial inquiry into RPF crimes and, as such, left the impression that these crimes are of no international importance.[119] In Rwanda, as Gerd Hankel argues, the Hutu has been officially acknowledged as the

113 Many women were exchanged for war prisoners held in captivity by the other side.

114 Interview with Božica Živković Rajilić, Banjaluka 5 July 2013.

115 Doris Buss, 'Rethinking Rape as a Weapon of War' (2009) 17 *Feminist Legal Studies* 145, 155.

116 Ibid.

117 See UNSC, *Report of the Secretary-General's Investigative Team Charged with Investigating Serious Violations of Human Rights and International Humanitarian Law in the Democratic Republic of the Congo*, UN Doc S/1998/581 (26 June 1998), https://daccess-ods.un.org/TMP/364274.494349957.html; see also African Union, *Rwanda – The Preventable Genocide: The Report of the International Panel of Eminent Personalities to Investigate the 1994 Genocide in Rwanda and the Surrounding Events*, Report, African Union (2000), www.refworld.org/pdfid/4d1da8752.pdf.

118 Marie Béatrice Umutesi, 'Is Reconciliation Between Hutus and Tutsis Possible?' (2006) 60(1) *Journal of International Affairs* 157–158.

119 Victor Peskin, 'Victor's Justice Revisited: Rwandan Patriotic Front Crimes and the Prosecutorial Endgame at the ICTR' in Scott Straus and Lars Waldorf (eds), *Remaking Rwanda: State Building and Human Rights after Mass Violence* (University of Wisconsin Press, 2011) 173, 181; see also Victor Peskin, *International Justice in Rwanda and the Balkans: Virtual Trials and the Struggle for State Cooperation* (Cambridge University Press, 2008).

only perpetrator group, and the genocide victims among the Tutsi as the only victim group.[120]

Richard Goldstone, the first chief prosecutor of the ICTY and ICTR, reportedly stated that the magnitude of genocidal crimes committed towards Tutsis by Hutu extremists outweighed his prosecutorial choice:[121]

> [m]y attitude . . . was to give priority in investigations and prosecutions to the most guilty . . . I wouldn't have issued an indictment against [Bosnian Muslims] for the sake of . . . saying what an even-handed chap I am. I think crimes have to be of the magnitude that justify doing so.[122]

A similar logic has been utilised by the BiH Prosecutor's Office, which in 2008 undertook a mapping of war crimes committed in the state which resulted in a list of the cases, the so-called 'catalogue of crimes', which identifies potential war criminals and witnesses. This is not a public document but is aimed at serving the prosecutors in resolving the problem of the massive backlog of war crime cases,[123] and assists them in making priorities among them.[124] It has been stated that the Prosecutor's Office will be 'oriented towards victims and the magnitude of crime' and that it will not engage itself in any attempt to 'artificially balance ethnic groups' when it comes to prosecuting war crimes.[125]

Although Croatian armed forces committed atrocities against Serbs, in particular during 1991 and 1992,[126] these acts did not equate to the magnitude of the Serbian crimes and,[127] as such, stayed outside of international scrutiny. It is thus unsurprising that the global attention on the rape of Bosnian women resulted in the construction of a hierarchy of crimes, a hierarchy of victims and a hierarchy of perpetrators; all based on ethnic identity. As Nancy Fraser

120 Gerd Hankel, 'On Victims and Non-Victims: Observations from Rwanda' in Throsten Bonacker and Christoph Safferling (eds), *Victims of International Crimes: And Interdisciplinary Discourse* (Asser Press, 2013) 29, 41.

121 Peskin, above n 119, 188.

122 Ibid., 189.

123 According to some estimates BiH has over 1,200 cases involving some 8,000 suspects in it backlog cases. See OSCE, *Accountability for War Crimes*, 2012, www.osce.org/bih/108141?download=true;
Denis Džizic 'Bosnia Struggles with War Crimes Investigation Backlog', *Balkan Insight* (online), 14 October 2014, www.balkaninsight.com/en/article/bosnia-failing-to-reduce-number-of-war-crimes-investigations.

124 Goran Šimić, *Suđenja za ratne zločine u Bosni i Hercegovini* [Trans: *War Crimes Trials in Bosnia and Herzegovina*] (Dobra knjiga, 2013) 92.

125 Balkan Investigative. Reporting Network, 'Katalog ratnih zločina', [Trans: 'The Catalogue of War Crimes'], 5 June 2008.

126 Ivo Goldstein, *Croatia: A History* (McGill-Queen's Press, 1999) 229, 236; Chris Hedges, 'Croatian's Confession Describes Torture and Killing on Vast Scale', *New York Times* (online), 5 September 1997, www.nytimes.com/1997/09/05/world/croatian-s-confession-describes-torture-and-killing-on-vast-scale.html.

127 Peskin, above n 119, 96.

argues, recognition based on identity has the effect of marginalising, eclipsing and displacing redistributive struggles, to 'drastically simplify and reify group identities . . . [encouraging] separatism, intolerance and chauvinism, patriarchalism and authoritarianism'.[128]

In line with such critiques, some feminist scholars have been hesitant about distinguishing between rapes in both peacetime and wartime contexts. Copelon, for example, noted that the condemnation of wartime rape has not been about crimes against gender but rather the mass rapes in the former Yugoslavia have only captured the world's attention because of their association with genocide or ethnic cleansing. The effect, she claims, is that a hierarchy around rape in wartime is created:

> The elision of genocide and rape in the focus on 'genocidal rape' as a means of emphasizing the heinousness of the rape of Muslim women in Bosnia is . . . dangerous. Rape and genocide are separate atrocities. Genocide – the effort to destroy a people based on its identity as a people – evokes the deepest horror and warrants the severest condemnation . . . to emphasize as unparalleled the horror of genocidal rape is factually dubious and risks rendering rape invisible once again. When the ethnic war ceases or is forced back into the bottle, will the crimes against women, the voices of women, and their struggles to survive be vindicated? Or will condemnation be limited to this seemingly exceptional case?[129]

Although the ICTY was, from the outset, careful about not pursuing the 'victor's justice' reminiscent at both the Nuremberg and Tokyo trials following WWII,[130] the court has been perceived by Serbs as biased and anti-Serb.[131]

128 Nancy Fraser, 'Rethinking Recognition' in Hans-Christoph Schmidt am Busch and Christopher F. Zurn (eds), *The Philosophy of Recognition: Historical and Contemporary Perspectives* (Lexington Books, 2010) 211, 212.

129 Rhonda Copelon, 'Gendered War Crimes: Reconceptualizing Rape in Time of War' in Julie Peters and Andrea Wolper (eds), *Women's Rights, Human Rights: International Feminist Perspectives* (Routledge, 1995) 197, 198–199.

130 The ICTY website: 'While the most significant number of cases heard at the Tribunal have dealt with alleged crimes committed by Serbs and Bosnian Serbs, the Tribunal has investigated and brought charges against persons from every ethnic background' UN ICTY, *About the ICTY*, www.icty.org/en/about.

131 Jelena Obradović-Wochnik, 'Revisionism, Denial and Anti-ICTY Discourse in Serbia's Public Sphere: Beyond the "Divided Society" Debate' in James Gow, Rachel Kerr and Zoran Pajic (eds), *Prosecuting War Crimes: Lessons and Legacies of the International Criminal Tribunal for the former Yugoslavia* (Routledge, 2014) 182, 197; Sanja Kutnjak Ivkovich, *Reclaiming Justice: The International Tribunal for the Former Yugoslavia and Local Courts* (Oxford University Press, 2011) 8; Patrice McMahon and Jennifer Miller, 'On a Wing and a Prayer: The Effect of the ICTY on the Balkans' (Paper presented at the Annual Meeting of the Midwest Political Association 67th Annual National Conference, The Palmer House Hilton, Chicago, IL, 2 April 2009) 19; Andrew A. G. Ross, *Mixed Emotions: Beyond Fear and Hatred in International Conflict* (University of Chicago Press, 2014) 131.

The ICTY prosecutes and punishes Serbs, Croats and Bosniaks, but over two-thirds of its indictees have been Serbs.[132] Although the substantial majority of cases have involved crimes of ethnic Serbs against non-Serb victims,[133] some Serbs deny these crimes, while others acknowledge them and believe that crimes committed against Serbs are war crimes too and, as such, should not be treated as a by-product or 'inevitable acts of war'.[134]

The focus on the wartime mass rapes in BiH as unique, exceptional and 'genocidal' paved the way, in part, for unprecedented global attention on the suffering of Bosniak women, and helped to place rape on the prosecutorial agenda of international war crimes courts. The hierarchy of crimes, including rape, reflects the hierarchy of victimhood, which places Serbs – the alleged perpetrators of majority of war crimes – at the bottom. As such, Serb victims are regarded as somehow less 'authentic' and less worthy of protection than others. As Karen Engle argues, assumptions that there are essential ethnic differences among Serbs, Bosniaks and Croats, and that women are powerless victims of war, have woven their way into various institutional responses to wartime rape.[135]

Despite these warnings from feminist scholars, an almost exclusive focus on Bosniak women and the suffering caused by Serb men, has been widely reinforced by researchers, scholars and media, which in turn has enabled other narratives to stay overlooked or ommitted.[136] Moreover, although some acts of 'goodness' by Serb soldiers towards Bosniak women were raised in the prosecutor's statements, they stayed buried in legal documents and archives and consequently have not been picked up and analysed in the context of of BiH war. For example, the prosecutor stated in the *Kunarac* case:

> Scattered throughout the testimony of exceedingly cruel acts were moments of goodness, and the witnesses told you about them: about the Serb woman who befriended those kept at Partizan and did what she could to protect them; about the guards at Partizan who did manage to turn away the soldiers when they came to take women; about the soldier who saved Witnesses 191 and 186 from the accused Kunarac, and who, as 191 poignantly put it,

132 For more discussion on the International Criminal Court's 'even-handedness', see Mark Drumbl, 'The Future of International Criminal Law and Transitional Justice' in William A. Schabas, Yvonne McDermott and Niamh Hayes (eds), *Ashgate Research Companion to International Criminal Law: Critical Perspectives* (Ashgate, 2013) 531; see also Rachel Kerr, 'Lost in Translation? Perceptions of the ICTY in the Former Yugoslavia' in James Gow, Zoran Pajič and Rachel Kerr (eds), *Prosecuting War Crimes: Lessons and Legacies of the International Criminal Tribunal for the Former Yugoslavia* (Routledge, 2013) 103, 110–122.

133 Diane F. Orentlicher, *Shrinking the Space for Denial: The Impact of the ICTY in Serbia*, Report, Open Society Justice Initiative (2008), www.opensocietyfoundations.org/sites/default/files/serbia_20080501.pdf 86.

134 Ibid.

135 Engle, above n 87, 778, 779–780.

136 Karen Engle, 'Judging Sex in War' (2008) 106(6) *Michigan Journal of Law* 941, 957.

> 'Didn't see me just as a Muslim but as a human being,' and whom she later married; and even about those Serb soldiers who refused to rape despite all the pressure from their peers.[137]

Some Serb soldiers paid high prices for not wanting to be part of gang rapes and for trying to save the lives of some women victims. In 1995, Kelly Dawn Askin in her book about the Balkans, *War Crimes Against Women*, used a footnote to record that there had been reports that commanders would castrate or kill their own soldiers for refusing to commit rapes under order.[138] A female eyewitness described what happened to a Serb soldier after he refused to rape a woman under direct orders:

> Unbutton your trousers and take it out, ordered Milan with a very sharp knife in his hand. The soldier started to fumble with his trousers. Milan tore his trousers away from his body in a single move. He grabbed his male organ and cut it off with one clean movement. A piece of flesh fell on the blanket and a blood stain appeared about it. I buried my face in my rags while Milan was pulling him towards the door. I could only image what would happen next. They would torture him as a coward and a traitor of his race until his last breath.[139]

Another account came also from a woman who survived a rape camp. She reported on the rape of herself and other women and girls in Doboj women's camp:

> I knew a lot of them; they were our friends and neighbours . . . [S]ome of them enjoyed doing it, and others were forced to do it . . . [A] few guys who used to work with me; they were forced to do it. You can tell, and one of them in particular, a close friend of my husband's, that's what he told me, too . . . There were three men I knew, they're dead now, they refused; they didn't want to go along with it, and so they killed them.[140]

However, these narratives of duress and acts of 'goodness' were often ignored and not further analysed by feminist scholars, activists or media. I agree with Dawn Askin that rapes under duress require special consideration in prosecution, but also special attention by researchers. Relegating such exepriences to a footnote, or not analysing them from feminist persepectives, does not do justice to the portrayal of the complex circumstances under which some CRSV occured.

137 *Prosecutor v Kunarac* (Transcript of proceedings) (International Criminal Tribunal for the former Yugoslavia, Trial Chamber, Case No. IT-96-23-T and IT-96-23/1-T. 6273–74.

138 Askin, above n 112, 283.

139 This eyewitness testimony was recorded by Tresnjevka Women's Group, cited in ibid.

140 Alexandra Stiglemayer (ed.), *Mass Rape: The War Against Women in Bosnia-Herzegovina* (University of Nebraska Press, 1994) 120.

Conclusion

Since the 1990s, when much attention was directed towards understanding the complexities of CRSV, local feminists have debated whether women were raped in wartime because of their sex, or because they belong to a particular ethnic/religious group. Has rape served as an 'ethnomarker',[141] or as an act of male violence against women that has no ethnic and religious boundaries? Can victims of rape experience justice other than justice through an ethnic lens?

By exclusively positioning and treating CRSV in BiH through an ethnic scope, feminist scholars unintentionally contributed to the further polarisation of rape discourse. As a consequence, feminist activists who tried to speak about crimes committed against women that belonged to the 'perpetrator' group (Serbs) were often denounced as traitors, nationalists, apologists or accused of being 'collaborators' with Serb forces.[142] As Tatjana Pavlović argues, being a woman was subsumed under a particular national identity, and attempts to express any form of solidarity and commonality with women across ethnic and national identity lines could be regarded as disloyalty.[143]

In such a complex political context, Bosnian Serb women survivors' experiences were often rejected and ignored, and the sources that draw on their testimonies deemed unreliable. As such, their stories were not used and made visible to local and international audiences, apart as a nationalistic Serb propaganda. There are several reasons why Bosnian Serb women victims were not attractive to international media and scholars. First, because they were perceived as mothers, daughters and wives of the 'perpetrator', Serb women were denied the status of victim;[144] their victimhood is either not acknowledged at all or is 'quantified' in a far lesser number that made their experiences appear insignificant in comparison to the mass rape of Bosniak women. Second, the discussion of Serb women by women from their own ethnic group puts them at risk of being regarded as 'Serb nationalists' and blacklisted by anti-nationalist feminists. This is because, as Elissa Helms argues, the collective war narratives (of innocence and victimhood) are so sacred that people cannot allow themselves to think about anything that might disrupt them.[145]

As a result, Serb feminists who consider themselves anti-nationalists have stayed largely silent about Serb women victims of rape. They felt morally responsible to publicly talk about the 'crimes committed in their own name' – primarily the rape of non-Serb women.[146] Due to such circumstances, the experiences of Serb women were readily appropriated and used by people who do in fact

141 Darius M. Rejali, 'After Feminist Analyses of Bosnian Violence' (1996) 8 *Peace Review* 365, 368.

142 Kesić, above n 93, 267, 275.

143 Tatjana Pavlović, 'Women in Croatia: Feminists, Nationalists and Homosexuals' in Sabrina P. Ramet (ed.), *Gender Politics in Western Balkans: Women and Society in Yugoslavia and the Yugoslav Successor States* (Pennsylvania State University Press, 1999) 131.

144 Stiglmayer, above n 140.

145 Helms, above n 107.

146 Such as 'Women in Black – Belgrade' and other groups in Serbia who have been more outspoken about CRSV crimes committed by Serbs, rather than against them.

adopt a pro-nationalist stand to advance nationalist politics. In consequence, these women's experiences have stayed largely muted and invisible, or misused and misinterpreted.

The continuous and ongoing efforts to minimise or neglect the suffering of Serb women have further divided women survivors along ethnic lines. As Linda Grant asserts: 'arguing how many women have been raped and why it was done has overshadowed another issue: What has happened to the women since the ordeal ended?'[147] Such questions have been raised, not to deny that Bosniak women were the most numerous among those who died, or survived rape, but, as Helms argues, to challenge existing and 'dominant representations' that depict them as 'the *only victims*'.[148] Gender intersects with other identitites – ethnic and religious – to produce both opportunities and oppression or multiple forms of discrimination.[149]

Transitional justice processes may reinforce a sense of victimhood leading to the continuum of negative attitudes towards those who have committed wrongs.[150] According to Dušan Jović, the narratives of victimhood have largely been constructed and reinforced by scholars[151] who often seek to hear and listen to particular voices. Naomi Roht-Arriza cautions that researchers and advocates need to pose and reflect on the question: 'Whose voices are we seeking out, and whose are we hearing when we ask the necessary questions?'[152] The research accounts can conceal the stories about the experiences of those who do not appear to be present in the research project. The academy functions to direct researcher questions and skills to explore certain human rights problems and not others.[153] It is the academy that sets the agenda in transitional justice societies, and politicians and governments rely on academic writing to pursue some issues and neglect others.[154] Due to unequal access to victims, the production of knowledge reinforces narratives of certain subjects that shape research agendas, which in turn inform the policies that shape the world.[155]

147 Linda Grant, as cited in, Nikolić-Ristanović, above n 96, 41, 44.

148 Helms, above n 107, 27 (emphasis in original).

149 Association for Women's Rights in Development, 'Intersectionality: A Tool for Gender and Economic Justice' (2004) 9 *Women's Rights and Economic Change: Facts & Issues* 1, https://lgbtq.unc.edu/sites/lgbtq.unc.edu/files/documents/intersectionality_en.pdf.

150 Harvey M. Weinsten, 'Victims, Transitional Justice and Social Reconstruction: Who Is Setting the Agenda?' in Inge Vanfraecham, Antony Pemberton and Felix Mukwiza Ndahinda (eds), *Justice for Victims: Perspectives on Rights, Transition and Reconciliation* (Routledge, 2014) 161, 162.

151 Center for European Studies, 'Dusan Jovic and Jelena Subotic, Fall 2013 CES Friday Lecture' 16 December 2013, www.youtube.com/watch?v=5fCdqVDfAu0.

152 Naomi Roht-Arriaza, 'Foreword' in Hugo van der Merwe, Victoria Baxter and Audrey R. Chapman (eds), *Assessing the Impact of Transitional Justice: Challenges for Empirical Research* (US Institute of Peace, 2009) vii, ix.

153 Charlie Carpenter, '"You Talk of Terrible Things so Matter-of-Factly in This Language of Science": Constructing Human Rights in the Academy' (2012) 10(2) *Perspectives on Politics* 363, 364.

154 Center for European Studies, above n 151.

155 Sarah M. H. Nowen, '"As You Set Out for Ithaka": Practical, Epistemological, Ethical, and Existential Questions about Socio-Legal Empirical Research in Conflict' (2014) 27(1) *Leiden Journal of International Law* 227, 258

While there has been considerable scholarly work on hierarchies of victimisation and how the notion of victim and perpetrator is produced and re-produced by governments and international constituencies, such work draws mostly on the fields of criminology and victimology, and has been relatively recent in the transitional justice field of study. Interrogation of 'the positionality of victimhood' is crucial in this relatively young and interdisciplinary field of studies that investigates how societies and victims attempt to come to terms with a legacy of large-scale past abuses.[156]

In transitional justice literature there is a tendency to theorise about women as a unified homogeneous category, as if there is no difference among them according to class, ethnicity or race. The gender analysis of wartime rape often focuses primarily on women's experiences only and then to *certain* women's experiences. The 'other' women excluded from analysis are classified as 'undeserving' victims; victims who are not designated as 'innocent' and who, as McEvoy and McConnachie argue, may not be able to lay claim to the term victim.[157] Indeed, those victims that the transitional justice field pays attention to are, as Susan Hirsch describes, 'deserving' of global justice.[158] Although many activists and scholars claim that the transitional justice field is 'victim centric',[159] the notion of victim is not holistic and the positionality of victimhood has not been of interest to many scholars in this field. Who the victims are in a given context is taken for granted and reproduced in the literature. Luc Huyse argues that 'the simple fact of having been physically, psychologically or economically harmed is a necessary but not sufficient element' to become a victim.[160] Although transitional justice literature acknowledges that the identity of victims is constructed by international law and judicial mechanisms,[161] the field has paid little attention to the politics of victimhood and the construction of victimhood in society, which evokes a contest over the identity and meaning of 'victim', and the status of different types of victims in a given context.[162]

156 Kieran McEvoy and Kirsten McConnachie, 'Victims and Transitional Justice: Voice, Agency and Blame' (2013) 22(4) *Social & Legal Studies* 489, 505.

157 Kieran McEvoy and Kirsten McConnachie, 'Victimology in Transitional Justice: Victimhood, Innocence and Hierarchy' (2012) 9(5) *European Journal of Criminology* 527–528.

158 Susan Hirsch, 'The Victim Deserving Global Justice: Power, Caution, and Recovering Individuals' in Kamari Maxine Clarke and Mark Goodale (eds), *Mirrors of Justice: Law and Power in the Post Cold* (Cambridge University Press, 2010) 149.

159 Simon Robins, 'Towards Victim-Centred Transitional Justice: Understanding the Needs of Families of the Disappeared in Postconflict Nepal' (2011) 5(1) *International Journal of Transitional Justice* 75.

160 Luc Huyse, 'Victims' in David Bloomfield, Theresa Barnes and Luc Hayes (eds), *Reconciliation After Violent Conflict: A Handbook* (International Institute for Democracy and Electoral Assistance, 2013) 57.

161 Michael J. Kelly, 'Definition of Victims' in Thorsten Bonacker and Christoph Safferling (ed.), *Victims of International Crimes: An Interdisciplinary Discourse* (Springer, 2013).

162 See Druliolle, above n 72, 320.

While it is impossible to 'do justice' to all of the voices of victims affected by past violence,[163] some 'complex interweaving' is required by transitional justice scholars and policy makers to minimise the danger of essentialising or silencing; in particular when it comes to issues such as gender, race, class and other variables that often play a key role in the construction of victim voices.[164] As the next chapters demonstrate, such interweaving failed in BiH where policy makers, feminist scholars and activists, to various extents, contributed to establishing and reinforcing a hierarchy of victimhood that reverberates today and will hardly be dismantled and deconstructed in the near future.

163 McEvoy and McConnachie, above n 157.

164 Fionnuala Ní Aoláin, 'Advancing Feminist Positioning in the Field of Transitional Justice' (2012) 6(2) *International Journal of Transitional Justice* 220.

2 Revisiting mass rape in Bosnia and Herzegovina

The numbers

Although CRSV is not a new phenomenon, its extensive use had become a key focus of the disastrous war in BiH and triggered the creation of the first ad hoc International Criminal Tribunal for the Former Yugoslavia (ICTY) since Nuremberg.[1] The stories of CRSV in BiH appeared to be different from what had been recorded in previous armed conflicts, in that the CRSV was reportedly systematic and specifically targeted against members of different ethnic groups, and on a larger scale.[2] As such, wartime rape has been recognised as a crime against humanity before the ICTY for the first time in history.[3]

The estimates of women victims of CRSV over the past two decades ranged from 20,000 and 60,000. The first report, released by the BiH government in September 1992, cited evidence of at least 13,000 Bosniak women having been raped by Serbs, hypothesising that the actual number was closer to 50,000.[4] According to a follow-up study by the European Commission (the *Warburton Mission Report*) that focused solely on rapes of Bosniak women in BiH, this number was reduced to around 20,000.[5] These numbers caught the attention of the media, activists and academics globally, who soon characterised the war in BiH as a war against women, in which rape was used as a 'weapon of war'.[6] At about the same time, in 1992, the Commission for War Crimes in former Yugoslavia alleged that 800 Serb women were victims of rape by the Bosniak forces.[7]

1 Louise Chappell, Andrea Durbach and Judge Elizabeth Odio Benito, 'Judge Odio Benito: A View of Gender Justice from the Bench' (2014) 16(4) *International Feminist Journal of Politics* 648.

2 Inger Skjelsbæk, *The Political Psychology of War Rape: Studies from Bosnia and Herzegovina* (Routledge, 2012), 64.

3 Established by UNSC Res. 827, 3217th mtg, UN Doc. S/RES/827 (25 May 1993).

4 Vesna Nikolić-Ristanović, 'Living Without Democracy and Peace: Violence Against Women in the Former Yugoslavia' (1999) 5(1) *Violence Against Women* 63, 67.

5 UNSC Res. 808, 48th sess., 3175th mtg, UN Doc. S/25240 (3 February 1993) annex I (*European Community Investigative Mission into the Treatment of Muslim Women in the Former Yugoslavia: Report to European Community Foreign Ministers*), para. 14.

6 Alexandra Stiglemayer (ed.), *Mass Rape: The War Against Women in Bosnia-Herzegovina* (University of Nebraska Press, 1994).

7 Nikolic-Ristanovic, above n 4, 67.

By 1993, the reported numbers varied widely, with estimates ranging from 12,000 to 70,000.[8] On 5 January 1994, the United Nations (UN) General Assembly adopted a special resolution stating that the

> systematic practice of rape was used as a weapon of war and an instrument of ethnic cleansing against women and children in the areas of armed conflicts in former Yugoslavia, and especially against the Bosniak women and children in BiH.[9]

In 1994, the Commission of Experts created by the United Nations Security Council (the *Bassiouni Report*), which had investigated allegations of sexual violence and other war crimes in BiH, asserted that probably about 20,000 women and girls had been raped.[10] According to the UN *Final Report of the Commission of Experts*, the majority of the cases were perpetrated by soldiers, paramilitary groups, local police and civilians, and occurred between the fall of 1991 and the end of 1993.[11] Still, even after this report was published, some scholars, such as Ruth Seifert, put the total figure of female rapes in BiH at 60,000.[12]

The *Bassiouni Report* also established that all parties of the war engaged in war rapes, but that Serb forces appeared most often among perpetrators, and Bosniak women most often among victims.[13] According to Bassiouni himself 'it is estimated that the large majority of reported victims were Bosnian Muslims . . . the second largest group of victims is unidentified as to ethnic background . . . the third group is Bosnian Serbs, followed by Croats'.[14] It was then established that while all parties to the armed conflict perpetrated CRSV, the largest numbers of reported victims were Bosniaks and the largest number of alleged perpetrators were Bosnian Serbs.[15] The *Bassiouni Report* remains today one of the most authoritative and comprehensive reports into the investigation

8 UNHCR, *Report of the Commission on Human Rights on Its First Special Session*, UN Doc E/CN.4/1992/2-1/8 (14 August 1992) annex 2, para. 30; UNGA, 'World Conference on Human Rights: Report of the Secretary-General' (World Conference on Human Rights Vienna, 14–25 June 1993) A/CONF.157/23 (13 October 1993).

9 UNGA, *Rape and Abuse of the Women in the Areas of Armed Conflict in the Former Yugoslavia*, A/RES/48/143 (5 January 1994).

10 UNSC, *Letter Dated 24 May 1994 from the Secretary-General to the President of the Security Council*, UN Doc S/1994/674 (27 May 1994). The Commission was established on 6 October 1992 by the UNSC Resolution 780.

11 UNSC, *Final Report of the Commission of Experts Established Pursuant to Security Council Resolution 780 (1992)*, Annex 241 n. 65, U.N. Doc. S/1994/674 (1994).

12 Ruth Seifert, 'The Second Front: The Logic of Sexual Violence in War' (1996) 19(1–2) *Women Studies International Forum* 35.

13 UNSC, above n 11, para. 563.

14 M. Cherif Bassiouni and Marcia McCormick, *Sexual Violence: An Invisible Weapon of War in the Former Yugoslavia, Occasional Paper No. 1* (International Human Rights Law Institute, DePaul University College of Law, 1996) 10.

15 UNSC, above n 10, para. 251.

of sexual violence during the war in BiH.[16] The European Commission, which was fully mandated to focus solely on the investigation of alleged abuses of Bosniak women in BiH emphasised that it is, 'important to place on record its view that rape and sexual assault are restricted to neither nationality nor gender'.[17]

Even today, more than 20 years since the war ended in BiH, there is no official data on the exact numbers of women victims of CRSV. While indicative, numbers remain approximations due to a number of factors: stigma, shame, political interference, migration and displacement, trauma and the killing of women after rape had been committed.[18] In addition, due to the paucity and loss of evidence, lack of witnesses coming forward, and also due to age, poor health or suicide by some women victims,[19] it is impossible to come to any conclusive and definite numbers. Nevertheless, from very early on reports were confirming suspicion of 'a deliberate pattern'.[20]

The fact that BiH does not have official statistics on women victims of CRSV is not, however, something unique to this post-conflict country. For example, almost 20 years after the so-called 'comfort women' spoke up for the first time about their ordeals, the precise number of women who went through the Japanese military sexual slavery system is still unknown.[21] Almost 20 years after the armed conflict in Kosovo ceased, the number of women victims also remains unknown. As Lepa Mladjenović, a long-term feminist activist argues: 'none of the statistics in the world register raped women – only women who are concerned for women talk about them'.[22]

Despite the improbability of asserting any accurate figure of women victims, the *numbers* played an important part in galvanising international attention on the issue of wartime rape in BiH. The early statistics released by the European Commission have been accepted as general knowledge and repeatedly cited in almost any local and international document, study and media outlet that discusses CRSV in BiH.

16 Sara Sharratt, *Gender, Shame and Sexual Violence: The Voices of Witnesses and Court Members at War Crimes Tribunals* (Routledge, 2011) 8.

17 Women Aid International, *Warburton Mission II Report: EC Investigative Mission into the Treatment of Muslim Women in the Former Yugoslavia: Report to EC Foreign Ministers*, Ministry of Foreign Affairs Copenhagen (1993), www.womenaid.org/press/info/humanrights/warburtonfull.htm, para. 9.

18 Amnesty International, *Bosnia and Herzegovina: Rape and Sexual Abuse by Armed Forces*, Report (1993), www.amnesty.org/en/documents/eur63/001/1993/en/ noted that 'according to some reports or allegations of rape, victims were later killed. Since few corpses are subject to autopsies in Bosnia and Herzegovina, it is probable that much evidence of rape . . . is hidden or lost', 3.

19 In July and December 2015 two Serb women victims of wartime sexual violence committed suicide in Sarajevo and Bratunac. Email from a representative of an association from RS who works with women victims of CRSV, 16 January 2016.

20 Women Aid International, above n 17.

21 The estimations are from 'several thousands to 200,000' women rounded up in rape camps by the Japanese army in WWII, Yoshimi Yoshiaki, *Comfort Women: Sexual Slavery in the Japanese Military During World War II* (Columbia University Press, 1995).

22 Lepa Mladjenović, 'Nacrt projekta za centar za žene silovane u ratu' [Trans: 'The Draft of Project for the Centre for Women Raped During the War'] *Žene za Žene* (1993) 108.

This was despite the fact that the report suggested that the numbers put forward are nothing more than an approximation, since some women were raped, tortured and then killed, some women disappeared and some never reported the crime. Statistics remains ambiguous and to this day neither the exact number of raped women, nor the ethnicity of each woman victim is known, and most likely will never be. Unlike data on battle deaths, the counts of acts of rapes or of the number of victims are only rarely available.[23] However, parallel with attempts to document these crimes, the estimation of numbers has been continuously used and misused for political purposes.[24] The numbers also preoccupied feminist scholars who wrote about CRSV in BiH.

Highly publicised rapes, followed by women victim's emerging stories, galvanised social and international community attention. The emphasis was on the quantity of crimes and the reportedly mass and systematic nature of the rapes, suggesting that these might have been committed pursuant to orders,[25] and this changed the international legal landscape and attracted global attention. The bureaucracy of counting women and grouping rape with 'ethnic cleansing' and later genocide, has been vital in identifying Bosniak women as the almost exclusive victims of rape. According to Vesna Nikolić Ristanović, the collection and publication of the high numbers of rapes sparked off a chain reaction of hostility and hatred in which all – Croats, Serbs and Bosniaks – took part and that, in turn, most likely led to more rape being committed.[26] As Renata Salecl argues:

> The question over the exact number of victims became a battle for the interpretation of the war. Scaling down the numbers or augmenting them became ways for the two sides, after the war, to continue the conflict by means of statistics.[27]

23 Dara Kay Cohen, *Rape During Civil War* (Cornell University, 2016) 66.

24 See, for example, Vesna Nikolić-Ristanović, *Women, Violence and War: Wartime Victimization of Refugees in the Balkans* (Central European University Press, 2000) 41–46; Dorothy Q. Thomas and Ralph E. Regan, 'Rape in War: Challenging the Tradition of Impunity' (1994) 14(1) *SAIS Review* 81, 93; Amnesty International noted that the issue of rape had 'been used as a propaganda weapon, with all sides minimizing or denying the abuses committed by their own forces and maximizing those of their opponents'. Amnesty International considers, therefore, that all estimates as to the number of women who have suffered rape or sexual abuse must be treated with caution. See Amnesty International, above n 18, 6.

25 On the role of international community in galvanising the topic of mass rape in BiH, see Grace Harbour, 'International Concern Regarding Conflict-Related Sexual Violence in the Lead-Up to the ICTY's Establishment' in Baron Serge Brammertz and Michelle Jarvis (eds), *Prosecuting Conflict-Related Sexual Violence at the ICTY* (Oxford University Press, 2016) 20–24.

26 Vesna Nikolić-Ristanović, 'From Sisterhood to Non Recognition: Instrumentalization of Women's Suffering in the War in the Former Yugoslavia' (Paper presented at Women's Discourses, War Discourses, Ljubljana Graduate School of the Humanities, 2–6 December 1997) cited in Skjelsbæk, above n 2, 65.

27 Renata Salecl, 'War Trauma Twenty Years After: From Bosnia to St. Louis' (2016) 28 *Journal of the Centre for Freudian Analysis and Research* 8.

The majority of international academic literature and media reports would often acknowledge the rape of all women, but often only in passing before concentrating on the 'bigger numbers': 'All sides in the conflict used this terror tactic, but by most accounts, rape was most inflicted on Muslim women by Bosnian Serb men as part of their "ethnic cleansing" campaign.'[28] Some authors, such as Elizabeth Kohn, went even further by reporting that 'Serbian forces [alone] have raped an estimated 20,000 to 50,000 Bosnian Muslim women during the armed conflict.'[29] Such reporting has exacerbated the difficulty of not only acknowledging but also emphasising and taking an interest in Serb women's experiences of CRSV. Although it is still questionable how many women survived wartime rape, according to Silva Meznaric:

> One could say that there is agreement in the sources concerning several important points: (1) mass rape had at least several thousand victims; (2) there have been many rapes of young girls between the ages of seven and fourteen; (3) rape is often committed in the presence of the victim's parents/children and generally the rape victim is raped by several assailants.[30]

The power of ***numbers*** continues to play an importance in today's BiH. For example, the statistical data on the numbers of civilian victims of CRSV in Federation of Bosnia and Herzegovina (FBiH) includes both women and men who were sexually tortured and abused during the war in BiH.[31] However, this number in official reports and other outlets is often not segregated by sex, but cited almost exclusively as 'women only'.[32]

The women victims

The rape of women was used as a weapon of war and a deliberate military strategy in order to spread terror, destabilise the civilian population, and

28 Marlise Simons, 'An Ex-Bosnian Serb Commander Admits rape of Muslims in War', *New York Times* (online), 10 March 1998, www.nytimes.com/1998/03/10/world/an-ex-bosnian-serb-commander-admits-rape-of-muslims-in-war.html.

29 Elizabeth A. Kohn, 'Rape as a Weapon of War: Women's Human Rights During the Dissolution of Yugoslavia' (1994) 24 *Golden Gate University Law Review* 199.

30 Silva Meznaric, 'Gender as Ethno-Marker: Rape, War and Identity in the Former Yugoslavia' in Valentine M. Moghadam (ed.), *Identity Politics and Women: Cultural Reassertion and Feminisms in International Perspectives* (Westview Press, 1994) 76, 92.

31 There has been hardly any scholarly analysis about male victims of wartime rape in BiH. See Dubravka Žarkov, 'The Body of the Other Man: Sexual Violence and the Construction of Masculinity, Sexuality and Ethnicity in Croatian Media' in Caroline Moser and Fiona Clark (eds), *Victims, Perpetrators or Actors? Gender, Armed Conflict and Political Violence* (Zed Books, 2001) 69; Olivera Simić, 'Wartime Rape and Its Shunned Victims' in Amy E. Randall (ed.), *Genocide and Gender in the Twentieth Century: A Comparative Survey* (Bloomsbury, 2015) 237.

32 Email from the government representative, who wanted to stay anonymous, and who works for the Federal Ministry of Labour and Social Policy, 25 December 2013.

reward soldiers.[33] It was a tool of ethnic cleansing where sexual violence against women, in particular Bosniak women, was used to humiliate their ethnic group.[34] In the *Kunarac* case, the ICTY found, for the first time in judicial history, that rape was 'used by members of the Bosnian Serb armed forces as an instrument of terror'.[35] Although CRSV in BiH had been systematically aimed at Bosniak women, Serb women too, according to Inger Skjelsbaek, were raped.[36] Yet, these rapes did not attract the serious attention of researchers.

The international community and the media quickly picked up the issue of rape in BiH, spreading the word around the world. In BiH, but also in the other countries of the former Yugoslavia, rape was made a national issue by the major nationalistic parties who used the rape of a woman as a metaphor for the rape of a country.[37] Vesna Kesic argues, for example, that 'a raped Croat or Bosniak woman stands for a raped Croatia or Bosnia'.[38] In this way, the women's bodies became part of male nationalist politics that strengthened sectarian ethnic identities. Rape was never a 'simple' rape of a woman by a man; it was always given a national context: it was rape of a Bosniak woman by a Serb man, or a Croat woman by a Serb man. The CRSV towards Bosniak women, in particular, has remained a focus of the international media and academia until today, prompting well-known feminist academics, such as Catharine MacKinnon, to lobby the international community to take up the cause.[39] This 'intellectual activism' together with civil society was able to keep the issue alive in the press, to shape how the situation was perceived, and defined who were considered the chief victims and who the chief perpetrators in the BiH war.

As former journalist and political analyst Diana Johnston argued:

> [a]s the war in Bosnia-Herzegovina got under way in mid-1992, American journalists who reported unconfirmed stories of Serbian authorities could count on getting published with a chance of a Pulitzer Prize . . . It became increasingly impossible to challenge the dominant interpretation in major media. Editors naturally prefer to keep the story simple: one villain, and as much blood as possible.[40]

33 Rhonda Copelon, 'Surfacing Gender: Reconceptualizing Crimes against Women in Time of War' in Lois Ann Lorentzen and Jennifer Turpin (eds), *The Women and War Reader* (New York University Press, 1998) 63, 64.

34 Jennifer Turpin, 'Many Faces: Women Confronting War' in Lois Ann Lorentzen and Jennifer Turpin (eds), *The Women and War Reader* (New York University Press, 1999) 32; Copelon, above n 33, 63, 69.

35 *Prosecutor v Kunarac et al.*, Case No IT-96-23, Judgment, 12 June 2002.

36 Skjelsbæk, above n 2, 63.

37 Vesna Kesić, 'Muslim Women, Croatian Women, Serbian Women, Albanian Women', *Eurozine* (online), 5 September 2003, www.eurozine.com/articles/2003-05-09-kesic-en.html.

38 Ibid.

39 Kate Ferguson, 'Masking Genocide in Bosnia' in Cathie Carmichael and Richard Maguire (eds), *The Routledge History of Genocide* (Routledge, 2015) 309, 316.

40 Diana Johnstone, 'Seeing Yugoslavia Through a Dark Glass' (1998) Fall *Covert Action Quarterly* 9.

Some of the reasons asserted as to why research into CRSV has been restricted to the experiences of Bosniak women, has been put forward by Inger Skjelsbaek:

> While it is a well-established fact that Serb and Croat women were also victims of similar forms of sexual violence during the war, this study draws its empirical findings from interviews with Bosniak women. There are pragmatic reasons for this choice. Though many of the local organizations I contacted aim to be multi-ethnic, there are simply more Bosniak women members of such organizations than members from other nationalities. It was therefore easier to get in touch with Bosniak women who were willing to talk than to contact similar women from other nationalities.[41]

Skjelsbaek's statement is important because it tells us that most women's local organisations in BiH gather mostly Bosniak women survivors. As a result, even if a researcher wanted to interview the 'other' women, it would be difficult or even impossible to locate them.[42] Until recently there was no local women's non-government organisation (NGO) in Republika Srpska (RS) that gathered women survivors of CRSV. Still, if researchers wanted to reach these women, they could do so through other women's NGOs that have the contact details of women survivors willing to talk about their experiences.[43]

Many women in BiH were imprisoned, tortured and raped repeatedly in private homes and units known as 'rape camps' – the term that was infamously introduced into the reporting and documenting of these acts of violence, that were far from being seeing as random.[44] Already in 1994, it was documented that camps were established by all sides: Bosniak, Croat and Serb alike.[45] Most women were subjected to gang rapes and often repeatedly raped, and usually released only when pregnant. Many women have never been identified as victims of rape by domestic or international courts. Women who were held in these places have often stayed invisible and were never identified and registered by international organisations such as the International Committee of the Red Cross.[46] They were sexually, and otherwise, abused in community properties such as schools, hotels, stadiums, military barracks or sports halls, by all of the

41 Inger Skjelsbæk, 'Victim and Survivor: Narrated Social Identities of Women who Experienced Rape During the War in Bosnia-Hezegovina' (2006) 16(4) *Feminism and Psychology* 373, 378.

42 See Janine Natalya Clark, 'Working with Survivors of War Rape and Sexual Violence: Fieldwork Reflections from Bosnia-Hercegovina' (2016) (online) *Qualitative Research*.

43 This study would not have been possible without these contacts.

44 Skjelsbæk, above n 2, 64.

45 Stiglemayer, above n 6, 115.

46 According to M. Đ., who was in a rape camp in Modriča (camp 'Strolit'), women and their children were exchanged just before the ICRC representatives came. She was 'released' and exchanged on 4 July 1992, together with 52 other Serb women and their children. The original copy of the exchange list, detailing the names of all women and children 'exchanged', is on file with the author. Interview with M. Đ. in Banjaluka, 15 July 2013.

warring parties.[47] In order to avoid their registration, women would be 'released' from these camps – exchanged for male war prisoners – often before the international journalists or aid workers were able to take any notice of them.[48]

Due to such tactics, the women were not recorded in any statistics, their victimisation stayed invisible. Since these rape camps were scattered throughout the country, many of them remained unidentified. Only a handful of notorious rape camps have become known to the local and international public. Some were even unknown to women activists I talked to in the course of my fieldwork. It seems that if these places had not been brought to the attention of the ICTY, they would have largely stayed unknown to the public outside BiH, and sometimes to locals too.[49]

Justice

Since the ICTY started its work, 78 individuals, or 48 per cent of the 161 accused, have had charges of sexual violence included in their indictments.[50] As of September 2016, 32 individuals had been convicted for their responsibility for crimes of sexual violence, as defined under Article 7(1) of the ICTY Statute.[51] Their sentences range from 3 to 40 years of prison. Four of them were additionally convicted for failing to prevent or punish the actual perpetrators of the crimes, under Article 7(3) of the statute.[52]

Between 2005 and 2013, only around 76 cases before domestic courts involved charges of sexual violence.[53] Out of these 76 cases, the BiH Court concluded 36 cases of wartime sexual violence, convicting 33 perpetrators and

47 It is a well-known fact that Serbs ran these camps for non-Serb women. There are also reports that Bosniak and Croat armies and paramilitary forces ran brothels and rape camps too. A number of reports also alleged the operation of private prisons controlled by various Bosniak and Croat forces or individuals. See: UNSC, above n 10, paras 151–305; Ivana Nizich, 'Violations of the Rules of War by Bosnian Croat and Muslim Forces in Bosnia-Herzegovina' (1994) 5(1) *Hastings Women Law Journal* 25.

48 Several Serb women interviewees told me the stories of 'release' or exchange with male war prisoners from the 'other side'. They had not seen any international representatives while held in captivity.

49 Rape camps such as 'Strolit' in Modriča, the primary school 'Bratstvo Jedinstvo', and other locations have not been analysed in scholarly work and were not known to many activists who I spoke to during my fieldwork in Serbia and Sarajevo. The well-known international organisation TRIAL, based in Sarajevo, did not know about rape camps for Serb women in Posavina either. Scholarly work on rape camps in BiH has been largely based on the ICTY jurisprudence.

50 UN ICTY, *In Numbers*, www.icty.org/sid/10586 (as at September 2016).

51 Ibid.

52 Article 7(3): 'The fact that any of the acts referred to in articles 2 to 5 of the present Statute was committed by a subordinate does not relieve his superior of criminal responsibility if he knew or had reason to know that the subordinate was about to commit such acts or had done so and the superior failed to take the necessary and reasonable measures to prevent such acts or to punish the perpetrators thereof.'

53 OSCE, *Combating Impunity for Conflict-Related Sexual Violence in BiH: Progress and Challenges: An Analysis of Criminal Proceedings before the Court of Bosnia and Herzegovina between 2005 and 2013*, OSCE Mission to Bosnia and Herzegovina (2014), www.files.ethz.ch/isn/179069/English.pdf.

acquitting 12 individuals. The rest of the cases – 30 in total – were prosecuted before entity courts in FBiH, the RS and the Brčko District. At the end of 2013, according to the Organization for Security and Cooperation in Europe (OSCE), indictments in a further 18 cases have been confirmed and 'many more such cases are under investigation'.[54] The vast majority of wartime rape crimes, however, remain unpunished and many have not even been acknowledged.[55] Although the BiH domestic jurisdiction has the highest completed number of cases involving CRSV, having in mind the magnitude of these crimes, the fact remains that the majority of perpetrators enjoy impunity,[56] and the thousands of victims have been denied access to justice, reparation and redress. According to the former UN Special Representative on Sexual Violence in Conflict, Margaret Wallstroem, there is a significant gap between the number of CRSV crimes committed during the war in BiH and the number of cases prosecuted over the years following the conflict.[57]

This, unfortunately, is not a surprise, since it is a well-known fact that prosecutions of CRSV remain the exception, and that they very rarely work as a deterrent.[58] Too often, CRSV crimes are removed from a list of indictments due to the difficulties of establishing evidence in these cases, which are resource-intensive.[59] These crimes have been neglected for too long due to historical silence, which is now combined with obstacles to prosecution. The institutional barriers equally impede their investigation and prosecution and make 'the legal process . . . painfully slow'.[60] For these reasons, CRSV continues to be under-represented in proceedings and judgements before international and domestic courts.[61]

54 Ibid., 8–9.

55 British Embassy Sarajevo, *Legacy of Wartime Sexual Violence in Bosnia Still Far From Addressed* (2013), GOV.UK, www.gov.uk/government/world-location-news/legacy-of-wartime-sexual-violence-in-bosnia-still-far-from-addressed.

56 OSCE, above n 52, 9.

57 Margot Wallstroem reportedly stated that 'there might be as much as 50,000 to 60,000 cases of sexual violence and only 12 have been prosecuted so far'. See Sabina Arslanagić, 'Justice for Wartime Rape Victims in Bosnia "Painfully Slow"', *Balkan Insight* (online), 29 November 2010, www.balkaninsight.com/en/article/justice-for-victims-of-war-time-rapes-in-bosnia-painfully-slow.

58 Rauði Krossinn Islandi, 'ICRC Lecture: Sexual Violence in Armed Conflict & Other Situations of Violence' 10 December 2013, www.youtube.com/watch?v=X4Iv9oMd-FQ.

59 On scholarly analysis of reasons why CRSV charges may be dropped from indictments see Michelle Jarvis and Kate Vigneswaran, 'Challenges to Successful Outcomes in Sexual Violent Cases' in Serge Brammertz and Michelle Jarvis (eds), *Prosecuting Conflict-Related Sexual Violence at the ICTY* (Oxford University Press, 2016) 33. The authors note that 'the simple reality of resource constraints in combination with the overwhelming volume of criminality at issue meant leaving out many sexual violence charges', 55.

60 Margot Wallstroem reportedly stated in Arslanagić, above n 57.

61 Saeeda Verrall, 'The Picture of Sexual Violence in the Former Yugoslavia Conflicts as Reflected in ICTY Judgments' in Serge Brammertz and Michelle Jarvis (eds), *Prosecuting Conflict-Related Sexual Violence at the ICTY* (Oxford University Press, 2016) 299. Jarvis and Vigneswaran, above n 59, 33. The authors note that 'the simple reality of resource constraints in combination with the overwhelming volume of criminality at issue meant leaving out many sexual violence charges' 55.

In contrast to Serbs, who had a policy of 'ethnic cleansing' that included the establishment of rape camps and forced impregnation of women, the Bosniak army did not have such a strategy, so these crimes were seen as random rather than as a tool of government policy.[62] As Jelke Boesten argues, if sexual violence does not fit 'the rape-as-a-weapon-of-war thesis' it stays largely invisible 'because they are not considered violence by either perpetrator or victims'.[63] Still, evidence exists that the Croatian army soldiers adopted a pattern of practising systematic rape in 1993, when engaged in wide-scale rape at the infamous Croat camp, Dretelj.[64] In Dretelj camp, women were told they would not be released until they had given birth to an *ustaša* (Croatian fascist).[65] The crimes of CRSV, committed by the Croatian army in the Posavina and Herzegovina regions against Serb women, have only recently started to be prosecuted before domestic courts. So far, they have not attracted international attention.

Victims of CRSV remain traumatised in many ways. Some of their perpetrators still walk free around the country, and in many cases live in close proximity to the victims. Often those responsible for their suffering – members of the military forces, the police, paramilitary groups and others (many of whom remained in positions of power) – live in the same community as their victims. Some perpetrators plea-bargained or were released after serving only two-thirds of their sentence because of 'good behaviour'.[66] The ICTY President, Theodor Meron, has granted release to the majority of convicted perpetrators 'particularly, where the person has served two-thirds of the sentence', despite being convicted of heinous crimes.[67] Anto Furundžija, for example, was the commander of a special unit of the Croatian Defence Council called 'the Jokers'. Furundžija was found guilty of aiding and abetting the war crime of outrages upon personal dignity, including rape.[68] The President granted his early release due to 'impeccable behaviour in prison and expression of remorse', which established 'the strong likelihood that Mr Furundžija will successfully reintegrate himself into the community upon the

62 Stiglemayer, above n 6, xii.

63 Jelke Boesten, *Sexual Violence During War and Peace: Gender, Power, and Post-Conflict Justice in Peru* (Palgrave Macmillan, 2014) 35.

64 See, for example, the case of *Ivan Zelenika and Others v Prosecutor*, Court BiH, 14 April 2015, Judgment for crimes against humanities in Dretelj camp; the case of Marjan Brnjić on going before the Court of BiH for the rape of Serb women in Odžak, see Srđan Kureljušić, 'Visestruka silovanja u Posavskoj Mahali' [Trans: 'Multiple Rape in Posavina Mahala'], *Justice Report* (online), 6 April 2016, www.justice-report.com/bh/sadr%C5%BEaj-%C4%8Dlanci/prije-optu%C5%BEenog-je-silovala-jo%C5%A1-%C4%8Detvorica.

65 Nikolić-Ristanović, above n 24, 61.

66 On the early release of war criminals see Barbora Holá and Joris van Wijk, 'Life After Conviction at International Criminal Tribunals: An Empirical Overview' (2014) 12(1) *Journal of International Criminal Justice* 109.

67 Gideon Boas, James L. Bischoff, Natalie L. Reid and B. Don Taylor, *International Criminal Law Practitioner Library Volume III* (Cambridge University Press, 2011) 417.

68 *The Prosecutor v Anto Furundžija*, Case No. IT-95-17/1-T Judgment, 10 December 1998.

release'.[69] The local media reported that Furundžija was released in August 2004 after serving two-thirds of his 10-year sentence.[70]

Once the perpetrators of CRSV are released, they often return to their community and women survivors can meet them on the street again. Lj. L., a recently deceased Bosnian Serb survivor of wartime CRSV and torture, was in the Posavina region rape camp in 1992 with her three young children and reported that she could see her perpetrators on a daily basis.[71] M.Đ. reported the same – whenever she goes to Odžak she can see her abusers walking freely in the town.[72] M. and other women survivors can meet their perpetrators in their villages or when they go to the shop or market.[73] She spent two months in the rape camp established by the Croatian Army in May 1992. She was forced to leave her village with her three young children, the youngest her baby daughter Lj.:

> None of them have been prosecuted so far. I see them when I go to Odžak. They walk around as if nothing has happened. I am always ready to give testimony before the courts. I want to see them accountable for what they did. I went through hell for two months . . . I weighed 68kg – when I was exchanged I was 48kg. I was two months in their hands but I cannot get status of civil victim and compensation. Only my youngest daughter who was nine months at the time has got that status and receives a pension.[74]

The histories of violence these women survived reverberate into peacetime daily life. Women's experiences in war shape their lives after the war, which can hardly equate to 'peace'.[75] Their lives are determined by the social framework they are part of and by the violent political structures of gender inequality that have not been addressed after the war.[76]

The silence

Many women survivors, regardless of their ethnic background, have never talked about their experience of CRSV and many will forever stay silent because they have no institutional and/or family support to speak up. They have many reasons to hide their stories and very few to tell them. Women survivors in RS have

69 *The Prosecutor v Anto Furundžija*, Case No. IT-95-17/1, 29 July 2004, Order of the President on the Application for the Early Release of Anto Furundžija.

70 Radio Široki Brijeg, 'Furundžija na slobodi' [Trans: 'Furundžija at Large'], *Radio Široki Brijeg* (online), 17 August 2004, www.radiosirokibrijeg.com/arhiv/1394-furundzija-na-slobodi-1394.

71 D. M., 'RS: Zaštita žena – žrtava ratnog nasilja' [Trans: 'RS: Protection of Women – Victims of War Violence'], *Večernje Novosti* (online), 16 January 2013.

72 Interview with M. Đ. (Banjaluka, 14 July 2014).

73 Arslanagic, above n 57.

74 Interview with M. Đ. (Banjaluka, 18 July 2014).

75 Chris Coulter, *Bush Wives and Girl Soldiers, Women's Lives Through War and Peace in Sierra Leone* (Cornell University Press, 2009).

76 Boesten, above n 63, 9.

only recently started to speak up; those who have remained silent for the past 20 years.[77] Many are unemployed with no access to health services and psychological support, particularly in remote areas of the country.[78] Many women still feel stigmatised and ashamed and need to be told that there is nothing to feel shame about – their perpetrators must bear all the embarrassment for what they have done. Unfortunately, a number of women survivors have died without any support and recognition, and many others do not have long to wait before it is also too late for them to see any form of justice. Despite a message by the ICTY that it is necessary to understand justice in a broader sense 'as something that transcends tribunals and as encompassing the need to somehow redress what had happened to the victims',[79] many victims in BiH are still in favour of retributive justice.

It has been more than two decades since the acts of CRSV were committed in BiH, and some women have also willingly or unwillingly relocated to other countries. As a long-term activist from the RS told me:

> Novi Grad is a town from which the majority of the population of former camp survivors migrated to Australia. Many women did not want to take part in proceedings and did not want to testify. The largest number of rape crimes occurred in that area; the towns of Modriča and Odžak. We worked with these women. I know a mother and daughter (who was 14 at the time) who were raped.[80]

As she explained, these women have little or no incentive to testify before the courts. Due to displacement and migration abroad, it has been difficult for the courts to locate witnesses and victims, but sometimes, even if they succeed in doing so, some women have not been willing to come and testify. In fact, some women who resettled in other countries have done so in order to avoid the possibility of testifying altogether and being part of criminal proceedings. Many potential witnesses have reportedly argued that they want to 'move on' with their lives and 'avoid stirring old antagonism'.[81]

The judges and prosecutors are well aware of the fact that with the beginning of a new life 'the people have a hard time deciding to testify'.[82] Many women

77 UNGA, *Report of the Special Rapporteur on Violence Against Women, Its Causes and Consequences, Rashida Manjoo*, A/HRC/23/49/Add.3 (4 June 2013), www.ohchr.org/Documents/HRBodies/HRCouncil/RegularSession/Session23/A-HRC-23-49-Add3_en.pdf.

78 Amnesty International, *Whose Justice? The Women of Bosnia and Herzegovina Are Still Waiting*, Report (2009), www.amnesty.org/en/documents/EUR63/006/2009/en/ 3.

79 Sara Sharratt, 'Interview with Elizabeth Odio Benito, Justice of the International Criminal Tribunal for the Former Yugoslavia' in Sara Sharratt and Ellyn Kaschak (eds), *Assault on the Soul: Women in the Former Yugoslavia* (Haworth Press, 1999) 39, 47.

80 Interview with Z. B. (16 December 2015).

81 Patricia M. Wald, 'Dealing with Witnesses in War Crime Trials: Lessons from the Yugoslav Tribunal' (2002) 5 *Yale Human Rights and Development Journal* 217, 220.

82 Vesna Kaknjo, 'Glavna Tužiteljica' ['The Key Prosecutor'], www.nasarijec.ba/index.php?option=com_content&view=article&id=2162:vesna-kaknjo-glavna-tuiteljica-kantonalnog-tuilatva-zenica&catid=69:interview&Itemid=86.

victims have no wish to expose themselves to any risk of being stigmatised or even threatened by perpetrators still enjoying their freedom,[83] but want to move on and not relive their experiences. The local judiciary offers little guarantee of safety for women who testify, or any form of compensation for the damage they have suffered.[84]

All women survivors of CRSV live with difficult traumatic experiences and long-lasting consequences of trauma. Those who live in RS, in particular, have no systematic, organised and free psychological (or other) support. They feel isolated, forgotten and neglected by the community and the government. They are the subject of both, formal and informal social ostracism.

Ethnic polarisation among women survivors

The stories of Serb women survivors were in the most part downplayed, trivialised and even justified as some sort of 'deserved' revenge.[85] As Kelly Askin argues: 'the crimes against them [Serb women] are excused, simply because they are associated with a group which has reportedly committed the majority of atrocities'.[86] Elissa Helms in her book *Innocence and Victimhood*, carefully problematises binary and simplistic representations of 'victim' and 'perpetrator' in BiH.[87] In the course of her field work, she finds that even some Bosniak women survivors blamed Serb women of nurturing their male children (later to become adult warriors) in a culture of violence and death and (Serb) nationalism: 'their wives/women simply bring up their children this way [encouraging violence] and they find those kinds of husbands'.[88] Serb women seem to be portrayed not only as collective 'guilty bystanders' but also as facilitators and active supporters of violence. Dubravka Zarkov, in her extensive media analysis of wartime press in Serbia and Croatia, in relation to rape victims and how they are linked to the definition of ethnicity, argues: 'The only status Muslim women had in these texts was the victim-status. Serb women were not only invisible as rape victims, but were explicitly denied victim-status, and were even described as instigators

83 Interview with a psychologist working with the victim support unit in one of the courts in RS (telephone interview, 12 December 2013).

84 Only three verdicts at state-level war crimes cases have ordered payment to victims of CRSV, but none of the victims have received any compensation yet. See Justice Report, 'Bosnian War Rape Victims Struggle for Compensation', *Balkan Insight* (online), 9 September 2016, www.balkaninsight.com/en/article/bosnian-war-rape-victims-struggle-for-compensation-09-09-2016.

85 Kelly Dawn Askin, *War Crimes Against Women: Prosecution in International War Crimes Tribunals* (Martinus Nijhoff, 1997) 287.

86 Ibid.

87 Elissa Helms, *Innocence and Victimhood: Gender, Nation, and Women's Activism in Postwar Bosnia-Herzegovina* (University of Wisconsin Press, 2013). See also, Elisa Helms, 'The Gender of Coffee: Women, Refugee Return, and Reconciliation Initiatives after the Bosnian War' (2007) 7 (57) *Focaal – European Journal of Anthropology*) 17–32.

88 Ibid., 136.

or even perpetrators of violence.'[89] There is a presumption of Serb collective guilt[90] that prevents seeing Serb women as potential victims of war crimes generally and CRSV in particular. While some Serb women may be reluctant to acknowledge the rape camps established for Bosniak women, Bosniak women also show 'little readiness' to speak about Čelebići or Dretelj camps where Serb women were detained and raped.[91]

According to Natalya Janine Clark, some Bosniak women reported that they had never heard of infamous Čelebići camp and insist that 50,000 Bosniak women were raped during the war.[92] Rape of Bosniak women has become a 'moral capital' for Bosniaks as a nation and for BiH as a state, and women's victimhood has been used for advancing the state's political and religious prospectus. For example, the recent launch of a movie about the rapes of Bosniak women[93] and a monograph about CRSV in BiH[94] were both organised in the library of Gazi Husrev-beg mosque in Sarajevo. Coupled with the Srebrenica genocide, the rapes of Bosniak women have become the foundation for building the fragile state of BiH and Bosniak national identity after the war. Enes Hotić, director of the movie *Pucanj u dušu* (A Shot in the Soul) reported:

> *Pucanj u dušu* was filmed in our homeland Bosnia and Herzegovina and is a shot in the soul for all those who truly embrace and love this country and consider it their homeland. My motivation, as a director was to archive the crimes that happened in our past so they do not happen to us again in future. Bosniaks as a people do not have the privilege or right to forget and it is on our shoulders to leave future generations a clear picture about the events that happened between 1992 and 1995.[95]

The production of this movie was possible with the support of the Association of Victims and Witnesses of Genocide and Mothers of Srebrenica through their

89 Dubravka Žarkov, 'Sexual Violence and War in Former Yugoslavia' (Paper presented at the Three Queens Debate: Gender-Based War Crimes, Cordaid, The Hague, January 2005), www.iccwomen.org/news/docs/CORDAID_Debate_Jan05_Zarkov.doc.

90 Robert Bideleux and Ian Jeffries argue 'there has been innumerable attempts to stigmatize the Serbs with collective guilt for the terrible atrocities carried out in their name by a vicious and callous minority of Serbs'. See Robert Bideleux and Ian Jeffries, *The Balkans: A Post-Communist History* (Routledge, 2007) 324.

91 Janine Natalya Clark, *International Trials and Reconciliation: Assessing the Impact of the International Criminal Tribunal for the Former Yugoslavia* (Routledge, 2015) 98.

92 Ibid., 99.

93 *Pucanj u dušu* (*Shot in the Soul*) (Directed by Enes Hotić, Exit Media Film, 2015); see Nedim Botić, 'Silovane žene – pucanj u dušu savjesti čovječanstva', *Aljazeera Balkans* (online), 12 December 2015, http://balkans.aljazeera.net/blog/silovane-zene-pucanj-u-dusu-savjesti-covjecanstva.

94 Vijesti.ba 'Promovisana monografija o ratnom silovanju i seksualnom zlostavljanju u BiH" [Trans. 'Promotion of the 'Monograph of War Rape and Sexual Abuse in BiH'], *Vijesti.ba* (online), 28 September 2015, http://vijesti.ba/clanak/279890/promovisana-monografija-o-ratnom-silovanju-i-seksualnom-zlostavljanju-u-bih.

95 *Pucanj u dušu* (*Shot in the Soul*), above n 93.

campaign 'With Film for Human Rights'. The aim of this campaign was to raise awareness in the community about the long-term consequences that such crimes left on Bosniak victims, witnesses and survivors of CRSV, committed during war.[96]

The movie serves as a reminder to the Bosniak population of crimes committed by their neighbours – Serbs – and is a tangible statement of a profoundly ethno-nationalist grievance about what happened to *Bosniak* women at the hands of *Serb* men. As such, it presents a political grievance about historical specificities and ethno-nationalist demand, not for reconciliation or forgiveness but to reflect the deep violence that Bosniaks, as Hotić stated 'have neither the privilege nor right to forget'.[97] The suffering of Bosniak women victims of rape is depicted and appropriated as the suffering of a whole ethno-nationalist group. The trauma of women is expected to be embraced as the collective trauma; as a key aspect of a Bosniak collective identity.

Božica Živković Rajilić, a Serb survivor of torture and director of the first-ever established NGO in RS that gathers primarily Serb women survivors of CRSV and torture, reported about her recent experience in one of her first meetings with Bosniak women victims:

> When we met with Brammertz[98]one Bosniak woman told him that she cannot be in the same room with genocidal Serbs and aggressors. When I asked her who is that aggressor, and why I was taken from my flat, sacked from my work and placed in detention, her comment and those of around her was: 'So, here you go, you deserved it.' From then on, when Brammertz is coming to visit we all go [Bosnia and Serb victim representatives] separately to talk to him.[99]

The division and ethnic polarisation between Serb and Bosniak women victims is seen also when it comes to the politics of supporting war criminals. In January 2016, the trial of Naser Orić started before the Court of BiH[100] and two groups of women came before the Court: one to support him and another with the hope that Orić would be found guilty for the crimes committed in the region of Podrinje. Radojka Filipović, director of the Association of Families of Detained and Killed Combatants and Missing Civilians from Bratunac stated:

96 Ibid.

97 Ibid.

98 Sergio Brammertz, the Chief Prosecutor of the ICTY.

99 Email communication with Božica Živković Rajilić, 10 September 2014.

100 Naser Orić is charged with killing Serb prisoners in 1992 in the area of Srebrenica and Bratunac, Eastern Bosnia. See Tanjug, 'War Crimes Trial of Naser Orić Begins in Bosnia', *Tanjug* (online), 26 January 2016, www.b92.net/eng/news/region.php?yyyy=2016&mm=01&dd=26&nav_id=96816. In 2008, the ICTY acquitted Naser Orić a former commander of the Army of Bosnia and Herzegovina from Srebrenica, of crimes committed between 1992 and 1993, crimes of killing Serb prisoners and wanton destruction of Serb villages. *Prosecutor v Naser Orić*, Case No. IT-03-68, Judgment, 3 July 2008.

> We came to the place where we could seek the truth about the killing of Serbs and where the final judgement has to be handed down for at least one killed Serb from the territories of Bratunac, Srebrenica, Milića, Sekovića, Vlasenice, Zvornik and for crimes committed by Muslims under the command of Naser Orić.[101]

On the other hand, Munira Subašić, the president of Mothers of Srebrenica and a representative of the other group that gathered reported: 'I don't want to say that there were not maybe some crimes [committed by Bosniaks], but these were committed in defence. The war crimes were not planned as it was the case from the Serb side.'[102] Assuming the role of the 'bigger' victim can entitle groups to justify their in-group violence, including what is viewed as defensive violence.[103] Such public reaction of Mothers of Srebrencia to Orić's arrest and lack of punishment for the crimes he committed can only be described as a reaffirmation that Bosniak survivors should not be accused of war crimes since their actions were only defensive or reactive.[104]

In post-conflict settings, this strategy can help groups deny responsibility for the harm done by them to the other group, given that competitive victimhood would portray their violence as provoked by the out-group.[105] The Bosniak-victim population largely consider themselves as 'innocent' or 'real' victims of war, which can perpetuate a powerful moral conception of victimhood.[106] The ICTY historical rulings and groundbreaking decisions have perhaps unintentionally contributed to fuelling further ethnic divisions and has created a hierarchy of crimes and victims that two decades later still holds strong. Downplaying the crimes committed by its 'own side' can drift into 'moral relativism', whereby groups or individuals blame the context, their situation or structural factors for committing atrocities.[107] As Luke Moffett argues, such perspectives and beliefs

101 Banjaluka.net, 'Završeno prvo ročište' [Trans: 'Finished First Hearing Oric: Mothers of Srebrenica Want to Testify'], *Banjaluka.net* (online), 26 January 2015, http://banjaluka.net/zavrseno-prvo-rociste-oricu-majke-srebrenice-zele-da-svjedoce/.

102 N1 BiH, 'Majke Srebrenice i porodice ubijenih Srba ispred Suda BiH' [Trans: 'Mothers of Srebrenica and the Families of Killed Serbs in Front of the Court'], *Vijesti* (online), 26 January 2016, http://ba.n1info.com/a78994/Vijesti/Vijesti/Majke-Srebrenice-i-porodice-ubijenih-Srba-ispred-Suda-BiH.html.

103 Daniel Bartal, Lily Chernyak-Hai, Noa Schori and Ayelet Gundar, 'A Sense of Self-Perceived Collective Victimhood in Intractable Conflicts' (2009) 91(874) *International Review of the Red Cross*, 229–258.

104 Jelena Subotic, *Hijacked Justice: Dealing with the Past in the Balkans* (Cornell University Press, 2009) 129.

105 Masi Noor, Nurit Shnabel, Samer Halabi and Arie Nadler, 'When Suffering Begets Suffering the Psychology of Competitive Victimhood Between Adversarial Groups in Violent Conflicts' (2012) 16(4) *Personality and Social Psychology Review* 351–374.

106 Erica Bouris, *Complex Political Victims* (Kumarian Press, 2007).

107 Kieran McEvoy and Kirsten McConnachie, 'Victims and Transitional Justice: Voice, Agency and Blame' (2013) 22(4) *Social & Legal Studies* 489, 502.

can impose collective guilt on groups and people, legitimise violence against individuals or deny recognition to certain victims.[108]

Bosniak survivors in Srebrenica and surrounding villages are reluctant to admit that Serb civilians had been killed and raped[109] in these areas too. The ICTY acquittal of Orić has been wrongly interpreted as meaning no crimes were committed against Serbs in the Srebrenica region. One Bosniak returnee was referring to the ICTY verdict as proof that Bosniaks were only defending themselves.[110] Overall, there seems to be a strong tendency to minimise crimes committed *against* the Serbs and compare them with a propensity to nullify their significance in relation to crimes committed *by* Serbs.[111] The culture of denial – 'the denial of truth about crimes that have been committed'[112] – and the lack of collective moral responsibility of members of a particular group for crimes committed against another group, is typical for members of all three ethnic groups in BiH. As Marko Milanović argues, 'denialism and revisionism are not just alive and well in the former Yugoslavia – they are thriving'.[113]

The crimes against Serbs in general, and against Serb women in particular, are perceived as 'less of a crime' and as something that was necessary to be done, in self-defence. As such, Serbs could not, and still are not perceived as victims. As a Serb woman survivor of CRSV told me:

> They [Bosniak women] will never say that Serb women were victims too but that we have 'blood ties' with perpetrators so we are perpetrators too. They think we 'deserved' what we got. They never said publically that members of their ethnic group committed crimes and I said that I am sorry for all women victims.[114]

These narratives align with surveys done in BiH, according to which in RS the dominant narrative is that everyone suffered and everybody is to blame, while 87 per cent of the respondents in the FBiH blame Serbs as 'the greatest perpetrators of crime during conflict'.[115] In her recent empirical research with Bosniak survivors from Srebrenica, Tuzla and Sarajevo, Sabina Čehajić-Clancy, a social psychologist, reported that '[Bosniaks] don't see a need for their group to apologise to others

108 Luke Moffett, 'Reparations for "Guilty Victims": Navigating Complex Identities of Victim-Perpetrators in Reparation Mechanisms' (2016) 10(1) *International Journal of Transitional Justice* 146, 149.
109 One of my interlocutors was a Serb woman, now in her early seventies, who was raped in Srebrenica.
110 Clark, above n 90, 98.
111 Ibid., 99.
112 See Nenad Dimitrijević, *Duty to Respond: Mass Crime, Denial and Collective Responsibility* (CEU Press, 2011).
113 Marko Milanović, 'The Impact of the ICTY on the Former Yugoslavia: An Anticipatory Post-Mortem' (2016) 110(2) *American Journal of International Law* 233, 236.
114 Interview with Serb woman survivor of CRSV (Banjaluka, 16 June 2015).
115 Milanović, above n 113, 16.

because they clearly see themselves as victims . . . and they think they should be apologised to without them necessarily apologising to others.'[116] She noted that Serbs are more ready to acknowledge their own crimes. Čehajić-Clancy also argues that Bosniak victims want acknowledgment from Serbs that crimes were committed, but they do not want to see them emotional about it.[117] She offers some explanation why this may be the case:

> Maybe the victims somehow think that feeling emotions is their exclusive right. 'Who are you as *a perpetrator* to feel emotional? It is my right. I should feel bad here. I am the victim here.' Maybe there is this unconscious motivation to preserve this dichotomy between victims and *perpetrators*. They [Bosniaks] are motivated to stay victims and they want to claim victimhood . . . That is a danger I observe with the Bosniak community and that is something we need to pull ourselves out of it.[118]

The victim–perpetrator dichotomy is entrenched among victims and is detrimental to the processes of reconciliation. Clark, in her in-depth interviews with Bosniak survivors, said that even when interviewees accepted that crimes were committed by all sides 'they [still] could never be compared'.[119] What differentiates them is that Serb crimes, including CRSV, were planned, systematic and organised. Still, this fact does not make the crime of others less significant or heinous. Judith Butler argues that bodily beings are shaped by social and political contexts that 'maximize precariousness for some and minimize precariousness for others'.[120] As a consequence, some lives are framed as valuable and others as expendable. Those deemed valuable are cared for, while others have been dismissed as collateral damage.

Conclusion

Many Serb women survivors self-censored their stories as they felt their testimonies were unwelcome and of no interest to anyone. Their construction as being 'less than victims' brought them stigmatisation, isolation and 'otherness'.

116 Sabina Čehajić-Clancy, 'Reconciliation in Bosnia and Herzegovina: Perspectives from Social Psychology' (Paper presented at the Humanity in Action, International Conference, Sarajevo, Bosnia and Herzegovina, 2012), https://vimeo.com/72300524.

117 Such views are in line with Thompson's arguments that some victims demand nothing more than acknowledgment of their suffering. Janna Thompson, 'Apology, Justice and Respect: A Critical Defence of Political Apology' in Mark Gibney, Rhoda E. Howard-Hassman, Jean Marc Coicaud and Niklaus Steiner (eds), *The Age of Apology: Facing Up to the Past* (University of Philadelphia Press, 2008) 31.

118 Čehajić-Clancy, above n 116; see also Johanna Kirchhoff and Sabina Čehajić-Clancy, 'Intergroup Apologies: Does It Matter What They Say? Experimental Analysis' (2014) 20(4) *Peace and Conflict: Journal of Peace Psychology* 430 (emphasis in original).

119 Clark, above n 91, 98.

120 Judith Butler, *Frames of War: When Is Life Grievable?* (Verso, 2009) 2.

Their experiences were suppressed and, as a result, their healing was deferred and never fully supported. By not being provided with the opportunity to talk about their suffering, they felt they were being forced into 'shame by violence and self-recrimination'.[121] The large absence of scholarship and interest into Serb women's stories has placed an additional layer of guilt, shame and feelings of injustice upon them. But rapes of Serb women occurred and must be understood and recognised as part of BiH women's experiences during the war. Enabling these women to reclaim their voice and narrate rather than sideline and silence their suffering is necessary in transitional societies 'to right the wrongs of the past'.[122] In the following Chapter, I provide in-depth analysis of ethnic politicisation of CRSV in BiH.

121 Veena Das, Arthur Kleinman, Mamphela Ramphele and Pamela Reynolds (eds), *Violence and Subjectivity* (University of California Press, 2000).

122 Kirk Simpson, 'Voices Silenced, Voices Rediscovered: Victims of Violence and the Reclamation of Language in Transitional Societies' (2007) 3(2) *International Journal of Law in Context* 89.

3 Ethnic politicisation of conflict-related sexual violence

Feminists split in the 1990s

In the 1990s feminists came together to lobby and demonstrate against the war. Between 1990 and 1993 many local feminist groups established anti-war groups and focused first on the prevention of war. Once the war started they offered assistance to female refugees and women victims of CRSV and of war violence generally.[1] Some of the new women's groups established in the 1990s identified themselves as feminist; some groups identified as nationalist, supporting nationalist political or religious groups.[2] Still, the news of mass rapes brought about protest activities organised by different grassroots women's groups. These actions had an effect on the international community and triggered the first fact-finding missions that were sent to investigate wartime rapes.

CRSV is primarily recognised as violence by men against women. Women's bodies become a target of violence, regardless of which ethnic group is, at some point, recognised as the aggressor and which as victim.[3] It is a message from one man to another;[4] a message of humiliation, underscoring the inability of men to protect their daughters, mothers, wives and sisters. Although rape affects all women in the same way and needs to be treated as a crime against women, the treatment of this crime in Bosnia and Herzegovina (BiH) has been divided along ethnic lines. The narration of rape in BiH and in international literature is a complicated enterprise, and some feminists and women's groups have been denounced as either 'traitors of the nation' for taking a position and treating all women – regardless of their ethnicity – as victims of CRSV, or as 'relativists' and 'apologists' for treating Serb women in the same way as Bosniak and Croat women.

1 Tanja Djuric-Kuzmanovic, Rada Drezgic and Dubravka Zarkov, 'Gendered War, Gendered Peace: Violent Conflicts in the Balkans and its Consequences' in Donna Pankhurst (ed.), *Gendered Peace: Women's Struggles for Post-War Justice and Reconciliation* (Routledge, 2007) 265.

2 Ibid., 273.

3 Vesna Kesić, 'Muslim Women, Croatian Women, Serbian Women, Albanian Women', *Eurozine* (online), 5 September 2003, www.eurozine.com/articles/2003-05-09-kesic-en.html.

4 Susan Brownmiller, *Against Our Will: Men, Women, and Rape* (Bantam Books, 1975) 119.

In 1993 feminists from Serbia issued a public appeal, protesting against an 'international campaign that instrumentalises women raped in BiH and Croatia'.[5] They issued several statements advocating for no distinction to be made between women according to their ethnic origin:

> Women who are raped in war in Bosnia are not to be distinguished and valued differently with respect to their nationality to which they belong. The question of Serb, Croat, Muslim and women of all other nationalities has for us the same value. Since the beginning of the war in Croatia and Bosnia, testimonies show that rape is widely spread; that victims of rape are of all nationalities, including Roma, Albanian and other women that do not belong to any warring parties. All the same, perpetrators belong to all military and para-military formations, as well as the civilian population.[6]

While there was no denial that women were the victims, and in spite of these public proclamations, some feminists and scholars persistently argued that rape was only happening to '*certain* women' [emphasis in original].[7] Those feminists who insisted that rape is a universal act of violence by men against women, were accused of downplaying the terror that Bosniak women suffered in the hands of the Serb army. They were blamed for 'aiding the Serbian aggressors because they failed to single out "Croatian" and "Muslim" women as the victims',[8] portrayed as disloyal and morally suspect, and exposed to public media accusations of 'concealing the Serbian rape of Muslim and Croat women'.[9]

Those feminists who have tried to speak about CRSV as crimes committed against all women, rather than as crimes against women of a particular ethnicity, have been portrayed as traitors, nationalists and/or deniers. Croatian feminists felt that Serbian feminists, who condemned men on all sides of the armed conflict for rapes, tried to equalise the phenomenon of rape on the different warring sides, thus equalising the responsibility.[10] Women in Black, a non-government organisation (NGO) based in Belgrade, responded to these accusations:

> The feminists of Belgrade and Serbia do not support the position about symmetrical suffering. They are conscious that the more powerful and

5 Lepa Mladjenovic, *Anti-ratni bilten SOS-a* [Trans: *Anti-War SOS Bulletin*] (SOS telefon za žene i decu žrtve nasilja, 1993).

6 Ibid., 111.

7 Elissa Helms, *Innocence and Victimhood: Gender, Nation, and Women's Activism in Postwar Bosnia-Herzegovina* (University of Wisconsin Press, 2013) 61.

8 Ibid., 61.

9 Maja Korac, 'Representation of Mass Rape in Ethnic Conflicts in What Was Yugoslavia' (1994) 36(4) *Sociologija* 495, 505.

10 Laura Pitter and Alexandra Stiglmayer, 'Will the World Remember? Can the Women Forget?' (1993) 3(5) *Ms. Magazine* 19, 21.

> better-armed military-political forces of Karadzic in Bosnia (the army of the self-declared Serbian Republic in Bosnia) have the largest number of rapes on their consciences. How many exactly, it will be difficult to know, even after the war. The high percentage of Muslim women raped in the war in Bosnia is not a reason to forget the suffering of women of other nationalities and religions, atheists, or those claiming no particular nationality.[11]

Feminists from Serbia, however, have been perceived as being on the 'perpetrator' side – as excusing and justifying crimes committed by their own group of people, and worse, as supporters of nationalist Serb politics.

Feminist nationalist groups in Croatia argued that

> [m]ass rapes under orders of the Serbian-occupied territories of Bosnia-Herzegovina and Croatia are part of a Serbian policy of genocide against non-Serbs. That means that non-Serbian women – most prominently Muslims and Croatians – are not only tortured by rape as are all women, but are being raped as a part of a Serbian policy of 'ethnic cleansing' on the basis of their sex and ethnicity; most of these rapes end in murder. And this is *not* happening to all women.[12]

The stand taken by feminist nationalists was that 'rape is a distinctly Serbian weapon for which all Serbs – even feminists who oppose the war – are culpable'.[13] Women in Black responded to such accusations:

> We refuse to be part of the debate: who is the real victim, or who has the greatest right to call themselves victims. We refuse the politics of instrumentalization of victims. A victim is a victim, and to her the number of other victims does not decrease her own suffering and pain. We happen to live in Belgrade and happen to work with women who happen to have Serbian names, and happen to be prisoners of war and victims of rape (we meet also Muslim and Croat women as well). Some of them have been months and months in camps where they have suffered all kinds of mental, physical and sexual violence. Facing these courageous, exhausted and traumatized women, we cannot in any way see them as less victims than any women of different nationality. They tell us of all kinds of atrocities, systematic rapes, death threats and other horrors. It is obvious that in war rapists are mostly of

11 As quoted in Donna M. Hughes, Lepa Mladjenovic and Zorica Mrsevic, 'Feminist Resistance in Serbia' (1994) 2(4) *European Journal of Women's Studies* 509, 519.

12 From the letter published in the special pull-out section of *Off Our Backs*, Kareta Feminist Group, International Initiative of Women of Bosnia-Hercegovina, Bosnia-Hercegovina Refugee Women's Group and Bedem Ljubavi [Wall of Love] Women's Group, 'Serbia's War Against Bosnia and Croatia' (1993) 23(5) *Off Our Backs* 1, 10.

13 Hughes et al., above n 12, 509–532.

> other nationality, but for many women it is not the nationality but the body of the men who have destroyed their joy of life. We must say that we are sad that some of our sisters from Croatia . . . do not want to communicate with us anymore. Even though we support their work for women, which in the long run should bring more freedom for everyone – they still see us as a part of the Enemy Body.[14]

While Women in Black did not want to discriminate among victims they felt 'responsible for the pain and suffering that the Serbian regime has inflicted upon others' and 'first want accountability for those who committed crimes in our name, and then all the others'.[15]

At the time, the wartime rape of non-Serb women had started to receive international attention. The lack of public attention for the war crimes committed by Croat and Bosniak forces was criticised by Kesić in 1994, who openly critiqued Catharine MacKinnon for supporting only non-Serb women victims of rape. Kesić argued that '[n]o side could stay innocent in this war. Muslims also committed war crimes and brutalized Serb and Croat women.'[16]

Feminist activists found themselves increasingly implicated within ethnic and nationalist discourses on CRSV. The debate among feminists as to whether the aggressors/rapists should be singled out according to their ethnicity or not, marked the most deadly years of the conflict – 1992 and 1993. As Kesić wrote about that time:

> Feminists and women's groups have been split into two relatively antagonistic groups: those who see rape as a universal problem of violence against women which needs to be identified and combated as such, and those who see the high incidence of rape in this particular war as being unique and the product of a contempt or hatred by one particular army (Serbian) for the women of a particular ethnic group (Muslim or Croatian).[17]

After rape was explicitly included as a crime against humanity in the Statute of the International Criminal Tribunal for the Former Yugoslavia (ICTY),[18] feminist scholars, legal professionals and activists were prompted to turn their attention to consider whether all rapes or only the 'worst' should be prosecuted in international

14 Women in Black, 1993 as cited in Jelena Batinić, 'Feminism, Nationalism, and War: The "Yugoslav Case" in Feminist Texts' (2001) 3(1) *Journal of International Women Studies* 1, 8.

15 Staša Zajović, *Women in Black: War, Feminism and Antimilitarism* (n.d.) Women's Feminist – Antimilitarist Peace Organization, http://zeneucrnom.org/index.php?option=com_content&task=view&id=78&Itemid=21.

16 Vesna Kesić, 'A Response to Catharine MacKinnon's Article "Turning Rape into Pornography: Postmodern Genocide"' (1994) 5 *Hastings Women's Law Journal* 276, 278.

17 Ibid., 194.

18 See Article 5(g) of the Statute of the ICTY adopted by UNSC Res 827, 3217th mtg, UN Doc S/RES/827 (25 May 1993).

war crimes courts. The acclaimed Western feminists, Catharine MacKinnon and Alexandra Stiglmayer, found themselves embroiled in internal struggles between feminist groups in the Yugoslav successor states. MacKinnon was openly hostile to Serbian feminists (even though they had condemned Serb crimes against Muslim and Croat women), accusing them of being pro-Serb nationalists and showing open condemnation and lack of trust towards them.[19]

Thus, from the beginning of the war to the present moment, the discourse surrounding rape as a weapon of war in BiH has been entirely positioned in terms of ethnicity and as part of a 'genocidal' strategy, while women, as Vesna Kesić argued a decade ago, have been turned into metaphors: 'A raped Croat or Bosniak woman stands for a raped Croatia or Bosnia.'[20] Women were raped regardless of their ethnic origin as punishment for having their husbands or partners fight for what was then considered 'an enemy'. Several women survivors, who were detained in different rape camps, confirmed that women from 'other' ethnic groups were detained and raped with them. Huzba Nukić, a 69-year-old Bosniak woman, was one of them. She was detained, together with Serb women and a few Croatian women, and repeatedly raped by Croatian military forces in Bosanski Brod.[21]

My interviewee, a Serb woman, was detained in the surroundings of Bradina, together with Croat women who were married to Serbs:

> We women were squashed in a school sports hall . . . the soldiers were came during the night and took women, girls and very young girls. We hid 12–13-year-old girls behind us so they could not see them. There were Croat women with their children too . . . they were married to Serbs . . . one of them was tortured, raped . . . they did terrible things to her. She survived. She lives now in Sydney . . . next to me was M.D. with her few-months-old baby. They came and took her away. I was trying to comfort the baby . . . when she came back I asked her 'Where have you been?' She said, 'You will know in the morning.' A doctor came in the morning and confirmed she had been raped. I don't know who brought the doctor in . . . they came with a night lamp and would flash it in our faces and choose . . . some women were jumping from stairs, wanting to kill themselves, because they knew what was awaiting them.[22]

19 A feminist activist, who was at an international conference organised to discuss women in war, in Zagreb in 1992, informed me that MacKinnon, doubting their anti-nationalist position, told her and a group of feminists from Serbia: 'if you were against Milošević, you would not be alive'. Personal conversation with L. J. in 2009; see also Ana Miškovska Kajevska, *Feminist Activism at War: Belgrade and Zagreb Feminists in the 1990s* (Routledge, 2017).

20 Kesić, above n 4.

21 Dragan Čolić, 'Tukli su me i silovanli' [Trans: 'They Beat and Raped Me'] *Blic* (online), 24 May 2002, www.blic.rs/stara_arhiva/reportaze/27076/Tukli-su-me-i-silovali.

22 Interview with M. A. (Brisbane, 13 July 2015).

Testimonies such as Huzba's and Mira's prove the feminist thesis that war is fought primarily over women's bodies; that women were raped to send a message to their enemy. As Brownmiller argues: 'rape is directed against all women who belong to other men'.[23] It is used with the intention of dehumanising and terrorising its victims. Rada Borić asserts, too, that:

> Women were often raped because of real or invented behaviour of the male members of their family ('guilty for the sins of others') . . . rape was performed with an intention to punish male relative(s). And indirectly, to punish all male members of a woman's ethnic group. In that manner, a woman's body ultimately becomes the place of interethnic 'communication'.[24]

In 1994, Stiglmayer reported on why Serb women had been ignored by foreign journalists, who flocked to BiH in search of a 'good' story:

> Because of the suffering of Muslim and Croat rape victims, we frequently forget that Serbian women in Bosnia-Herzegovina are also being raped. Of course, they are not affected by rape as frequently as the Muslims . . . the real reason that Serbian women seldom appear in the reports of rapes in Bosnia might be a different one: they are the wives, sisters and daughters of the aggressors. There is hardly a journalist who feels motivated to seek them out, to check up on what has happened to them and thus offer propaganda material to the Serbian side – that is, the bad side, the side 'responsible for the war'.[25]

Despite these acknowledgments, the discourse on CRSV in BiH was reduced exclusively to the dynamics between Serb males, as the aggressors, and Croat and Muslim women as the victims.[26] This is how rapes were constructed in literature too: the body of a Serb man against the body of a Croat or Muslim woman. Any other bodily combination is almost excluded from the scholarly analysis. As a result, the rapes have become a symbol of the suffering of Bosniaks and Croats and, further extrapolated, of the suffering of the Federation of BiH and the Republic of Croatia,[27] while experiences of 'other' women were at best downplayed and at worst, ignored. However, 'rape camps', where women were often impregnated and then kept in confinement until the last stage of their pregnancies, were organised by all warring parties.

23 Brownmillier, above n 5, 181.

24 Rada Boric, 'Letter of Intention' quoted in Rada Boric, *Gendered Violence in the Balkans, Sexualized Violence Against Women*, paper on file with author, 1.

25 Alexandra Stiglmayer, 'The Rapes in Bosnia-Herzegovina' in Alexandra Stiglmayer (ed.), *Mass Rape: The War Against Women in Bosnia-Herzegovina* (University of Nebraska Press, 1994) 82, 138.

26 Darius M. Rejali, 'After Feminist Analyses of Bosnian Violence' (1996) 8(3) *Peace Review* 365, 366.

27 See Marija Slišković, *Sunčica* (Hrvatsko društvo logoraša srpskih koncentracijskih logora, 2011).

The foreign media played a powerful role in shaping new Bosnian identities, by deciding what constitutes a crime, whose suffering would be recognised and how women's suffering should be portrayed and addressed. Some victims were valued more than others and quickly gained the top status on the Bosnian pyramid of victimhood. There were extensive rapes of Serb women in camps run by Bosniak and Croatian authorities in several areas of BiH, particularly in 1992 at the very beginning of the war.[28] These events also had an organised character and had been documented in the reports, but scholarly literature on these instances of CRSV is scarce. The media and international organisations did not show much interest in these stories, but searched for stories of the most visible women victims – Bosniak and Croat women – raped by Serb men. If Serb women were mentioned, it was usually in passing, but without thorough analysis, as it is the narrative of wartime rapes experienced by Bosniak women that has been collectively remembered locally and internationally.

A few feminist scholars have noted that Serb women have not been on anyone's agenda (locally and internationally) because they have been viewed as ultimately belonging to the 'rapists' (the Serbs).[29] Today, more than 20 years since the war ended in BiH, it seems that it is still not possible to dismantle ethnicity from gender. Due to the complex political and social landscape, CRSV has become a 'characteristic' only ascribed to Serb men. Serb women have thus felt doubly victimised and betrayed – by the men who raped them, and further by their own government and community who have done next to nothing for them. For many women, it is precisely the denial of their victim status, and the social and political silence surrounding their victimisation, that are most difficult to bear.[30] The silence then becomes a new form of violence that preoccupies the mind and the body of victims. As Bernstein argues, by silencing the victims they suffer an additional layer of injustice – misrecognition – they are 'ignored, silenced, smothered, and suppressed from the public eye'.[31] Their suffering becomes reduced to clandestine experience – forgotten and overlooked.[32]

28 To name a few: Dretelj-Čapljina, camp Čelebići, camp Strolit- Modriča, Odžak, Brod, Bradina and camp Musala-Mostar. See Rachel Kerr, 'Peace Through Justice?' The International Criminal Tribunal for Former Yugoslavia' (2007) 7(3) *Southeast European and Black Sea Studies* 373; Ivana Nizich, 'Violations of the Rules of War by Bosnian Croat and Muslim Forces in Bosnia and Herzegovina' (1994) 5(1) *Hastings Women Law Journal* 25.

29 Such as Dubravka Zarkov and Vesna Nikolić-Ristanović.

30 Brandon Hamber and Ingrid Palmary, 'Gender, Memorialization, and Symbolic Reparations' in Ruth Rubio-Marin (ed.), *The Gender of Reparations: Unsettling Sexual Hierarchies While Redressing Human Rights Violations* (Cambridge University Press, 2009) 324, 364.

31 J. M. Bernstein, 'Suffering Injustice: Misrecognition as Moral Injury in Critical Theory' (2005) 13(3) *International Journal Philosophy Studies* 303, 311.

32 Martha Minow, 'The Hope for Healing: What the Truth Commissions Can Do?' in Robert I. Rotberg and Dennis Thompson (eds), *Truth v. Justice the Morality of Truth Commissions* (Princeton University Press, 2010) 235.

The role of religious leadership

From the beginning of the war, Muslim religious leaders supported Bosniak women victims. In 1992, Muslim religious leaders issued a fatwa, a religious decree, which appealed to the Muslim community to recognise and embrace raped women as victims and treat them with respect. According to Gabriela Mischkowski and Gorana Mlinarevic, the young imam in Zenica, where Medica Zenica, the first and largest NGO[33] and therapy centre was established in 1993 to support women victims of CRSV, did this to support their work.[34] The Muslim religious community also called Muslim men to marry the raped women and to raise children born out of these rapes as Muslims.[35] The imam told to refugee women from the countryside to seek advice from Medica Zenica, and he explicitly allowed rape survivors to abort up to the fourth month of their pregnancy.[36] In the same year, the Bosnian government was claiming that 200,000 people were killed in '15 months of nationalistic aggression'[37] and banned international adoption of war orphans and the children born of rape. The hope was that the relatives of these children would take care of them, but also that they would be a means of repopulating the country.[38] Some nationalist leaders viewed these children as a 'lesser evil' than those who would be born from mixed marriages. In such marriages there was a threat that the children would not be raised as Muslims, since 'every marriage of a Muslim woman to a non-Muslim means loss of her and her children for Islam and Muslims'.[39]

Muharem Omerdić, the Counsellor for Religious Issues in BiH, undertook a study of the status of women under Sharia Law with the intention of making sure that women victims of CRSV were protected. Omerdić stated that 'it was particularly painful when some of the raped women were left by their husbands, even by

33 Gabriela Mischowski and Gorana Mlinarevic, '. . . *And That It Does Not Happen to Anyone Anywhere in the World' The Trouble with Rape Trials – Views of Witnesses, Prosecutors and Judges on Prosecuting Sexualised Violence during the War in the former Yugoslavia*, Report, Medica Mondiale (2009), www.medicamondiale.org/fileadmin/redaktion/5_Service/Mediathek/Dokumente/English/Documentations_studies/medica_mondiale_and_that_it_does_not_happen_to_anyone_anywhere_in_the_world_english_complete_version_dec_2009.pdf, 6.

34 Ibid.

35 Duska Andric Ruzicic, 'War Rape and Political Manipulation of Survivors' in Wenona Gils, Malathi de Alwsi, Edith Klein, Kuluka Siva and Maja Korac (eds), *Feminists Under Fire: Exchanges Across War Zones* (Between the Lines Press, 2003) 103.

36 Ibid.

37 Carol J. Williams, 'Bosnia's Orphans of Rape: Innocent Legacy of Hatred', *Los Angeles Times*, 24 July 1993, http://articles.latimes.com/1993-07-24/news/mn-16356_1_bosnian.

38 Patricia Weitsman, 'The Discourse of Rape in Wartime; Sexual Violence, War Babies and Identity' (Paper presented at the Annual Meeting of the International Studies Association Portland, OR, 26 February–1 March 2003) 19; Muharem Omerdić 'The Position of the Islamic Community on the Care for Children of Raped Mothers' in Mirsad Tokača (ed.), *Plucked Buds* (Commission on Gathering the Facts on War Crimes in Bosnia and Herzegovina, 2002) 428.

39 Mustafa Mujki Spahić, 'Gore od silovanja: zlo mješovitih brakova' [Trans: 'Worse than Rape: The Evil of Mixed Marriages'], *Ljiljan*, 10 August 1994, 22.

their fathers. Cruel gossip about some women spread through their neighbourhoods, especially when they were left pregnant.'[40]

The local Muslim leaders were supported by former sheik of Al-Azhar, Cairo, who wrote and published a fatwa entitled *Fatwa on Children Born by Raped Women in BiH*.[41] According to Joana Daniel-Wrabetz, this fatwa, translated and published in BiH, provides important guidelines for the conduct of both women and local communities in the acceptance and integration of these women and their children as important members of society.[42] The programs initiated by the Islamic community were available only to Bosniak children, and not to children who were born to Serb or Croat women survivors of rape. The programs were initiated to ensure that the identity of the Bosniak community, as a victim, was sustained.[43]

From very early on, the threat of suffering and rape to the collective body of a nation, rather than individual women's bodies, is seen as more important. The Bosniak women survivors of rape embraced this collective identity and insisted on collectivisation of their experiences and on ethnic identification.[44] For example, Bakira Hasečić, a Bosniak woman survivor, reportedly stated,

> I am only one among thousands and thousands of raped and sexually abused women . . . The crime against Bosniak women was a planned attack on the dignity of Muslims, a destruction of the biological substance of Muslims in Bosnia and Herzegovina.[45]

In 1993, Pope John Paul II addressed a letter to Catholic Archbishop Vinko Puljić of Sarajevo with a message to Bosnian women who had been raped in the conflict. The aim of this letter was to appeal for these women to 'transform an act of violence into an act of love and welcome' by 'accepting' the enemy inside them and making him 'flesh of their flesh' by carrying their pregnancies to term.[46] Now, 20 years later, the NGO *Sunčica* from Croatia,

40 Omerdić, above n 38, 428.

41 Ál-Šajh D'allulakk, Ali D'allulakk, al Ima al akbar, Hukmu at fali n-nisa I al-mugtesibati fi l-Busneti wa l-Harsaki [Trans: 'Regulations Related to the Children of Raped Women in BiH'] (Buhnus wa fatawa islamiyya fi qadaya al-mu asira, 1994) 175–186. Other Islamic theoreticians, experts in Sharia Law and commissions for scientific research, decreed their fatwas relating to this issue: Omer Nakičević, *Fetva o djeci silovanih žena u Bosni i Herzegovini* [Trans: *Fatwa on Children Born by Raped Women in BiH*] (Glasnik Rijaseta IZ u BiH, 1996) 1–3, 41–44.

42 Joana Daniel-Wrabetz, 'Children Born of War Rape in Bosnia-Herzegovina and the Convention on the Rights of the Child' in R. Charlie Carpenter (ed.), *Born of War: Protecting Children of Sexual Violence Survivors in Conflict Zones* (Kumarin Press, 2007) 29.

43 Donna Seto, *No Place for a War Baby: The Global Politics of Children Born of Wartime Sexual Violence* (Routledge, 2013) 168.

44 Tamara Banjeglav, *Gender, Nation, Rape. Intersections of Gender and Ethnic Violence During the War in Bosnia and Herzegovina* (MA Thesis, Central European University, 2009) 61.

45 Irfan Ajanović (ed.), *I Begged Them to Kill Me: The Crimes Against Women in Bosnia and Herzegovina* (Center for Investigation and Documentation, 2007).

46 'Pope Urges Bosnian Rape Victims Not to Have Abortions', *Los Angeles Times*, 28 February 1993, http://articles.latimes.com/1993-02-28/news/mn-234_1_bosnian-serbs.

which works with women survivors, has decided to work with the Catholic priests and use their influence to encourage women to speak up about their ordeal.[47]

While the Muslim religious community supported Muslim women who were raped and their children (albeit for nationalist reasons), and the Catholic Church issued at least one public declaration of support to Bosnian women who were raped, the Serbian Orthodox Church has, until recently, stayed silent. This should not be that surprising since the Bosnian Serb government, contrary to the Bosniak and Croatian, has not yet acknowledged these women either. On 29 June 2017, the Inter-Religious Council in BiH adopted the landmark 'Declaration on Denouncing Stigmatization of Survivors of Conflict-related Sexual Violence'. The signing of the Declaration was part of a campaign run by the United Nations Population Fund (UNFPA) and the British Embassy in BiH to alleviate the stigmatisation of survivors.[48] Although symbolic in its nature, it is significant for being the first time the leaders of the four religious communities[49] came together to publically denounce stigma of CRSV.

Feminist disagreements now

> [W]e have discussed a lot that it would be good, that after 20 years, at least one story in which the perpetrator is from the BiH army is published . . . or has the time for that not yet come?[50]

Over time, the divisions among feminists in BiH, Croatia and Serbia grew stronger. In Croatia the feminist movement split into nationalist and anti-nationalists, with

47 The representative of this organisation, *Ružica Ramljak*, reported about the new project work with Catholic priests. The idea is to visit some of the Croatian villages where women survivors live, and fight the stigma and shame by enabling women to hear directly from priests that there is nothing to be ashamed of and that it is important they speak up in order to help bring justice. Presentation given at the workshop on reparations for victims of conflict related sexual violence, Sarajevo, 9–10 June 2016. On the potential of religious actors to lend their special legitimacy to transitional justice and make them valuable allies to NGOs and others, see Ioana Cismas, 'Reflections on the Presence and Absence of Religious Actors in Transitional Justice Processes: On Legitimacy and Accountability' in Roger Duthie and Paul Seils (eds), *Justice Mosaics: How Context Shapes Transitional Justice in Fractured Societies* (International Center for Transitional Justice, 2017), 302.

48 See United Nations in Bosnia and Herzegovina, 'Declaration on Denouncing Stigmatization of Survivors of Conflict-related Sexual Violence adopted by BiH Inter-Religious Council', http://ba.one.un.org/content/unct/bosnia_and_herzegovina/en/home/presscenter/declaration-on-denouncing-stigmatization-of-survivors-of-conflic.html; Igor Spaic, 'Bosnian Clerks Unite to Condemn Wartime Sexual Violence', *Balkan Insight* (online), 30 June 2017, www.balkaninsight.com/en/article/bosnian-clerics-unite-to-condemn-wartime-sexual-violence-06-30-2017.

49 The Bosnian Islamic, Jewish, Orthodox and Catholic Community.

50 A long-term feminist from Serbia posted this question in an email she sent to the web group list that gathers feminist NGOs from ex-Yugoslavia that have been working for years on sexual violence in war and peace. No one from the list replied to her question. Email on file with author, 8 November 2014.

the former insisting on including only Croat and Muslim women as victims, and only Serb men as perpetrators. The latter insisted on the acknowledgment that 'other women', albeit to a lesser degree, were also victims and that all men raped. The earlier political stance had consequences on assisting women victims of rape. Djuric-Kuzmanovic et al. argue that because of such a context there were times when

> politicisation of rape was done at the expense of the women who were raped; when it was opportune to identify with specific victims and forget the others, and when the struggle of other women was appropriated for advancement of one's own agenda.[51]

A creation of a hierarchy of victims, which started very early on and has been reinforced over time, has been both 'dangerous and inhibits reconciliation'.[52]

The debates and opposing views on ethnic identity of victims and perpetrators peaked by the end of the war and progressively contributed to institutionalising silence among ex-Yugoslav feminists on this topic. There are still many 'silent' disagreements and a deliberate avoidance of discussing openly how much ethnicity, rather than gender, has been an issue when it comes to CRSV. The Croatian forces used rape as a tool of ethnic cleansing against Serb women in the Croatian region of Western Slavonia. Serb civilians from the Posavina region were besieged and driven out by members of the Croatian Army. This huge exodus of Serbs was accompanied by a large-scale campaign of raping Serb women, burning their homes, and destroying their cultural and religious institutions.[53]

In December 2014, a long-term feminist and activist from RS told me:

> I know a lot of women from the region of Modriča and Odžak. Many of them came to Belgrade where I was during the war and I know that babies

51 Djuric-Kuzmanovic, Drezgic and Zarkov, above n 2, 286.

52 Janine Natalya Clark, *International Trials and Reconciliation: Assessing the Impact of the International Criminal Tribunal for the Former Yugoslavia* (Routledge, 2015) 98.

53 Alexandra Stiglmayer (ed.), *Mass Rape: The War Against Women in Bosnia-Herzegovina* (University of Nebraska Press, 1994) 140; *Crimes Against Serbian Civilians* (Produced and Directed by Bosnian Serbs' Television, 1993) 00:57:00 (Video); Dragomir Djokić, 'Memorandum on War Crimes and Crimes of Genocide Committed Against the Serbian People in the Area of the Former Commune of Odžak by Ustashi-Fundamentalist Paramilitary Formations and Members of the National Guard of the Republic of Croatia, Samac, 21 May 1993', A Letter to the Secretary-General from Dragomir Djokić, the Chargé d'affaires of the Permanent Mission of Yugoslavia to the United Nations (6 August 1993), UN Doc. A/48/299-S/26261; *Raping Serbian Women* (Produced and Directed by Tanja Peternek-Aleksić, 1993) 00:55:00 (Video); UN Commission on Human Rights, *Report on the Situation of Human Rights in the Territory of the Former Yugoslavia Submitted by Mr Tadeusz Mazowiecki*, UN Doc. E/CN.4/1993/50 (10 February 1993) 16; Vesna Nikolić-Ristanović, 'Sexual Violence' in Vesna Nikolić-Ristanović (ed.), *Women, Violence and War: Wartime Victimization of Refugees in the Balkans* (Central European University Press, 1999) 41.

> were born in 'Narodni Front' hospital; babies conceived in rape, unwanted kids. So I know another story and dimension of the war in BiH. If we want to talk about peace in this country and region, it is necessary to acknowledge that Serb women were victims of the war crimes too. Why do feminists from Serbia only go to Srebrenica? They never come to visit women in Posavina or Hercegovina where Serb women victims live. To tell you the truth, I think Women in Black and feminists from Serbia are doing more damage than good. They reinforce ethnic divisions by only visiting Muslim graveyards; visiting their victims . . . They should stop dealing with us from Bosnia. They have nothing to do with us and they should stop doing their activism here, or if they do, they must do it for all women not only Muslim women.[54]

Such opinions and reflections on feminist activism are primarily spoken and shared in mono-ethnic and confidential, private spaces. Feminist activists across the borders do not necessarily discuss them among themselves, in public. It would be like opening a wound that has never fully healed. In this complex political context, Serb women's experiences have often been rejected or ignored. Over time, it has become for anti-nationalist feminists almost impossible to talk about crimes committed against Serb women, and at the same time, not be perceived as a Serb nationalists. Serb victimhood is 'quantified' in far smaller numbers than the victimhood of Bosniak and Croat women and, as a result, their voices have not been able to generate concern or interest in crimes committed against them. Their bodies collectively present the geographies of violence and 'ethical loneliness', which is the experience of being abandoned by humanity, compounded by the experience of not being heard when wanting to testify to what happened.[55]

As a 'smaller' group of victims, living alongside a larger group of victims, Serb women were marginalised and disappeared from the public discourse on wartime rape almost entirely. Any discussion about these women by women from their own ethnic group, runs the risk of them being characterised as 'nationalist' and, even worse, as a denial of the crimes committed by Serbs.

Within such a complex political environment, it has become impossible to challenge the dominant views and clear-cut division between victims and perpetrators. The Western media too, which shaped the global image of the BiH war, was not interested in reporting that Serb women were being raped along with Croat and Bosniak women. According to Paul Mojzes, feminist legal scholars (such as Catharine McKinnon) and journalists (such as Allan Little) seemed to be '[un]interested in the fate of all women in Bosnia, since they focus almost exclusively on victims of mass rape by Serbs'.[56] Such reporting had the effect of concealing the suffering and hardship experienced by Serb women victims.

54 Telephone interview, 17 June 2015.

55 Jill Stauffer, *Ethical Loneliness: The Injustice of Not Being Heard* (Columbia University Press, 2016).

56 Paul Mojzes, *Balkan Genocides: Holocaust and Ethnic Cleansing in the Twentieth Century* (Rowman & Littlefield, 2011) 184

As a result, apart from the nationalist propaganda, international agencies, and others, have wittingly or unwittingly chosen not to talk about Serb women. The apparent lack of interest in Serb women victims of rape has raised bitterness and feelings of injustice among Serb women survivors and some feminist activists. According to one long-term female activist:

> If internationals wanted to find out about these women, they could have done so during the war and today. But, they did not and do not. Foreign media did not welcome Serb women from Bosniak/Croat camps after they were exchanged for soldiers who were prisoners of war from the 'other' side. They were interested in victims of rape, but only of particular ethnic group(s).[57]

In order to distance themselves from the Serb nationalist politics, some Serb feminists felt morally responsible to talk primarily about rape of 'other' women – non-Serb – and crimes committed in their 'own name'. As one activist from Serbia told me, talking about Serb women has not been politically correct or popular. Even 20 years after the war ended, a long-term feminist from Belgrade told me: 'today, if you speak about them [Serb women], your speech cannot be seen as anything else but nationalist propaganda'.[58] It seems that any public support for Serb women victims has always been at risk of being hijacked by Serb nationalist discourses, and as such, being silenced. Due to these circumstances, it is of no surprise that the experiences of Serb women have been muted or appropriated and used by people with a pro-nationalist stance to advance their nationalist politics. For these reasons, the wartime experiences of Serb women have become a difficult and contested topic, avoided by many and excluded almost entirely from academic literature on mass rapes in BiH.

'Oh really, so few?': discarded accounts of Serb women's testimonies

Ongoing one-sided attention has not only relativised women's experiences of CRSV but excluded the spaces where rapes of 'other' women could be publically discussed and acknowledged. As a consequence of selective representation, the silencing of Serb female experiences has become the norm. The omission of this group of women's experiences has had serious implications for the entrenchment of ideological, political and social divisions within cultures of memory.

The master narratives of BiH have established one class of victims (Bosniaks) and another of perpetrators (Serbs), since they fail to delve more deeply into the complexities within the binary position of victim–perpetrator. International organisations and researchers have put little effort into identifying Serb women

57 Interview with S. T., Banjaluka, 19 June 2015. Many Serbs distrusted outsiders and resented world opinion. The US, while seemingly sympathetic to all victims, provided little help to Serb refugees. See Swanee Hunt, *Worlds Apart: Bosnian Lessons for Global Security* (Duke University Press, 2011) 113.

58 Telephone interview with A. Z., 18 July 2015.

victims of CRSV, both during the war and in its aftermath. Their stories did not trickle into the formation of the Bosnian state, which still does not recognise Serb women victims' claims to victimhood, or their accounts of CRSV. There was simply no interest in *these* victims because Serbs as an ethnic group were demonised from the very beginning of the war. As Vesna Nikolić-Ristanović argues, talking about Serb women victims was understood as a denial of Serb culpability for the crimes, or was often received with ironic remarks, such as: 'Oh really, so few?' or 'That is nothing in comparison with thousands of raped Muslim women.'[59]

Some 20 years later, Serb women victims are still forgotten and there are hardly any local and foreign journalists or researchers seeking to uncover their experiences. Despite acknowledgment that all women were exposed to rape, irrespective of ethnicity, their gender has inevitably been 'blurred' by national, ethnic and religious 'representations'.[60] In its 2012 report concerning rape survivors,[61] Amnesty International acknowledges that they 'did not talk to Bosnian Serb women survivors of rape and other sexual abuse crimes' because it is 'difficult for these women to come out in public and speak up'.[62] The constant and dominant focus on Serb (male) perpetrators and Bosniak (female) survivors by researchers and others has further marginalised Serb women and has not allowed them the opportunity to speak up. While it may be true that it is difficult for Serb women to talk about their experiences, this is not an exclusive problem for Serb women but for all women victims of rape.[63] What is more difficult for them, I would argue, is not 'speaking up' per se, but being listened to.

It is well known that victims of CRSV experience fear, stigma and shame and often never reveal their experiences as they have no support from family, community or the power elites. According to a Serb female activist from Banjaluka, 'these women do not have a reason to talk because they will be judged and stigmatised not only by their family but collectively by the whole Republika Srpska'.[64] As M. Dj., a woman survivor of gang rape by the Croatian Defence Forces in 1992 from Posavina told me:

59 Vesna Nikolić-Ristanović, *Women, Violence and War: Wartime Victimization of Refugees in the Balkans* (Central European University Press, 2000) 46. In 2013, I attended a feminist conference on South Eastern Europe in Norway. I received a similar remark on my comment that Serb women were also raped in the war. The feminist academic from Germany turned to me and asked: 'What numbers are we talking about? The numbers cannot be compared with the number of Muslim women.'

60 Rada Boric, *Gendered Violence in the Balkans, Sexualized Violence Against Women*, paper on file with author.

61 Amnesty International, *Bosnia and Herzegovina: Old Crimes Same Suffering: No Justice for Survivors of Wartime Rape in North-East Bosnia and Herzegovina*, Campaign for International Justice, Paper (2012), www.amnesty.org/en/documents/EUR63/002/2012/en/, 4.

62 Ibid.

63 On the challenges of gaining access to women survivors of CRSV in BiH, see Janine Natalya Clark, 'Working with Survivors of War Rape and Sexual Violence: Fieldwork Reflections from Bosnia-Hercegovina' (2016) (online) *Qualitative Research* 1.

64 Interview with A. S., Banjaluka, 17 May 2015.

> No one has ever come to visit me or ask me about my ordeal. I told my story only once to an NGO from Banjaluka who helped me after I was released from camp, and once to some Serb journalist whom I never saw again. That was in 1993. Since then no one was ever interested in my story.[65]

On the other hand, Bosniak women have been in the spotlight for the past two decades and some have become prominent leaders of their communities. These women survivors have been constructed as perpetual victims; fixed in their social positions of inferior and vulnerable victim.[66] In BiH, a common past of violence has become obligatory to remember, so groups are inclined to transform individuals' past suffering into an 'icon of identity' and an instrument of community power and cohesion.[67] 'Suffering and ethnic cleansing,' argue Elzar Barkan and Belma Bećirbasić, produced 'a strong victimhood narrative and are constitutive of Bosniak ethnic identity'.[68] Bosniak women victims of CRSV are in many ways what Thorsten Bonacker would describe as a group who have obtained 'widespread charismatic authority' from the international community.[69]

The media uncovered the rape camps in which Bosniak and Croat women were held in 1992, and thanks to the bravery of these women, the first stories of CRSV reached the world.[70] The stories of 'mass rape of Bosnian women by Serbian forces went on the front pages of western media in 1992 and 1992'.[71] The stories of rapes by Croat and Bosniak soldiers of Serb women were not the focus of international media attention. These women did not have the satisfaction of experiencing public condemnation of the crimes that had been perpetrated against them. Due to a lack of political will and selective remembrance and narratives, documenting war crimes perpetrated against Bosniak – and to some extent Croat – women has become the norm, on both the local and international stages.

While there have been locally produced and published books, documents and reports that include Serb women CRSV survivors' testimonies, because of the

65 Interview with M. Dj. (Banjaluka, 23 June 2015). M. Dj. was detained with her three young children in Strolit camp in Modriča for two months where she was repeatedly raped before being released.

66 See Olivera Simić, 'Challenging Bosnian Women Identity as Rape Victims, as Unending Victims: The "Other" Sex in Times of War' (2012) 13(4) *Journal of International Women's Studies* 129.

67 Barbara Misztal, *Theories of Social Remembering* (McGraw-Hill Education, 2003) 75.

68 Elazar Barkan and Belma Bećirbasić, 'The Politics of Memory, Victimization, and Activism in Postconflict Bosnia and Herzegovina' in Klaus Neumann and Janna Thompson (eds), *Historical Justice and Memory* (University of Wisconsin Press, 2015) 95, 101.

69 Thorsten Bonacker, 'Global Victimhood: On the Charisma of the Victim in Transitional Justice Processes' (2013) 9(1) *World Political Science Review* 97, 110.

70 Mischowski and Mlinarevic, above n 33, 6.

71 Lene Hansen, 'Gender, Nation, Rape: Bosnia and the Construction of Security', *International Feminist Journal of Politics* 3(1) 2000, 56; Allen Baverly, *Rape Warfare: The Hidden Genocide in Bosnia-Herzegovina and Croatia* (University of Minnesota Press, 1996); Penny Stanley, 'Reporting of Mass Rape in the Balkans: *Plus Ca Change, Plus C'est Même Chose*? From Bosnia to Kosovo', *Civil Wars* 2(2) 1996.

nature of these sources, the stories have mostly been rejected as 'ultra nationalist', 'politically motivated', 'ideologically coloured' and 'suspicious' by feminist activists who consider themselves anti-militarist and anti-nationalist in their orientation.[72] Although such sources are almost the only available accounts of Serb women's experiences, they have not been reproduced in feminist writings on CRSV in BiH. According to one activist from Serbia:

> I am aware that there are a few really good collections about Serb women testimonies of wartime rape and violence. These were made by the Documentation Center of the Commissariat for Refugees in Republic of Serbia, but these sources we did not want and could not use. They are considered pro-nationalist because women and their testimonies were used to promote a nationalist propaganda. The whole discourse and rhetoric was ultra-right so we did not want to use these sources in our writings . . . We did not accept sources which were suspicious in terms of their authenticity or nationalism. That still does not mean that there are no correct facts or authentic stories in them. We used the same principle when it comes to the documents published by Bosniak or Croatian ultra-right organisations.[73]

Such decisions to not reproduce these materials have had their implications, the most important being that Serb women's voices have been silenced. D.O., a woman survivor of CRSV, told me that she vividly remembers 'someone from Belgrade, a woman historian who came down to Herzegovina to collect testimonies from people who spent time in rape and other camps around the year 2000'.[74] That woman was Dušica Bojić, a historian with the Museum of History, Belgrade, who has produced five volumes of oral history by interviewing thousands of Serb women and men about their experiences of torture and abuse.[75]

This is probably the most comprehensive archival collection of testimonies of Serbs, males and females, about injustices inflicted upon them. Since these archives were produced and supported by the Slobodan Milošević regime, they were perceived as being used to advance a nationalist agenda and as such, anti-nationalist feminist activists did not want to reproduce them in their writings. There are also a number of testimonies by Serb women who spent their time

72 Another activist from Serbia told me that the NGO she worked for had access to such testimonies, but they had not used them for the reasons mentioned. Interview with R. A., 18 August 2015.

73 Interview with S. O., 18 August 2015.

74 Interview with K. S., 7 June 2015.

75 Dušica Bojić was a part of the Documentation Center located as a section in the Commissariat for Refugees of the Republic of Serbia. The Documentation Center carried out its investigations from April 1992 to the end of 1997. They gathered a large archive of materials such as personal testimonies, video materials, audio tapes and objects found during fieldwork. Although people from all ethnic groups came to the Center to tell their stories, Serb refugees were the most numerous. The database was created to reveal the truth about the suffering of the Serbs in the war. See Dušica Bojić, 'The War in Bosnia with a Description of Events in the Tuzla Region (1992–1995)' (2003) 17(2) *Journal of the North American Society for Serbian Studies* 225, 226–227.

in the psychiatric hospital Laza Lazarević in Belgrade, but these documents 'are quite possibly still sitting in the filing cabinets of some women's NGOs'.[76] With the fear that if made public, these files would serve only for the purpose of advancing nationalist discourse, the files with these stories were never published:

> I remember once, during the war, a psychiatrist personally came to our offices and handed us one file with all the medical and other details of one female patient. He wanted us to use the data and publish it so Serb women victims of wartime rape would gain visibility in public and advance Serb nationalist propaganda of victimhood. We refused to do so because he only wanted to use us and our status to support Milošević's machine. We also did not want to use the confidential info from the file and reproduce it without the woman's consent. We have never done anything with that file. I think we still have that file somewhere in our office.[77]

Another female activist told me that the people who worked for the government took testimonies from women who had suffered wartime rape as soon as women would cross the border of Serbia: 'they literally were grabbing the stories from them . . . These were all heavy cases and many of them were sent abroad for rehabilitation, but they did not care about the women. They wanted a story of Serb suffering.'[78] These fears of being accused of supporting the nationalist cause still exist and they are not to be underestimated. Still, the combination of feminists' reluctance to publicise the stories, and the lack of interest by the local and international public in hearing the perspectives of 'other women' – women who belong to ethnic groups other than Bosniak and Croat – has had further consequences: the testimonies of Serb women, whether oral or audio-visual, do not occupy public space and have been systematically excluded from the discourse on CRSV in BiH. Testimonies, fragmented narratives (taken out of context and used in ethnic and nationalist discourses) and facts about CRSV against Serb women have been scarce and scattered among various archives, court files and cases, or stayed buried in local media papers, books, and the drawers of local and international organisations.

These testimonies were also not documented separately, but often together with male experiences of torture, which were distorted, misused or taken out of context to serve the aims of the nationalist propaganda. To extract these stories from, what these activists considered to be, the right-wing sources was simply not acceptable to women activists and, as such, they were dismissed as legitimate sources that could be used. These testimonies, another female activist told me, have stayed 'silent'. She elaborated:

76 Interview with R. K., 14 May 2015. Bosnian Serb women who crossed the border to Serbia, often in the late months of their pregnancies, were accommodated after abortion or delivery in the psychiatric hospital Laza Lazarević.

77 Interview with S. O., 18 August 2015.

78 Telephone interview with S. B., 12 June 2014.

> We heard that Serb women were systematically raped in so-called brothels in Sarajevo, for example, but I never read these testimonies. I think that it would be good to bring together these stories in the name of justice and fairness.[79]

From my conversations, it seems that many feminist activists, both Bosnian Serbs and Serbians, agree that something needs to be done, and that it would be good that someone writes about this issue and perhaps documents and archives women's testimonies. To my question whether Bosniak feminists are ready to talk about crimes committed by their own group, a long-term feminist from Serbia told me:

> I really don't believe that the time has come because it is somehow systematic – it [Serb women's rape cases] is always invisible. I just read this detailed research from Medica Zenica and Medica Mondiale,[80] it is all very important, but even there, there is nothing about it. I think two things here . . . One, it is difficult for them [the researchers] to find a woman who wants to talk about her experience of rape in the context of all other experiences . . . Second, I think they [the researchers] do not make much effort to find these women . . . Unless they found at least one woman who would talk about her experience where the perpetrator was from the Bosnian army, the researchers should not label their study feminist. Third, none of the groups is feminist anymore so we cannot expect that. Fourth, Republika Srpska with its totalitarian politics just hinders this process and it does that systematically . . . the time has not come yet, since people still cannot accept each other . . . but only 20 years has passed. The Tokyo Women's Tribunal happened 50 years after WWII.[81]

The materials that contain Serb women survivors' testimonies include documentary films made by the Association of Camp Inmates Republika Srpska, Bosnian Serb or Serbian journalists who have circulated them in local public spaces, including the Internet. However, these movies are not commercial and are often made with scarce funds and publicity. Further, they are traumatic and difficult to watch and, as such, unattractive even to Serb local media. Most have not been

79 Ibid.

80 Medica Zenica and Medica Mondiale, '*We Are Still Alive': Research on the Long-Term Consequences of War Rape and Copying Strategies of Survivors in Bosnia and Herzegovina*, Report (2014), www.medicamondiale.org/fileadmin/redaktion/5_Service/Mediathek/Dokumente/English/Documentations_studies/141128_Research_We-Are-Still-Alive_CR-Medica-Zenica_medica-mondiale.pdf, 63. The Bosnian organisation Medica Zenica was established in 1993 and is known for its work with women survivors of wartime rape. Out of 51 women survivors who participated in the study, only 2 were Serbs. One explanation for such a low number is that Medica Zenica is based in the Federation of Bosnia and Herzegovina entity with predominantly a Bosniak population. So, the study is not representative of the whole territory of the state as suggested in its title, but rather limited to the specific demographic area.

81 Email correspondence, 13 January 2015. On file with author.

translated into English or any other foreign language and as such remain inaccessible to foreign journalists and researchers. These movies remain unpopular with, or unknown to, either local or international audiences – only survivors, their families and some nationalist journalists know of them.

Anti-nationalist groups generally dismiss such movies as trying to promote a Serb nationalist agenda.[82] Regardless of their aims, the multimedia and documentary archives emphasise the importance of creating 'alternative bodies of evidence'[83] that capture women's testimonies where dominant systems of representation have failed to do so, and where the listener engages in 'an act of remembering that . . . obliges us to receive rather than repress inhumane events'.[84]

(Lack of) recognition as (in)justice

Transitional justice measures seek to provide recognition for victims as individuals and as bearers of rights.[85] In his work on 'justice as recognition'; Frank Haldemann talks about the human need for validation and recognition.[86] He argues that feelings of being ignored and a failure to recognise another's dignity or equal worth are internalised as a lack of respect. Acknowledging the fact and wrongfulness of the violations is a precondition to 'de-victimization'.[87] As Albie Sachs commented, there is a need 'to move from knowledge to acknowledgment . . . Knowledge is just knowing the facts, the details, but it's abstract . . . acknowledgment means it enters into your emotional world, your world of responsibility.'[88]

Possibly one of the most serious consequences of the one-sided representation of CRSV is the lack of recognition, which in turn affects the lack of support, empathy and assistance to survivors who live in RS. Women's NGOs in this entity stayed without donor-driven support to develop programs to help women to recover from trauma and regain their life. As a result, more than 20 years after the war ended, none of the NGOs or governmental institutions in RS

82 The movie about 8-year-old Mirjana Dragičević, who was raped by Mujahidin, was made by the Association of film workers *Vizantija* in 2005. The movie travelled internationally to depict Serb suffering. Radmila, Mirjana's mother, has not received any profit from the movie and even found it on sale on the streets of the town where she lives, together with a DVD of local folk singers. See the movie with English subtitles, *Mirjana dokumentarni film* [Trans: *Mirjana Documentary Film*] 7 December 2011, www.youtube.com/watch?v=A4sirVibWkI>.

83 See Olivera Simić, 'But I Want to Speak Out: Making Art From Women's Testimonies' (2014) 40(1) *Australian Feminist Law Journal* 51.

84 Hartman Geoffrey, 'Memory, Com: Tele-Suffering and Testimony in the Dot Com Era' (2000) 19(3) *Raritan* 1, 13.

85 Pablo de Greiff, 'Theorizing Transitional Justice' in Melissa S. Williams, Rosemary Nagy and Jon Elster (ed.), *Transitional Justice: NOMOS LI* (New York University Press, 2012) 31, 42.

86 Frank Haldemann, 'Another Kind of Justice: Transitional Justice as Recognition' (2008) 41(3) *Cornell International Law Journal* 675.

87 Merryl Lawry-White, 'The Reparative Effect of Truth Seeking in Transitional Justice' (2015) 64(1) *International and Comparative Law Quarterly* 141, 151.

88 Cited in ibid.

have programs and strategies for women's recovery and rehabilitation. Women have been left to deal alone with the feelings of shame and guilt for being raped.[89] They have collectively become 'collateral damage', an unfortunate by-product of war; sometimes a number and a statistic, often faceless and nameless, only occasionally remembered by politicians when they wish to emphasise the crimes of 'the other side' (and in the case of the RS government, not even that). Rarely, if ever, have such women been on the political or other agenda of the politicians. One would assume that it might be in the interest of the RS government to say 'our women were raped too', but that has not been the case.

It is hard to think of reasons why the RS government does not want to recognise its women survivors of CRSV. Is it about the excessive budgeting and funding that would be necessary to cover claims for reparation? Is it about a fear of a wave of compensation claims coming from 'other' non-Serb women survivors living in the entity? Ironically, as time passes by, there are fewer and fewer women survivors because they are aging and consequently dying. Or does this attitude reflect a lack of interest in women's lives more generally? Or perhaps Serb males do not want to admit that they 'failed' to protect 'their' women and in that way, Serb women's feeling of shame does not become their shame too? Whatever may be the reason, the overall ignorance and lack of recognition of women survivors' basic human rights and freedoms have led to the different treatment of women geographically, depending on which territory of BiH the women live in.

In that respect, the UN Committee on the Elimination of Discrimination Against Women (the CEDAW Committee) published its concluding observations on BiH in July 2013 and expressed its deep concern due to

> long delays in adopting measures to address the needs of a large number of women victimised by the conflict . . . [as well as] [w]omen's inadequate and unequal access to compensation, support and rehabilitation measures for violations suffered during the war, including enforced disappearances, such as sustained psychological and medical support, as well as financial and social benefits, which are regulated differently in the entities.[90]

Different regulation of victim status in the BiH government is unacceptable since a victim is a victim bearing the same physical and psychological scars, irrespective

89 See Gorana Mlinarević, Jakov Čaušević and Jasmina Čaušević, *Prosecution of Wartime Sexualized Violence at the Court of Bosnia and Herzegovina: What Happened to the Interest of Justice? An Analysis and Recommendations of Gender Sensitive Trial Monitoring for Wartime Sexualized Violence Cases in Bosnia and Herzegovina for the Period 23/05/2011–25/05/2012* (Report, Association Alumni of the Centre for Interdisciplinary Postgraduate Studies, 2012), www.civilsocietylibrary.org/CSL/529/Prosecution-of-Wartime-Sexualized-Violence-at-the-Court-of-Bosnia-and-Herzegovina-What-Happened-to-The-Interest-of-Justice>.

90 UN Committee on the Elimination of Discrimination Against Women, *Concluding Observations on the Combined Fourth and Fifth Reports of Bosnia and Herzegovina*, CEDAW/C/BIH/CO/4–5, 30 July 2013, para. 9 (f) 3.

of ethnic and entity borders. In RS women victims feel forgotten, stigmatised and betrayed by their community; they have no influence on the political and social transformation of the country in which they live.

Conclusion

Almost 20 years after the war, one of the biggest obstacles to reconciliation and long-lasting peace in BiH is the ignoring of the thousands of women victims of CRSV and the persistence of discriminatory practices regarding the exercising of their rights to material and symbolic reparation.[91] Given these dynamics, international media and academic attention has been preoccupied with Bosniak women and during the war and, in particular, its aftermath, international organisations and donors largely supported Bosniak victims and assisted in the foundation and establishment of dozens of NGOs in the Federation of BiH (FBiH),[92] enabling them to offer much-needed assistance to women survivors of CRSV. The polarised and strongly established view concerning CRSV as exclusively perpetrated by Serb males has had enormous consequences on the lives of women survivors in both entities. It has, to some extent, advanced the situation of women victims in the FBiH, in the sense that at least the government in this entity has shown a political will to move, albeit slowly, towards acknowledgement and support. For example, as a result of joint local and international women's campaigns, women survivors in the FBiH have been able to exercise the right to material reparation as civilian victims of CRSV since 2006.[93]

On the other hand, in RS, polarised views concerning Serb women and the marginalisation of their experiences as victims of CRSV have closed the door to foreign donors. Such views have produced a permanent obstacle that still seems impossible to overcome; large proportions of women victims in RS have not succeeded in gaining the status of civilian victim of war and differential treatment has exacerbated the divisions between the two entities and women survivors. The women survivors in RS who I spoke to, feel bitter and forgotten about, not only by their government but by civil society too. They feel that their experiences have been downplayed and less valued than the experiences of other women, in particular Bosniak women.

91 Selma Korjenić, 'Preventing Sexual Violence in Conflict' on *Prevent Sexual Violence in Conflict* (12 April 2012), http://preventsexualviolenceinconflict.tumblr.com/post/37183224957/bosnia-trial>.

92 Max Stephenson and Laura Zanotti, 'Implementing Liberal Peace in Post-Conflict Scenarios: The Case of Women in Black Serbia' (2012) 3(1) *Global Policy Volume* 46, 53.

93 The women's movement for recognition of female survivors of CRSV gained its momentum after release of the famous film *Grbavica* made by Jasmila Žbanić. With her film, Žbanić, the director of the movie, gave a boost to the 'Dignity Campaign' and renewed interest in the issue of wartime rape and its survivors. Its popularity triggered legislative changes, but only in the Federation of BiH, not Republika Srpska. See Helms, above n 8, 197; Charlie Carpenter, *Forgetting Children Born of War: Setting the Human Rights Agenda in Bosnia and Beyond* (Columbia University Press, 2010) 159.

An effort to cross carefully constructed, and over the years, well-cemented ethnic bridges, and bring all women victims together has most recently been seen by the Women's Court that was held in Sarajevo in May 2015. Although the work on the establishment of the Women's Court was a long-term commitment of the feminists from across ex-Yugoslavia, the Court failed to bring Serb women survivors of CRSV from RS to share their experiences. In Chapter 5, I analyse the events in Sarajevo that, unfortunately, confirmed entrenched ethnic divisions in BiH.

4 Becoming a victim in Bosnia and Herzegovina

The judicial system in BiH

Although BiH is a small country with under 4 million inhabitants, it is divided into four territorial and administrative units: Republika Srpska (RS), the Federation of Bosnia and Herzegovina (FBiH), the internationally supervised Brčko District and the State of BiH. Each unit has its legislative, judicial and executive powers. The prosecution of war crimes, including the cases of CRSV, takes place before 15 different courts and prosecutor's offices and under different criminal legislations. Both entities (RS and FBiH) and the Brčko District have a Prosecutor's Office for indictments of war crimes. Since the 2003 legal reform, the State Court of BiH has jurisdiction over the most serious war crime cases.[1] The Special Department for War Crimes of the Prosecutor's Office was established by The Law of the Prosecutor's Office of Bosnia and Herzegovina.[2]

The War Crimes Chamber (WCC) operates under the Criminal Code of BiH, which includes sexual violence offences. With its official start in 2005, the WCC was tasked with a backlog of war crimes cases. In 2009 it was estimated that between 6,000 and 16,000 war crimes cases, at different stages of prosecution, remain unresolved.[3] In 2014, according to the High Judicial and Prosecutorial Council, which is responsible for supervising the BiH justice system, the number of open investigations of war crimes against known suspects was around 1,300.[4] The low number of suspects, lack of evidence and perpetrators' unavailability during investigations impedes the progress of inquiries. Statistics of how many unresolved cases are related to rape and other forms of CRSV crimes are

1 OSCE, *War Crimes Trials Before the Domestic Courts of Bosnia and Herzegovina: Progress and Obstacles*, Human Rights Department (2005), www.nuhanovicfoundation.org/user/file/2005_osce_report_war_crimes_trials_before_domestic_courts_in_bih.pdf_-_to_be_added%21.pdf, 17.

2 The Law on the Prosecutor's Office of Bosnia and Herzegovina, *Official Gazette of Bosnia and Herzegovina*, Nos 24/02, 3/03, 37/03, 42/03, 9/04, 35/04, 61/04, https://advokat-prnjavorac.com/legislation/Law-on-The-Prosecutors-Office-of-BH.pdf.

3 Amnesty International, *Whose Justice? The Women of Bosnia and Herzegovina Are Still Waiting*, Report (2009), www.amnesty.org/en/documents/EUR63/006/2009/en/, 18.

4 Denis Džidic, 'Bosnia Struggles with War Crimes Investigation Backlog', *BalkanInsight* (online), 14 October 2014, www.balkaninsight.com/en/article/bosnia-failing-to-reduce-number-of-war-crimes-investigations.

not available and have never been collected by authorities.[5] According to the European Commission 'the overall number of indictments for sexual violence is low in comparison to the prevalence of such crimes during the conflict'.[6] In its report on 10 years of prosecuting war crimes before the WCC, the authorities did not provide the number of prosecuted cases, or those still in backlog, but stated that 2,700 witnesses testified before the Court.[7] Despite the progress that has been made, the WCC acknowledged that they 'are far away from bringing all perpetrators before the justice system'.[8]

RS, FBiH, Brčko District and the BiH State each has its own legal system. Only a small number of laws are implemented at the state level. The majority of the laws that were in force in the former Yugoslavia are enforced at entity levels, in most cases without major alterations. Each entity has wide legislative competencies and may adopt completely different laws. The challenge of having a plethora of different entity laws that regulate the same matters prompted the Office of the High Representative to encourage the entities to start adopting so-called 'mirror laws' – laws that are identical but enacted separately by the Parliaments in each entity.[9]

In BiH, there are 13 jurisdictions in which war crimes and crimes against humanity can be prosecuted with a referral from the State Prosecutor's Office. The war crimes trials can take place in one of the 10 cantonal courts in FBiH, in five District Courts in RS and in the Basic Court of Brčko District. Appeals can be made at the Supreme Courts in RS, FBiH and the Appellate Court of Brčko District. The WCC has a concurrent jurisdiction, since under the 2008 *National War Crimes Strategy* (*National Strategy*) cases are grouped and divided into jurisdictions according to where the crime was committed.[10] Only the most sensitive war crimes cases are prosecuted at the state level, while cases initiated before the 2003 Criminal Code, and lower-ranking indictees, are to be prosecuted before the entity and district courts.

5 Amnesty International, above n 3, 18.

6 European Commission, *Bosnia and Herzegovina Progress Report* (2014), https://ec.europa.eu/neighbourhood-enlargement/sites/near/files/pdf/key_documents/2014/20141008-bosnia-and-herzegovina-progress-report_en.pdf, 14.

7 Sud Bosne i Hercegovine, *10 godina rada Odjela za ratne zločine Suda Bosne i Hercegovine: 2005–2015*, Sarajevo (2015) [Trans: *The Court of Bosnia and Herzegovina: 10 Years of Work of the War Crimes Chamber: 2005–2015*], www.sudbih.gov.ba/files/docs/brosura/10_anniversary_of_Section_I.pdf, 15.

8 Ibid., 16.

9 European Bank for Reconstruction and Development, *Commercial Laws of Bosnia and Herzegovina: An Assessment by the EBRD*, Report (2014), www.ebrd.com/downloads/legal/concessions/pppreport.pdf, 2.

10 *National War Crimes Strategy Adopted by the Council of Ministers of Bosnia and Herzegovina on 28 December 2008*, Ministry of Justice of Bosnia and Herzegovina. English translated version available as Annex 2 in Morten Bergsmo, Kjetil Helvig, Ilia Utmelidze and Gorana Žagovec, *The Backlog of Core International Crimes Case Files in Bosnia and Herzegovina* (Torkel Opsahl Academic EPublisher, 2008), www.fichl.org/fileadmin/fichl/documents/FICHL_3_Second_Edition_web.pdf.

Due to the large backlog of cases, BiH failed to meet its *National Strategy* targets and resolve the most sensitive cases by December 2015. According to some predictions, the country may not be capable of tackling the thousands of unresolved remaining cases by the final deadline of 2023.[11] From 2008 till December 2015 only 30 per cent of cases had been resolved. A total of 750 people have been charged, but investigations into alleged war crimes committed by at least 7,000 more people remain to be resolved.[12] Some reasons for such a small number are lack of political will to prosecute war crimes, the complexity of the investigations and the fact that some suspects and witnesses have either left the country or passed away.[13] In some cases, parallel investigative procedures at the state and entity levels have been conducted, which is a waste of resources and time. The judiciary also requires more staff to help resolve the most complex war crime cases.[14]

Between 2003 and 2015, definitions within the Criminal Code of BiH for CRSV crimes as war crimes and crimes against humanity, contained the element of 'use of threat or force' and as such they were not fully compliant with international standards and the jurisprudence of international courts.[15] The international tribunals and jurisprudence have established that lack of consent for sexual activity may be demonstrated by other means of coercion, such as duress, detention, abuse of power, psychological oppression or fear of violence, all of which are particularly relevant during periods of armed conflicts.[16]

11 Marija Tausan, 'Huge War Crimes Case Backlog Overwhelms Bosnia', *Justice Report* (online), 23 October 2015, www.justice-report.com/en/articles/huge-war-crimes-case-backlog-overwhelms-bosnia.

12 Ibid.

13 By September 2009, 139 individuals had been indicted for war-related crimes before the WCC at the state court, most of them of Serb ethnicity. By the end of the same period, 72 of the defendants had received a final verdict. Yaël Ronen, *Prosecutions and Sentencing in the Western Balkans* (with the assistance of Sharon Avital and Oren Tamir), DOMAC (2010), http://en.ru.is/domac/domac-reports/; Justice Report, 'Bosnian War Crimes Strategy 'Failing', *BalkanInsight* (online), 29 January 2016, www.balkaninsight.com/en/article/bosnia-drowning-in-war-crimes-backlog-01-29-2016?utm_source=Balkan+Transitional+Justice+Daily+Newsletter+-+NEW&utm_campaign=cfbd6cb52c-RSS_EMAIL_CAMPAIGN&utm_medium=email&utm_term=0_a1d9e93e97-cfbd6cb52c-319752573.

14 Tausan, above n 11.

15 Article 172 (1)(g), governing crimes against humanity prescribed: 'Coercing another by force or by threat of immediate attack upon his life or limb, or the life or limb a person close to him, to sexual intercourse or equivalent sexual act (rape), sexual slavery, enforced prostitution, forced pregnancy, enforced sterilization or any other form of sexual violence of comparable gravity.' Article 173(1)(e), governing war crimes, prescribes, in the relevant part: 'Coercing another by force or by threat of immediate attack upon his life or limb, or the life or limb a person close to him, to sexual intercourse or equivalent sexual act (rape) or forcible prostitution.'

16 The *Akayesu* Trial Chamber provided the clearest explanation of 'coercive circumstances', when it stated: 'Coercive circumstances need not be evidenced by a show of physical force. Threats, intimidation, extortion and other forms of duress may constitute coercion, and coercion may be inherent in certain circumstances, such as armed conflict or the military presence of Interahamwe among refugee women.' *Prosecutor v Jean-Paul Akayesu*, Trial Judgement (International Criminal Tribunal for Rwanda), Chamber 1, Case No. ICTR-96-4-T, 2 September 1998, 688.

Definitions of such crimes in BiH were unduly narrow and resulted in a low number of indictments in relation to CRSV.[17] The BiH judiciary ignored the wartime context – abuse of power, exploitation, slavery and general environment of fear that prevailed in wartime society.

While the Criminal Code of BiH's narrow definition encouraged impunity and unnecessary interrogation of the sexual conduct of women testifying,[18] in some cases the judges overcame these legislative shortcomings by interpreting the relevant provisions in line with international standards. In 2005, in *Prosecutor v Simsic*, the first BiH Court case to address sexual violence as persecution, the BiH Court relied upon *Kunarac* and recognised that not only force, or threat of force, but also coercive circumstances may negate consent. Quoting *Kunarac*, it found that 'resistance is not a requirement'.[19] In 2010 the UN Committee Against Torture recommended amending the definition of CRSV in BiH legislation and removing the condition 'of force or threat of immediate attack'.[20] This groundbreaking change and shift in definition, which is now consistent with international law, came in 2015 after years of lobbying by local and international organisations.[21]

Another problem for prosecution of CRSV has been the problem of inconsistency of entity and state laws. Due to the number of war crimes cases to be prosecuted, responsibility for prosecuting less complex cases, such as single acts of rape, has been passed down to entity level courts. However, there are five criminal laws that are being implemented in BiH: the Criminal Law of BiH, the Criminal Law of FBiH, the Criminal Law of RS, the Brčko District Criminal Law and the Criminal Law of the Socialist Federal Republic of Yugoslavia (SFRY).

The major difference between these laws is that the Criminal Law of BiH contains war crimes and crimes against humanity provisions, while the entities' laws

17 OSCE, *Combating Impunity for Conflict-Related Sexual Violence in BiH: Progress and Challenges: An Analysis of Criminal Proceedings before the Court of Bosnia and Herzegovina between 2005 and 2013*, OSCE Mission to Bosnia and Herzegovina (2014), www.files.ethz.ch/isn/179069/English.pdf, 23.

18 Annika Björkdahl and Selma Mannergren Selimovic, 'Gender Justice Gaps in Bosnia-Herzegovina' (2014) 15(2) *Human Rights Review* 201, 209.

19 *Prosecutor v Simsic Boban* (The Court of Bosnia and Herzegovina), Trial Judgment, Case No. X-KR-05/04, 11 July 2006, 49.

20 UN Human Rights Office of the High Commissioner, *Consideration of Reports Submitted by State Parties Under Article 19 of the Convention: Concluding Observation of the Committee Against Torture*, Committee against Torture, Forty-Fifth Session (1–19 November, 2010), www2.ohchr.org/english/bodies/cat/docs/CAT.C.BIH.CO.2-5.pdf, 3 [9].

21 On 18 May 2015 the BiH Parliament adopted the necessary changes and removed the elements of threat/force from definition of sexual violence. The Criminal Code of BiH was amended, but none of the criminal codes at the entity level were amended and significant pitfalls remain. The amendments to the Criminal Code of BiH were approved by the House of Peoples under urgent procedure on 18 May 2015, published in the *Official Gazette* no. 40/15, entered into force on 28 May 2015. Art. 172, para. 1 (g), and 173, para. 1 (e) of the Criminal Code of BiH were amended and the requirement that the victims is coerced 'by force or by threat of immediate attack upon his or her life or limb, or the life or limb of the person close to him or her' has been removed.

and the laws of the Brčko District do not. Accordingly, the courts in the entities do not necessarily use the Criminal Code of BiH in their indictments and trials of the individuals for crimes committed in war, but the Criminal Law of SFRY.[22] Yet, the SFRY Criminal Code does not include CRSV crimes, such as forced pregnancy and sexual slavery, which increases the possibility of impunity for these crimes. Due to such inconsistencies, prosecuting crimes of CRSV under the SFRY Criminal Code result in different sentencing. A person convicted of a wartime rape under the SFRY Criminal Code is sentenced to between 1 and 10 years of imprisonment, while under the BiH Criminal Code a minimum sentence of 10 years is applied. Consequently, due to such variations in code implementation, survivors of CRSV do not have fair and equal access to justice.

BiH authorities also failed to adopt the Programme for Victims of Sexual Violence that was jointly launched by the Ministry for Human Rights and Refugees and United Nations Population Fund (UNPFA) and aimed to help ensure access to reparations for the survivors. The Programme defines the basis for realising survivors' rights to social welfare and health care, and provides measures for economic empowerment. Failing to receive a positive response on the Programme from the government of the RS, the Ministry of Human Rights and Refugees never submitted it to the BiH Council of Ministers for adoption.[23] In the following two sections, I provide an overview of the regulation of CRSV at entity levels.

Regulation of conflict-related sexual violence at entity levels

Republika Srpska

RS does not have a specific legal framework for survivors of CRSV. In the territory of RS, survivors could become recognised as 'civil victims of war' under the *Law on Protection of Civil War Victims in the Serb Republic* (the *Law*).[24] The *Law* guaranteed special measures of social protection, mainly in the form of financial assistance, however, only to victims who could prove 60 per cent of bodily damage as a result of torture, assault, rape or other crimes committed in the course of the armed conflict. Those who qualified under the *Law* were entitled to a pension, as were all civilian victims of war and disabled persons. The pension was not compensation, but a social welfare scheme, which covered all disabled persons under the same line in the RS budget.

In RS, according to the Ministry of Labour, War Veterans and Disabled Persons' Protection, by the end of 2013, 587 women and 965 male victims of

22 *Meddžida* Kreso, '(Ne)jednakost pred zakonom' [Trans: '(In)equality Before the Law'] (2006) 5 *Pravda u tranziciji* 1; Amnesty International, above n 3, 30.

23 Amnesty International, *Bosnia and Herzegovina: Submission to the United Nations Human Rights Committee 119th Session, 6–29 March 2017*. Document on file with author.

24 *Official Gazette of the Republika Srpska*, Nos 25/93, 32/94, 37/07, 60/07, 111/09 and 118/09.

war had obtained the status of civilian victims of war.[25] While it is not known how many beneficiaries received their status on the basis of having survived CRSV and torture (since the data is not segregated), in official correspondence with the Assistant of the RS Minister for Labour, War Veterans and Disabled Persons, I have been told that an 'insignificant number of women victims of wartime sexual violence received their status of civilian victim of war'.[26] The *Law* did not recognise survivors of CRSV as a special category of victims, and the RS government has been criticised by international non-government organisations (NGOs), such as Amnesty International, who reported that the government 'have never made a meaningful attempt to collect data on this population, to understand and quantify their problems or to develop policies that would address their specific needs'.[27] According to Milenko Savanović, Minister of Labour, War Veterans and Disabled Persons' Protection in RS, the government 'had a large number of killed soldiers, of invalids and perhaps we focused more on this population who came out from the war directly from the front'.[28] The government was primarily concerned with the combatant population, consisting of almost exclusively males, while women and other civilian victims were pushed to the margins. Savanović's statement was made in 2017, 22 years after the war ended, and as such can hardly serve as a legitimate reason as to why the Ministry has failed, for more than two decades, to regulate the status of women survivors of CRSV.

One of the key problems faced by women who reside in the RS territory were the deadlines for applying for the status of civilian victim and assistance. The first deadline for claiming the status of civilian victim of war expired in 2001. This deadline was extended until December 2007 with all claims made after this deadline being automatically rejected.[29] The *Law* should be amended and the requirement, stipulating the submission of applications for obtaining status be made by 31 December 2007, abolished. Many victims were not informed about

25 Official letter from the *Ministry of Labour, War Veterans and Disabled Persons No. 16-03/1-56-1052/13*, Banjaluka, 14 November 2013, on file with the author. I should say that this number has probably not changed much today since the Law expired in December 2007 and after this deadline victims could not apply for the status any more. Some of the victims had appealed on decisions and if successful their numbers would be added, but according to one government official, that would not have significantly changed the number from 2013, which I officially received. Email communication from RS government official, 14 April 2017. On file with author.

26 Letter from the Assistant to the RS Minister for Labour, War Veterans and Disabled Persons, 26 December 2013, on file with the author. The largest number of the victims received the status on basis of wounding.

27 Amnesty International, *When Everyone Is Silent: Reparations for Survivors of Wartime Rape in Republika Srpska in Bosnia and Herzegovina*, Report (2012), www.amnesty.org/en/documents/EUR63/012/2012/en/.

28 RTV Oko, 'Sjećaš li se mene u ropstvu' [Trans: 'Do You Remember Me in Slavery?'], 7 February 2017, www.youtube.com/watch?v=w98DAtuTUYw.

29 International Centre for Transitional Justice, Submission to the Universal Periodic Review of the UN Human Rights Council, Seventh Session, ICTJ (2009), www.ictj.org/publication-type/un-universal-periodic-review-submission, 3.

the legal requirement to meet the deadline for submissions and missed the opportunity to apply for the status:

> Many women who were with me in the same camp did not know about the deadlines: deadlines to submit claims and to appeal if rejected. They also did not know that they could appeal if their claim was initially rejected. There was a window of two weeks to appeal but they did not read the documents carefully. Many of them are illiterate and they thought once they were rejected that was final. Only a handful of us received the status after years of fighting the system.[30]

Survivors should not be restricted in exercising their lawful rights subject to meeting a specific deadline. Their rights to achieve reparation must not be limited either by a fixed timeline or geographical location. Women victims who were not officially recognised as civilian victims of war, have no access to free legal aid, health care, and are not eligible for education, rehabilitation or psychological support.

Apart from the expiry date for the submission of applications, in order to acquire victim status, a person had to prove that he or she had bodily damage of at least 60 per cent – which made obtaining the status extremely challenging. Health commissions conducted the assessment of bodily damage on the basis of the *Rulebook on Establishing Levels of Veterans' Disability*, which does not refer to mental health. According to the *Rulebook*, full medical documentation, which must be dated within a year of the injury being sustained or within a year of the war ending, was required to make a claim as a civilian victim of war.[31]

It is obvious that such conditions would deter many survivors from applying for the status, either because they could not provide the required medical documentation or because their damages are primarily psychological.[32] Obtaining medical documentation in the midst of war and in its immediate aftermath would be, if not impossible, extremely difficult for the large majority of survivors. They simply did not have an opportunity to seek medical help at the time, and those who sought it were often not given medical certificates that described the nature of their injuries as a result of the sexual assault they had survived. As Božica Živković Rajilić, a Serb woman survivor from RS, reported:

> [T]he procedure to prove detention in the camp within RS lasted a full sixteen-and-a-half years because I could not fulfil their absurd conditions that the then government had made – conditions that none of the victims could fulfil. They asked us to bring to them medical documentation about

30 Interview with M. Đ., Banjaluka, 9 July 2016.

31 Linda Popić and Belma Panjeta, *Compensation, Transitional Justice and Conditional International Credit in Bosnia and Herzegovina: Attempts to Reform Governments Payments to Victims and Veterans of the 1992–1995 War*, Royal Norwegian Embassy in Bosnia and Herzegovina and Embassy of Switzerland in Bosnia and Herzegovina (2010), www.norveska.ba/PageFiles/417487/Study_Linda_Popic_english.pdf, 7.

32 Amnesty International, above n 27.

> our suffering and torture in concentration camps. Do you really think that someone will beat you, torture you, rape you and then give you a certificate that will confirm that?[33]

M. Đ., a survivor of gang rape by the Croatian army in the Posavina region, told me that when she was taken to the hospital in Banjaluka in 1993, together with a group of women with whom she and her three young children had been held in a rape camp, she never told any of the doctors (including gynaecologists) what she had survived. M. Đ. reported: 'no one asked me what happened to me, but everyone knew it since the transport was organised for us, women, who were sexually abused'.[34] These group visits to Banjaluka hospital were organised by the NGO 'Duga' from Banjaluka.

Dragiša Andrić, President of the Association of Detainees in Višegrad, reflects on the fact that the *Law* requires that women possess medical documentation from wartime:

> We know that 90 per cent of violations happened in 1992, with maybe only 10 per cent during the rest of the war, and that many people were killed or they lost their homes. They couldn't even keep the space where they lived, let alone some medical documentation. So, a lot of profiteers have gained from this law, and there are those who managed to buy some kind of support, instead of those who are the real victims of war.[35]

Similarly Dr Olga Draško, a survivor, reports:

> The problem is that medical commissions will only take into account medical documentation that is obtained two years after an individual was released from the camp. If you don't have that documentation, you cannot exercise any rights. The fact that many of the former camp inmates suffer from PTSD [post-traumatic stress disorder] is not taken into account either. The majority of women could not achieve the status for these reasons. Also, some women who went to do medical examinations after being released never told to anyone what had happened to them.[36]

Benefits that were provided under this law did not extend to psychological care either – this is despite the well-known fact that survivors of rape suffer from severe trauma and mental illnesses, rather than bodily damage alone, and that they face particular risk of re-traumatisation when they cooperate with investigating officers

33 RTV Oko, above n 28.

34 Interview with M. Đ., Banjaluka, 19 June 2014.

35 Ivan Katavić, 'BiH: Ko koči usvajanje zakona o pravima žrtava torture' [Trans: BiH: 'Who Hinders the Adoption of the Law on the Rights of Victims of Torture'], *Radio Slobodna Evropa* (online), 26 May 2013, www.slobodnaevropa.org/content/bih-ko-koci-usvajanje-zakona-o-pravima-zrtava-torture/24996602.html.

36 Telephone interview, 15 May 2014.

or testify at trial. In this way, the *Law* excluded a great many survivors of CRSV because of the strict deadlines and by not taking into account psychological harm. The social stigma attached to CRSV makes survivors of such crimes vulnerable if they are identified publically, due to the social and cultural norms that operate to marginalise and shame victims of violence.[37] They feel humiliated and ashamed by what has happened to them. Women identified as victims of CRSV may not marry and may be divorced by their husbands or outcast from their families. As a result, without support, they may shy away from reporting the crime, thinking that such efforts would be pointless and bring them further stigma and isolation. Due to these difficulties, only insignificant numbers of women have managed to exercise their rights under the *Law*.

Unlike RS laws, in August 2012 Brčko District promulgated a regulation that enables women to receive the status of civil victim of war. This regulation does not stipulate any deadline and it takes into account psychological trauma, which is certainly an improvement in comparison with entity laws.[38] Why has the RS government been reluctant to abolish the 2007 deadline and open up the possibility of continuing to receive claims for civilian victims' status? Why has it never publically recognised its women victims? The women survivors in RS were ignored by the authorities, possibly because of government fears that it will receive a wave of compensation claims that would have to be paid from the entity budget, which is in deficit, if not bankrupt.[39]

It is also possible that the RS authorities simply do not want to receive claims from non-Serb women and pay them compensation. Yet, they are not in a position to promulgate laws that would favour only Serb women since that would be unconstitutional. Nusreta Mujkić is a Bosniak woman who lives in RS. Bosniak soldiers raped her because she lived with a Serb man who fought with the Serb army. Nusreta was captured and detained for several months. She feels bitter and disappointed by the treatment she and other women survivors have received by the RS government:

> I think that we as civilian victims of war contribute something to this state too. We also gave this state a name. I do not understand why they do not want to acknowledge us. I just cannot understand it and explain it to myself. Why can't women be civilian victims of war? Don't we exist at all? They would not exist either if there was no us, women.[40]

37 Mofidul Hoque (ed.), *Colloquium on Accountability of Sexual Violence Crimes and Experiences of the International Tribunals* (Dhaka Liberation War Museum, 2012).

38 'Odluka o zaštiti civilnih žrtava rata (2010), 7 [Trans: 'Decision on the Protection of Civilians'], Službeni glasnik Brčko Distrikta, broj 33, 15 August 2012 [Trans: 'Victims of War'], *Official Gazette of Brcko District* No. 33, 15 September 2012).

39 Milovan Matić, '"Bolji" dio BiH pred bankrotom: Godina u RS počinje slavlje, a završava ekonomskim krahom?' [Trans: '"Better" Part of BiH Before Bankruptcy: Year of the RS Begins Celebration and Ending the Economic Collapse?'], *BUKA* (online), 8 January 2016, www.6yka.com/novost/96978/bolji-dio-bih-pred-bankrotom-godina-u-rs-pocinje-slavljem-a-zavrsava-ekonomskim-krahom.

40 RTV Oko, above n 28.

The commencement of new claims for receiving the status of civilian victim of war would require the creation of a database with the personal data of women victims of CRSV from all ethnic groups. My presumption is that the RS authorities have no interest in creating such a database because non-Serb women would come forward too and perhaps outnumber Serb women victims. In this case, it would be impossible for the RS government to continue its denial that women from all ethnic groups were sexually abused in the war, and that Bosniak women perhaps are in the majority. In 2012 the RS Minister for Labour and Veterans' Affairs, Petar Đokić, reported that his government was exploring ways to resolve the issue while safeguarding against the possibility of 'false claims and attempted abuse of the social support system'; and that 'all victims will have to prove exposure to sexual violence, though not necessarily medical confirmation of the level of bodily damage'.[41] This statement implies that the government treats women victims with no respect; as someone not to be trusted. As such, women survivors stay at the margins of society, unrecognised by the law, and excluded from the social welfare system. Until today, the RS government has not yet shown any commitment towards assisting women survivors in exercising their rights to reparation.[42]

Witness protection and support

Although domestic courts began trying war crimes in 2005, the organised system of a witness protection and support program was officially non-existent till 2014. In April 2014 the *Law on Witness Protection Program* in BiH was adopted. However, this law only applies to witnesses testifying before the Court of BiH and not to district courts in RS, cantonal courts in the Federation of BiH, or courts in the Brčko District.[43] This essentially means that all women who decide

41 Maja Zuvela, 'Bosnian War Rape Victims Suffer in Silence, Wait for Justice', *Reuters*, 19 December 2012, www.reuters.com/article/us-bosnia-rape-idUSBRE8BI0SD20121219.

42 I should note that at the time of this book going into production, the *Law on Victims of Wartime Torture* has been drafted by the RS Ministry of Labour and Veterans' Affairs. The draft has not yet entered into the parliamentary procedure. The women victims feel betrayed yet again, since the promise that the draft law will enter into the parliamentary procedure keeps being postponed for the past two years. The draft law is problematic since it provides a very narrow and restrictive definition of victims that may exclude many survivors and their families. It excludes the persons 'who had been members of enemy forces'. Given the complexity of war in BiH, this provision allows for broad interpretation to exclude many victims. The draft law with the latest amendments from December 2016 on file with author. See also Amnesty International, *Bosnia and Herzegovina: Submission to the United Nations Human Rights Committee 119th Session, 6–29 March 2017*. On disappointment of Serb women victims with slow and inefficient procedure see Vida Đukić, 'Žene žrtve rata zaboravljene u Srpskoj: Dijaspora za jedno veče više pomogla od Vlade RS za dve godine' [Trans: 'Women Victims of War Forgotten in Srpska: Diaspora Helped More in One Evening than the Government of RS Had Helped in Two Years'], *Blic Online*, 18 February 2017.

43 A year before promulgation of this law, the Committee on the Elimination of All Forms of Discrimination against Women (CEDAW), recommended 'that the State Party ensure the effective implementation of the new law on the witness protection program and establish sustainable

to bring their cases before their local courts, will not be afforded witness protection. Until November 2016, they did not also have free legal aid.[44]

Disappointment in the RS government's attitude and lack of support towards women survivors, led some women to decline the Courts' offered witness protection program while standing trial. Irena Antić, a journalist at Federal Radio in Sarajevo, reported that it is quite common that witnesses withdraw their testimony after the procedure has already begun 'because all witnesses, especially victims of wartime rape, give up on reappearing before the courts because that is traumatic for them and they do not get the protection that they expect'.[45] In April 2014 four former members of the Croatian army were arrested under suspicion that they had committed crimes against humanity, including CRSV, against Serb women from the Odžak and Modriča regions. On 27 July 2014, the Prosecutor's Office issued an indictment and the trial began in September of the same year. The trial ended in November 2015, convicting one accused and acquitting the rest. This was the first case that dealt with the rape of Serb women from the Posavina region. However, the RS government has done little to nothing to provide much-needed support to women who decide to come forward to testify. According to M Đ., one of the key witnesses in this trial, she has been offered no legal or psychological support. She was asked by the Prosecutor's Office whether she wanted to be a protected witness, but she declined:

> I want to look at them [the perpetrators] in the eye. I have nothing to be afraid of. What worse could happen to me than what happened in 1992? I had no protection back then, I don't need it now.[46]

Since she had never been in court before and had no one to explain to her what she could expect once the trial started, M. Đ. decided to go on her own to the local court to familiarise herself with the courtroom and get a sense of the court procedure. She also told me that she worries that other women, who were also not familiar with courts procedures, will have to go through the process alone. A few women from her neighbourhood, who were detained in the same camp with her and who initially agreed to act as witnesses, decided to withdraw. One of them has recently died.

and operational witness protection measures at the district and cantonal levels'. UN, *Concluding Observations on the Combined Fourth and Fifth Periodic Reports of Bosnia and Herzegovina*, Committee on the Elimination of All Forms of Discrimination against Women (CEDAW), CEDAW/C/BIH/CO/, 4–5 (26 July 2013) [10(d)].

44 *The BiH Law on Free Legal Aid* was adopted in November 2016, but remains fragmented overall. *Official Gazette*, 4 November 2016, www.mpr.gov.ba/biblioteka/zakoni/default.aspx?id=5655&langTag=en-US

45 On the lack of witness support and protection, see the movie, *Unprotected* (Directed by Post-Conflict Research Centre, Sarajevo, PCRC and Pinch Media, 2011) and Rachel Irwin and Velma Šarić, *Poor Protection for Balkan Trial Witnesses (Special Report, Institute for War and Peace Reporting*, Report (2012), https://iwpr.net/global-voices/poor-protection-balkan-trial-witnesses

46 Interview with M. Đ., Banjaluka, 18 March 2016.

Another example of the blatant disinterest of the RS government for the female witnesses, is the case in which Rasim Delić was charged with, among other crimes, the wartime rape of Serb women in the mujahedeen camp in Kamenica in September 1995.[47] The female victims gave their statement and were expected to go to The Hague to testify before the International Criminal Tribunal for the Former Yugoslavia (ICTY). They sought the assistance from the RS authorities. The assistance was refused with the explanation that the matter in case 'was their private thing'.[48] This decision by the RS government not to assist in the processes that would bring justice for women victims and shed light on crimes committed against Serb women is perplexing. Delić was acquitted of the rape charges since there was 'not enough evidence to corroborate rape'[49] and thus support his conviction.

Federation of Bosnia and Herzegovina

In contrast to RS, the Federation of Bosnia and Herzegovina (FBiH) has some specific measures of compensation available to survivors of CRSV. In FBiH, survivors may apply to be recognised as civilian victims of war under the *Law on the Basis of the Social Protection, Protection of Civilian Victims of War and Families with Children* (the *Law*).[50] The *Law* is the first in the world to recognise women victims of CRSV as a specific group of victims that can claim reparation for the harm done to them. Lepa Mlađenović, a feminist and psychologist, argues that the *Law* is important to women survivors because it tells them that:

> [T]he state has taken responsibility and recognised that women were victims because they [the government] had fought for their independence, national integrity and so on. That is the key message to women: 'yes, we know that this happened to you, yes it is important to us to acknowledge your pain. That is in fact an acknowledgment of the pain.[51]

Similarly, Irma Šiljak, an activist with long experience working with CRSV, stated that through exercising the right to obtain the status of civilian victim of war 'the crime that women survived will be documented and serve as prevention for

47 *Prosecutor v Rasim Delić* (Judgment) (International Tribunal for the Prosecution of Persons Responsible for Serious Violations of International Humanitarian Law Committed in the Territory of the Former Yugoslavia since 199) Trial Chamber I, Case No. IT-04-83-T, 15 September 2008.

48 Official document from the meeting held between the institutional representatives of the RS government on file with author. The document dated as of 6 October 2009.

49 Sense Tribunal, 'Defense Wants Delic Acquitted of Rape Charges', *Sense Tribunal*, 14 February 2008, www.sense-agency.com/icty/defense-wants-delic-acquitted-of-rape-charges.29.html?cat_id=1&news_id=10750.

50 Law on Basic Social Protection, Protection of Civilian Victims of War and Protection of Families with Children, *Official Gazette of the Federation Bosnia and Herzegovina*, Nos 36/99, 54/04, 39/06 and 14/09.

51 RTV Oko, above n 28.

future generations'.[52] The *Law* stipulates that all survivors of CRSV are entitled to reparations regardless of their level of bodily damage. This is in contrast to all other civilian victims of war who must prove 60 per cent of bodily damage.[53] The removal of the requirement to show the high-threshold evidence for 60 per cent of bodily damage for women and men survivors of CRSV is to be commended, and something that the RS government should mirror if it promulgates new laws. By the end of 2013 in FBiH, 779 individuals – victims of rape and other forms of CRSV – had obtained the status of a civilian victim of war. Out of 779 survivors, 104 are males and 675 females.[54] Dobrica Jonjić, reportedly stated that the FBiH government

> knows well that [CRSV] was a mass phenomenon and it is not just 800 people, it is more, and I think only a fraction of people registered with us. Why don't they register? I think the whole society is to blame because we do very little to encourage women, and also men, to come out and identify as victims.[55]

The fact that the Federal Ministry of Labour and Social Policy has sex-disaggregated data, is a welcome and much-needed step forward.[56] This is in contrast again to RS, which does not have official data on the number of survivors of CRSV, let alone sex-disaggregated figures. With respect to the amount that welfare survivors ought to receive monthly, it is not the same in the entire entity, as 70 per cent of funds come from the state budget of FBiH and 30 per cent from local cantons.[57] Also, the *Law* states that those who receive benefits should not lose them if they return to their pre-war residence in RS. However, RS does not

52 Ibid.

53 Popić and Panjeta, above n 31.

54 Official letter from Ministry of Labour and Social Policy No. 06-41/3-3338/13, Sarajevo, 13 December 2013. On file with the author.

55 Assistant of Minister for Protection of People with Disabilities statement in RTV Oko, above n 26.

56 If sexual violence against women is surrounded by silence, then sexual abuse of men is a total taboo and receives almost no attention. The overwhelming preoccupation with the rape of women, rather than the wider patterns of gendered and sexualised violence that affect men too, has reinforced the identification of 'the raped victim' with females only. There is the tendency to conflate 'gender' with 'female', which means that violence against males is often not contextualised specifically as a gender-based crime. As a consequence, when one thinks of rape, we 'inevitably see a raped woman'. In BiH, there are no men's organisations, NGOs or institutional agencies that focus on male survivors of sexual torture and abuse. See Žarkov, Dubravka, 'War Rapes in Bosnia: On Masculinity, Femininity and Power of the Rape Victim Identity' (1997) 39(2) *Tijdschrift voor Criminologie* 140; Nicola Henry, 'The Fixation on Wartime Rape: Feminist Critique and International Criminal Law' (2014) 23(1) *Social & Legal Studies* 93, 99; Sharon Marcus, 'Fighting Bodies, Fighting Words: A Theory and Politics of Rape Prevention' in Judith Butler (ed.), *Feminists Theorize the Political* (Routledge, 1992) 385, 386.

57 Michaelina Jakala, *Wartime Rape: War's Worst Experience? A Feminist Grounded Theory Study of Female Non-Raped and Wartime Rape Survivors in Sarajevo, Bosnia and Herzegovina* (Unpublished Doctoral Dissertation, University of Bradford, 2010); Popić and Panjeta, above n 29.

recognise this provision since it has its own separate laws and social welfare system, which are not harmonised with the FBiH laws and system.[58] Such regulations are discriminatory as they prevent CRSV survivors' freedom of movement and are a disincentive for those with pre-war homes in RS to return.[59] The gaps and discrepancies that exist in and between entity level legislation, result in discrimination between survivors depending on where in BiH they live.[60] Such discrimination is extended to women victims of rape and other forms of CRSV who cannot get the status of the civil victim of war if they live abroad – outside of BiH, or, if they have obtained such a right, they can lose it if they reside outside of BiH for more than three months. Such an approach is in breach of victims' human rights – the freedom of movement.[61]

The *Law* recognises survivors of CRSV as civilian victims of war under certain conditions, which are friendlier than those stipulated in RS. Medical documentation issued immediately after the act of CRSV occurred is considered valid evidence, but also other relevant documents issued by either government or non-government organisations (NGOs). According to the *Instructions* given by the Ministry of Labour and Social Politics in the Federation of Bosnia and Herzegovina,[62] authorisation for issuing certificates of the status and repercussions of abuse and rape in war, is given to the local association of women based in Sarajevo called 'Women – Victims of War' (Žene-Žrtve Rata). A woman survivor can begin the procedure with the association if she has two witnesses or thorough documentary evidence, although there are situations when both witnesses and material evidence have been required to enter into the process of gaining the status. The procedure is demanding on women, considering that the women need to tell what happened to them in front of the Committee, and access to psychological support is very limited.[63] The association does not

58 Medica Zenica and Medica Mondiale, '*We Are Still Alive': Research on the Long-Term Consequences of War Rape and Copying Strategies of Survivors in Bosnia and Herzegovina*, Report (2014), www.medicamondiale.org/fileadmin/redaktion/5_Service/Mediathek/Dokumente/English/Documentations_studies/141128_Research_We-Are-Still-Alive_CR-Medica-Zenica_medica-mondiale.pdf, 11.

59 TRIAL, 'Violence Against Women, Its Causes and Consequences after Her Mission to Bosnia and Herzegovina', *Track Impunity Always* (2014) 17.

60 TRIAL, *Written Information for the Consideration of Bosnia and Herzegovina's Combined Fourth and Fifth Periodic Reports by the Committee on the Elimination of Discrimination against Women*, Track Impunity Always (2013), tbinternet.ohchr.org/Treaties/CEDAW/. . ./INT_CEDAW_NGO_BIH_13143_E.pdf.

61 Sabiha Husić, '*'Women Victims of War': Annex to the Shadow Report on the Implementation of the CEDAW Convention and on Women's Human Rights in Bosnia and Herzegovina* (2013), www.ecoi.net/file_upload/1930_1375090959_jointngosubmission-forthesession-bih-cedaw55.pdf.

62 'Uputstvo o postupku priznavanja statusa civilne žrtve rata', *Službene novine FBiH*, br. 62/06) [Trans: 'Instructions on the Procedure for Recognition of the Status of Civilian Victims of War'], *Official Gazette of BiH*, No. 62/06.

63 Briony Jones, Alex Jeffrey and Michaelina Jakala, 'The "Transitional Citizen": Civil Society, Political Agency and Hopes for Transitional Justice in Bosnia-Herzegovina' in Olivera Simić and Zala Volčič (eds), *Transitional Justice and Civil Society in the Balkans* (Springer, 2013) 87.

have the capacity to provide psychological support or counselling services, even though women have to relive experiences they may have already had to recount several times during their lives.[64]

In this way, women are at risk of being re-traumatised even though there is a possibility that they will not even receive the necessary certificate that would enable them to obtain the victim status. Amnesty International has raised concern that the association is ethnically biased and not physically accessible to all survivors, in particular to those who live in rural areas. Despite these concerns, the association is still one of the four NGOs licensed to issue certificates without any sanctions or monitoring.[65]

In May 2015 I met S. A., a Serb woman who was denied the status of victim of CRSV by 'Women – Victims of War' association and felt that the only reason for the negative outcome of her case was that she 'is not a Bosniak'.[66] S. A. resides in the territory of FBiH, so she has to submit her claims to the NGO residing in this entity. She reported that she was exposed to sexual, physical and psychological violence from May to October 1993. After spending five months collecting her evidence that she was a survivor of CRSV by Croatian, and later Bosnian army soldiers, having an interview on the association's premises and providing several witnesses, S. A. received a letter of rejection from the association. S. A. did not get any oral explanation as to why her application was rejected, and the reasons for such a decision were not clearly articulated in the letter that she received.[67] According to S. A, during the procedure she was asked to provide four witnesses, although usually only two witnesses are required in such cases. S. A. was also rejected despite the fact that she submitted all necessary documentation, including a certificate from the Association of Camp Inmates of Republika Srpska, acknowledging that she survived CRSV.[68] S. A. told me:

> I am bitter and angry. How is it possible that they turned me down? They dragged me along for six months. I brought four witnesses and told them my story several times and they said there is not enough evidence to support my story?![69]

S. A. felt like she was 'victimised for the second time'.[70] The procedure before the association lasts between six and eight months, although in some cases this is extended to several years.[71] According to some reports, many women who came

64 Amnesty International, above n 3; Jakala, above n 57.

65 The other three are: the Association of Former Camp Inmates BiH (Savez logoraša BiH); Croatian Association of Former Camp Inmates in a Homeland War (Hrvatska udruga logoraša domovinkog rata) and Medica Zenica.

66 Interview with S. A., Banjaluka, 17 June 2015.

67 Original document on file with author.

68 Ibid.

69 Interview with S. A., Banjaluka, 17 June 2015.

70 Ibid.

71 Jones, Jeffrey and Jakala, above n 63, 99.

to the association were forced to speak publically about their experiences and to agree to the public use of their written statement in order to get welfare.[72] All survivors are required to sign a statement authorising their testimonies to be used as part of criminal proceedings against those charged with war crimes.[73] Once they receive the certificate, they have to collect other documentation to further substantiate they have experienced CRSV, such as medical records from the medical service providers that treated them: private doctors, NGOs, mental health centres, hospitals.[74] Once they have all the documentation, they need to submit it to the Municipal Level Commission for its consideration.

The Commission invites survivors for an interview, reviews their case and issues a response within a few months. The Commission is usually comprised of only one person, who is not a psychologist, and who serves on a rotating basis with other individuals. If a survivor receives a negative response, s/he can appeal to a commission at the Cantonal level.[75] This recognition is very important to survivors as a form of 'symbolic acknowledgment' of the crimes that have been committed against them,[76] but also because they are entitled to monthly pensions of around EUR250, health care, psychological aid, medical help and free legal aid. However, FBiH is unable to provide many of these rehabilitative services, and NGOs are trying to fill this gap in services with their projects.

Women who live in RS can only seek advice about their rights from a few NGOs based in this entity, since the key NGOs who support women survivors of CRSV are all based in FBiH, such as Medica Zenica (Zenica), Vive Žene (Tuzla) or TRIAL (Sarajevo). However, the Serb women I met (most of them living in the countryside) have never heard about these organisations. Those rare ones who had, told me that they do not have the financial means to travel to visit them (or even call them) or were not willing to have contact because the organisations are based in the 'other' entity. Some women literally never travelled to FBiH after the war and were afraid that something 'bad' may happen to them; that someone may 'attack' them for 'being a Serb'.

They were obviously anxious even to think about the possibility of going there due to the unprocessed trauma they live with. Others fear that the associations they are already members of, such as the Association of Camp Inmates of Republika Srpska, will not approve of them seeking assistance from NGOs based in FBiH. Women victims told me that they were afraid of being perceived as 'traitors' for receiving support from those NGOs and consequently being

72 Amnesty International, above n 3; Jakala above n 57.

73 Amnesty International, above n 3, 44–46.

74 Victoria S. Rames, *Healing the Spirit: Reparations for Survivors of Sexual Violence Related to the Armed Conflict in Kosovo*, UN Human Rights Office of the High Commissioner (2013), www.ohchr.org/Documents/Issues/Women/WRGS/PeaceAndSecurity/StudyHealingTheSpirit.pdf, 31.

75 Ibid., 31.

76 Amnesty International, *Bosnia and Herzegovina: Old Crimes Same Suffering: No Justice for Survivors of Wartime Rape in North-East Bosnia and Herzegovina*, Campaign for International Justice, Paper (2012), www.amnesty.org/en/documents/EUR63/002/2012/en/.

ostracised from their own community of survivors. They have been told by its representatives that they should not seek any assistance in an 'other' entity. This mentality of fear overwhelms women and paralyses them from crossing the ethnic borders and meeting women and men from the 'other' side.[77]

None of the NGOs in RS has ever been authorised to issue the certificate that confers the status of 'civilian victim of war' and 'victim of sexual abuse'. Stanojka Tešić, a long-term feminist and activist, and director of Forum Žena Bratunac thinks that

> the regulation of status of civilian victims of war should be under institutional competence, which would be established by the expert committee, consisting of experts in the field of psychology, psychiatry, law and other fields . . . it would be degrading for women to be interrogated by some NGOs and reduced to a second-class citizen that is not worthy of institutional time and engagement. This is the job and responsibility of the governmental institutions.[78]

In theory, the rights that survivors of CRSV may exercise if given the status of civilian victims of war are: welfare and other material support, health care rights in accordance with laws on health care, the right to professional rehabilitation and (in the territory of the FBiH only) preference in employment and psychological and legal support.[79] The amount of welfare for survivors of CRSV is not uniform between entities and varies from around BAM100 in RS, to BAM500 in the FBiH.[80]

According to some estimates, almost 80 per cent of women victims have chronic post-traumatic stress disorder: they experience psychological and physical symptoms of distress and their recovery may be lifelong.[81] These women's traumatic experiences also affect their whole family and may trigger inter-generational trauma. It is important to keep in mind that many women survivors were in rape

77 Whether this fear is realistic or not, it should not be underestimated. As it operates with no financial means and largely on a volunteer basis, the Association of Camp Inmates of Republika Srpska gathers survivors and many of them have met each other for the first time through this network.

78 Telephone interview with Stanojka Tešić, 18 November 2015.

79 While this is to be applauded, unfortunately in practice victims can exercise only very few of these rights. The right to preference in employment, for example, has never been taken up due to confidentiality issues. Namely, the governmental department for employment asks for public disclosure of the identity of the victim and her status, which many victims do not want to agree to. Some 10 years after the laws were enforced, the relevant authorities are still not able to resolve this issue, which prevents victims from exercising this particular right. Presentation by Dobrica Jonjić, Ministry of Social Policy of the Federation of BiH, the Workshop on Reparations for Victims of Conflict Related Sexual Violence (Sarajevo, 9–10 June 2016).

80 BAM100 is equivalent to EUR50, and BAM500 to EUR250.

81 UN Population Fund (UNFPA), 'Dealing with a Legacy of Rape and Torture in Bosnia and Herzegovina, Bosnia: Rape a Legacy of War', UNFPA, 20 October 2010, www.unfpa.org/news/dealing-legacy-rape-and-torture-bosnia-and-herzegovina.

camps with their young children, who are now adults and must have traumatic experiences and memories of the past events.[82] These children have not necessarily been direct victims themselves, but witnesses of the crimes committed against their family members and other people. So far, no one has done any comprehensive assessment of these (then) children and their needs.

Redress and compensation

Transitional justice encompasses a myriad of judicial and non-judicial measures to redress massive human rights abuses, including criminal prosecutions, truth commissions and reparations, as well as policy reforms. Reparations specifically seek to recognise and address both the physical and psychological harms suffered by victims of systematic human rights violations. The right to reparations is recognised in international law[83] including the recent affirmation of a woman's right to adequate and effective reparations in the *Convention on the Elimination of Discrimination against Women General Recommendation No. 30* (2013).[84]

Reparation is the term for the concrete measures that should be taken to address the suffering of the survivors and to help them rebuild their lives. There are five recognised forms of reparation: restitution, compensation, rehabilitation, satisfaction and guarantees of non-repetition. Restitution denotes measures aimed at re-establishing, as much as possible, the situation that existed before the violation happened, including restoration of property rights, employment, liberty, citizenship or residency status. Compensation involves monetary payment for 'any economically assessable loss', such as physical or mental harm, lost opportunities, material damage or loss of earning. Rehabilitation aims to address any physical or psychological harm caused to victims including medical and

82 On 25 May 2015 the Court of BiH convicted Zaima Laličić, a former member of the Bosnian Army's First Corps and a guard at the prison camp in an abandoned building in Hrasnica, for the multiple rape of a female prisoner and the abuse of another civilian detainee in 1992 and 1993. In the case, the Trial Chamber took into account the seriousness of the crimes and 'the persistence of Lalicic, who raped S. M. several times, using the situation that she was detained [at the improvised prison] with her child . . . reminding her that her son was detained as well – [a threat] through which Laličić showed particular ruthlessness'. See Denis Džidic, 'Bosniak Soldier Convicted of Wartime Rape', *BalkanInsight* (online), 25 May 2015, www.balkaninsight.com/en/article/ex-bosniak-fighter-sentenced-for-wartime-rape.

83 See UN, *Guidance Note of the Secretary General, Reparations for Conflict-Related Sexual Violence* [Hereinafter: 'Guidance Note'] (2014), www.ohchr.org/Documents/Press/GuidanceNoteReparationsJune-2014.pdf, 3–4, FN 9 (including Article 8 of the Universal Declaration of Human Rights, Article 2 of the International Covenant on Civil and Political Rights, Article 14 of the Convention Against Torture and Other Cruel, Inhuman or Degrading Treatment or Punishment, Article 39 of the Convention on the Rights of the Child, Article 3 of the Hague Convention (Convention IV), Article 91 of the Protocol Additional to the Geneva Conventions of 12 August 1949, Article 75 of the Rome Statute for the International Criminal Court.

84 UN, *General Recommendation No. 30 on Women in Conflict Prevention, Conflict and Post-Conflict Situations*, Convention on the Elimination of Discrimination against Women, [Hereinafter 'General Recommendation No. 30'] CEDAW/C/GC/30 (13 October 2013) [79].

psychological care as well as legal and social services. Satisfaction includes important symbolic measures such as: verification of the facts and full and public disclosure of the truth; an official declaration or a judicial decision restoring the dignity, the reputation and the rights of the victim and of persons closely connected with the victim; a public apology, including acknowledgement of the facts and acceptance of responsibility; judicial and administrative sanctions against persons liable for the violations; and commemorations, memorials and tributes to the victims. Finally, guarantees of non-repetition involve measures aimed at ensuring that victims are not subject to other crimes or that the crimes are not committed again.[85]

At the BiH state level, there is no legislation that can enable reparation or recognition of survivors of CRSV. Survivors can only apply for reparation at the FBiH level once they meet certain requirements. In May 2006, the United Nations Committee on the Elimination of Discrimination Against Women (CEDAW) Committee adopted a line of recommendations referring to women victims of CRSV in BiH during 1992 to 1995. The Committee requested that the BiH State recognise and protect women who were civil victims of sexual violence through a State law and allocate funds for adequate social measures, including health insurance and accommodation/housing, in such a way that their rights and benefits would be guaranteed throughout the entire country.[86] This recommendation was issued in 2006, but the state has still not acted upon it.

In 2012 the United Nations Human Rights Committee noted the lack of a 'strategy on transitional justice'.[87] The Bosnian authorities have prepared a *Draft National Strategy on Transitional Justice* (the *Strategy*) and the related action plan, which notes that states are obliged to prosecute individuals for war crimes, crimes against humanity and genocide, and to provide effective reparations to victims.[88] However, the RS government and its NGOs withdrew from the process of drafting the *Strategy* claiming that their views have not been respected.[89] As Pantelija Ćurguz, the President of the Republika Srpska War Veterans Association reportedly stated:

85 UNGA, *Basic Principles and Guidelines on the Right to Remedy and Reparation for Victims of Gross Violations of International Human Rights Law and Serious Violations of International Humanitarian Law*, Res. 60/147, 60th sess., 64th plen. mtg, Agenda Item 71(a), A/RES/60/147 (16 December 2005) arts 19-21.

86 UN, *Concluding Comments of the Committee on the Elimination of Discrimination Against Women: Bosnia and Herzegovina*, Committee on the Elimination of All Forms of Discrimination Against Women (CEDAW), CEDAW/C/BiH/CO/3 (2 June 2006) [38].

87 UN Human Rights Committee, *Concluding Observations on the Second Periodic Report of Bosnia and Herzegovina Adopted by the Committee at its 106th session (15 October–2 November 2012)*, CCPR/C/BIH/CO/2 (13 November 2012) [8].

88 Ministry of Justice, *Strategija tranzicijske pravde u Bosni i Hercegovini 2012–2016* [Trans: *Draft Strategy of Transitional Justice in Bosnia and Herzegovina 2012–2016*], www.mpr.gov.ba/aktuelnosti/propisi/konsultacije/Strategija%20TP%20-%20bosanski%20jezik%20fin%20doc.pdf.

89 Denis Džidic, 'Bosnian Transitional Justice Strategy Hits First Bump', *BalkanInsight* (online), 1 November 2012, www.balkaninsight.com/en/article/bosnian-transitional-justice-strategy-hits-first-bump.

> The document is heavily biased towards one viewpoint, and has only one aim – which is to legalize the commonly held perception that all the victims were on one side and all the aggressors on the other. This is an offensive document with a threatening tone.[90]

The *Strategy* is meant to provide a comprehensive framework for dealing with the legacy of human rights violations and war crimes, to build the foundations for a peaceful future. The purpose of the *Strategy* is to form a sustainable platform for establishing facts about the past, providing redress for injustice and war-related trauma, protecting individual and collective memory, and reforming and regaining trust in institutions.[91] The *Strategy* covers non-judicial transitional justice mechanisms – truth seeking and truth telling, reparations, memorialisation and institutional reforms. When it comes to reparations, the *Strategy* deals particularly with compensations and rehabilitation – psychosocial support, employment and organising socio-cultural and sport activities. It does not deal with women victims of CRSV as a separate category, although women are considered within the category of 'civilian victims of war'. It stresses the different roles of women in war, not only as victims of CRSV, but witnesses, soldiers, and even perpetrators.

The *Strategy* was submitted to the entities for their consideration, but the RS authorities have never publicly voiced their opinions on it, and the process seems to be paralysed. The lack of response by RS on the *Strategy* since 2012 makes it impossible for this piece of legislation to be presented to the State Parliament.[92] Obviously, there is an absence of political will at the RS entity level to adopt it, while for many survivors, who have been waiting for redress for over 20 years, this document represents the top priority.[93]

As of September 2017 no comprehensive program to provide redress and compensation for the harm suffered during the war has been adopted in BiH. At the state level, there has been a failure on the part of the authorities to establish an effective mechanism that would ensure reparation for all victims of war-related crimes and their families. A few employees in governmental bodies in RS told me: 'RS has to draft its own reparation laws. We do not want to have a joint legislation with them [FBiH].'[94] Amnesty International has also urged BiH to develop 'the BiH Law on the Rights of Victims of Torture and Civilian Victims of War' but there is no political consensus at a federal state level to adopt comprehensive a law.[95]

90 Ibid.

91 Goran Šimić, 'Transitional Justice Strategy for Bosnia and Herzegovina: An Overview', *Peace Direct*, 7 May 2013, www.insightonconflict.org/2013/05/transitional-justice-strategy-bosnia-herzegovina/.

92 TRIAL, *General Allegation on the Situation in Bosnia and Herzegovina to the Special Rapporteur on Truth, Justice, Reparations and Guarantees of Non-Recurrence*, Track Impunity Always (2014), https://trialinternational.org/wp-content/uploads/2016/05/TRIAL_BiH_GA_SRTJ_Feb2014.pdf, 6.

93 Ibid., 7.

94 Banjaluka, 18 June 2016.

95 Gentian Zyberi and Jernej Letnar Černič, 'Transitional Justice Processes and Reconciliation in the Former Yugoslavia: Challenges and Prospects' (2015) 33(2) *Nordic Journal of Human Rights* 132, 150.

Even where legal basis for reparation and compensation exists, the claims of victims have not been fully executed, or executed at all. On 20 January 2015 the European Court of Human Rights (ECHR) found in *Đurić and Others v Bosnia and Herzegovina* that BiH had violated Article 6 and Article 1 of Protocol No 1 to ECHR, concerning the non-execution of final judgements awarding compensation to war victims under the terms of the *War Damage Act 2005* of RS.[96] In the leading judgement, *Čolić and Others v Bosnia and Herzegovina*, the ECHR concluded that 'the State respondent is to secure enforcement of the domestic judgements'.[97]

The ECHR noted that:

> [T]he Court is well aware of Republika Srpska's significant public debt as well as of the number of non-enforced judgements and the number of cases pending before the domestic courts . . . it reiterates that it is not open to a state authority to cite lack of funds as an excuse for not honouring a judgement debt.[98]

In July 2013 RS extended the time frame to 20 years for the enforcement of the final judgement ordering payment of war damages, which the ECHR finds 'too long in the light of the lengthy delay which has already occurred'.[99] In December 2013 the aggravated debt was around EUR85 million, the number of unenforced judgements 4,089, and around 3,030 cases pending before domestic courts.[100]

Further, with respect to compensation, it is almost impossible for women to obtain it in criminal proceedings. Although criminal courts have the option to award whole or part of a claim for compensation to the injured parties or to refer them to civil actions, until recently victims have been referred to civil actions. This practice hampers the access to compensation for the majority of victims, given that to launch a civil action they would need a lawyer to represent them, and, in almost the totality of cases, they cannot afford it and free legal aid is not granted by the State.[101] Another, possibly more serious, problem for their personal safety, is that while filing civil claims for compensation, victims would need to disclose the identity they had as a protected witness during criminal trial. In this way, they would need to put at risk their own safety and that of their families. While such a

96 Case of *Đurić and Others v Bosnia and Herzegovina* (Judgment) (European Court of Human Rights), Applications Nos 79867/12, 79873/12, 80027/12, 80182/12, 80203/12 and 115/13, 20 January 2015.

97 Case of *Čolić and Others v Bosnia and Herzegovina* (Judgment) (European Court of Human Rights) Applications Nos 1218/07, 1240/07, 1242/07, 1335/07, 1368/07, 1369/07, 3424/07, 3428/07, 3430/07, 3935/07, 3940/07, 7194/07, 7204/07, 7206/07 and 7211/07, 10 November 2009, [B(20)].

98 Case of *Đurić and Others v Bosnia and Herzegovina*, above n 90, [30].

99 Ibid.

100 Ibid. [23].

101 UNGA, *Report of the Working Group on the Universal Periodic Review: Bosnia and Herzegovina*, Human Rights Council, A/HRC/28/17 (4 December 2014) [52]–[53].

disclosure is a criminal offence under BiH legislation, this has already happened in a number of cases.[102] Such a legal situation places victims in a paradoxical and impossible situation in which they are asked to endanger their own and their families' safety in order to exercise their right on compensation.

In 2015 a Sarajevo-based organisation, TRIAL, filed for the first time a compensation claim for moral damages suffered by a victim of rape in a criminal proceedings pending before the Court of BiH. On 24 June 2015, the Court of BiH issued a landmark ruling in which it not only sentenced two defendants to 10 years imprisonment[103] for having repeatedly raped a Croat woman during the Serb attack on the northern village of Orahova, but also ordered them the payment of BAM26,500 (approximately EUR13,500) to the victim as compensation for damages. In this case, the defendants, Bosiljko Marković and Ostoja Marković, while members of the Army of Republika Srpska, were found guilty of raping a 14-year-old girl from the town of Kotor Varoš. The survivor – 'S-4' – was awarded non-pecuniary damages: BAM20000 (approximately EUR10,000) for 'mental pain caused by violation of liberty or rights of personality', and BAM6,500 (approximately EUR3,500) for 'mental pain caused by diminished quality of life'.[104]

A few days later, on 29 June 2015 a former Bosnian Serb soldier was sentenced to eight years imprisonment for a rape committed in 1993, and ordered to pay roughly BAM30,000 (approximately EUR15,000) to the Bosniak woman he raped. A defendant, Slavko Savić, was found guilty of raping a woman twice, impregnating her on the first occasion and then abusing her violently on the second occasion – the trauma of which resulted in a miscarriage. In both instances, the victim's 11-year-old daughter was present and witnessed her mother being taken from their home.[105] Out of BAM30,000, Savić was asked to pay BAM16,000 (approximately EUR8,000) for 'mental pain caused by violation of liberty or rights of personality', and BAM14,000 (approximately EUR7,000) for 'mental pain caused by diminished quality of life'.[106]

102 TRIAL, *Follow-Up Report on the Implementation by Bosnia and Herzegovina's of the Recommendations Issued by the Committee on the Elimination of Discrimination Against Women in July 2013*, CEDAW/C/BIH/CO/, 4–5 (2015), http://tbinternet.ohchr.org/Treaties/CEDAW/Shared%20Documents/BIH/INT_CEDAW_NGS_BIH_21073_E.pdf, [39].

103 See Court of Bosnia and Herzegovina, 'First Instance Verdict Pronounced in Bosiljko Marković et al.' (News Release, 24 June 2015), www.sudbih.gov.ba/index.php?id=4065&jezik=e; TRIAL, 'BiH: Groundbreaking Court Decision Paves the Way for Wartime Victims to Get Compensation' *Trial International*, 24 June 2015, https://trialinternational.org/latest-post/bih-groundbreaking-court-decision-paves-the-way-for-wartime-victims-to-get-compensation/

104 Court of Bosnia and Herzegovina, above n 103.

105 Denis Džidic 'Bosnian Serb Fighter Convicted of Wartime Rape', *Balkan Insight* (online), 29 June 2015, www.balkaninsight.com/en/article/ex-bosnian-serb-fighter-sentenced-for-war time-rape.

106 Court of Bosnia and Herzegovina, 'Slavko Savić Sentenced to 8 (eight) Years in Prison' (News Release, 29 June 2015), www.sudbih.gov.ba/index.php?id=4075&jezik=e; Julian Borger, 'Bosnia Rape Victims May Claim Compensation For First Time', *Guardian* (online), 30 June 2015, www.theguardian.com/world/2015/jun/30/bosnia-victims-compensation-landmark-ruling.

Prior to these decisions, not a single case involving CRSV had resulted in a reparation award, and not a single victim had ever obtained compensation through criminal proceedings. But now that the BiH Court is willing to include reparations: 'it is expected that many more women will come forward'.[107] While these decisions are an important and welcomed step ahead, which may encourage other women to come forward and testify, the payment and actual receiving of compensation has already witnessed obstacles. In the same judgements that obliged defendants to pay compensation for damages, it was stated that they were released from paying legal costs and received free legal aid since they live in very difficult economic situations.

Nevenka Vitomir, the attorney for Savić, reportedly stated: 'He [Slavko] owns no property, has nothing in his own name, so it is going to be difficult to obtain that payment.'[108] The lawyer for Bosiljko Marković and Ostoja Marković similarly stated that the two men have no money or property, so it remains unclear how victims will get the compensation ordered in the verdict.[109] While one battle with ordering compensations has been won, the other of its actual payment still needs to be resolved.

As of September 2017, all of the victims have yet to receive any compensation.[110] Bearing in mind that the Constitutional Court of BiH has ruled that compensation cannot be obtained from the state or from one of the country's two entities, but only from the immediate perpetrator, TRIAL suggested the establishment of special state funds that would be used to cover ordered payment to victims.[111] In the cantonal and district courts, two victims of CRSV have so far managed to get compensation as a result of a plea agreement between the defendants and the cantonal prosecution in Bihać. Both defendants made the payments of EUR25,000 (approximately EUR12,000) each[112] and in return

107 Ashley Binetti, *Gender-Sensitive and Transformative Reparations in Bosnia*, Georgetown Institute for Women, Peace & Security (2015), https://giwps.georgetown.edu/sites/giwps/files/I2A%20-%20Gender-Sensitive%20and%20Transformative%20Reparations%20in%20Bosnia.pdf.

108 Amer Jahić, 'Upitna odštete žrtvama silovanja u BiH' [Trans: 'Questionable Payment for Compensation to Victims of Rape in Bosnia and Herzegovina'], *BalkanInsight* (online), 14 August 2015, www.balkaninsight.com/en/article/upitna-naplata-od%C5%A1tete-%C5%BErtvama-silovanja-u-bih-08-13-2015.

109 Justice Report, 'Bosnian War Rape Victims Struggle for Compensation', *Balkan Insight* (online), 9 September 2016, www.balkaninsight.com/en/article/bosnian-war-rape-victims-struggle-for-compensation-09-09-2016.

110 Ibid.

111 TRIAL, 'Ostvarivanje zahtjeva za naknadu štete žrtava ratnih zločina u okviru krivičnih postupaka u Bosni i Hercegovini – stanje, problem, perspective' [Trans: 'Enforcement of Damage Compensation Claims of Victims of War in Criminal Proceedings in Bosnia and Herzegovina: Situations, Challenges and Perspectives'] (2015), http://trial.ba/wp-content/uploads/2015/10/ENG_Ostvarivanje-zahtjeva-za-naknadu-%C5%A1tete-%C5%BErtava-ratnih-zlo%C4%8Dina-u-okviru-krivi%C4%8Dnih-postupaka-u-Bosni-i-Hercegovini-%E2%80%93-stanje-problemi-i-perspektive-.pdf, 27.

112 The Final Judgment against Amir Ćoralić. Presuda kantonalnog suda u Bihaću, broj 01 0 K 009451 15 K, Bihać, 19 October 2015. On file with author.

received only one year in prison for raping minors. According to amendments to criminal laws in BiH, it is now possible to pay the fine instead of serving one year in prison – with each day in prison costing around EUR50 (approximately EUR25).[113] For the war crimes that are considered as the most serious breaches of international criminal law, in BiH there have been several cases in which cantonal courts in FBiH allowed the payments to be made by the convicted men. Such 'deals' are paradoxical and morally and ethically unacceptable. Allowing war criminals to 'pay off' the war crime of rape of minors rather than serve the sentence in prison, not only goes against key sentencing principles and purposes, such as just punishment and deterrence, but it 'encourages committing of such difficult acts since those who are wealthy can allow themselves to commit the crimes and later "pay them off"'.[114]

Conclusion

The relevant legislation at the level of the entities aimed at establishing victims' status provides different recognition and treatment of women victims. Such unjust treatment of victims depending where they live needs to be abolished. The relevant legislation at the level of the entities and cantons aimed at providing reparation to the victims of the war provides further different treatments for war veterans than civilian victims. Laws in both entities treat war veterans differently and considerably more favourably than civilian victims.[115] Civilian victims receive less in monthly payments than war veterans, namely, 70 per cent of war veterans' compensation.[116]

Reparations, however, should not be understood as a form of 'social support' (as the authorities often describe them) but funds that the state has to secure for the citizens it failed to protect. The existing reparative system can be at best described

113 Amendments on criminal law from 2010 (čl. 42a KZ BiH, 43a KZ FBiH, čl. 33. st. 2. KZ RS i čl. 43a KZ BD BiH). In RS only conviction to six months in prison can be 'paid off' by monetary penalty.

114 Nermina Avdukić, 'Osuđene za ratni zločine otkupili kazne za 18.300 eura' [Trans: 'Convicted of War Crimes Bought Penalties for 18,300 euros'], *Aljazeera Balkans* (online), n.d., http://balkans.aljazeera.net/vijesti/osudeni-za-ratne-zlocine-otkupili-kazne-za-18300-eura.

115 See art. 9, Law on Changes and Amendments to the Law on Basis of Welfare, Care for Civilian War Victims, Care for Families with Children, *Official Gazette of Federation of Bosnia and Herzegovina*, No. 39/06; See art. 2, Law on Rights of Veterans, Disabled Veterans and Families of Killed Veterans of the Defence and Homeland War of Republika Srpska, *Official Gazette of the Republika Srpska*, No. 46/04 and 53/04, art. 4; Law on the Protection of Civilian War Victims, *Official Gazette of the Republika Srpska* No. 25/93, 1/94, 32/94, 37/07 and 60/07)

116 In Republika Srpska veterans' benefits are centrally managed within the Ministry of Labor and Veterans' Affairs', with the budget coming from general entity revenues. Kendra G. Gregson, *Veterans' Programs in Bosnia-Herzegovina*, European Stability Initiative (ESI) (2000), www.esiweb.org/pdf/bridges/bosnia/WB-KGregsonVeterans.pdf. According to the Law on the Entitlements of War Veterans, Militaries with Disabilities and Families of Soldiers Fallen in the Fatherland War of the Republika Srpska, the basis for the calculation of monthly benefits is established by law at BAM500.

as 'a hybrid of social welfare and reparation' that marginalise civilian victims and privilege the military.[117] It is a system captured and led by ethno-nationalist elites, based on politically and ethnically sponsored rights and privileges.[118] The authorities must identify the approximate number of survivors of CRSV in RS and cater for their current needs, as well as provide them with the necessary medical and psychological care. Further, they must reopen the applications procedure and abolish the requirement of the specific percentage of bodily damage, in addition to taking into account psychological damage. Symbolic reparation in BiH, such as a public apology, acknowledgement of the facts and acceptance of responsibility (which is one of the forms of satisfaction that may comfort victims) has been entirely absent. In RS, the recognition of past atrocities by state officials would help reconciliation by signalling that governments are able to break with the past politics of their states: the politics of denial and silence.

117 Jessie Hronešová, 'Might Makes Right: War-Related Payments in Bosnia and Herzegovina' (2016) 10(3) *Journal of Intervention and Statebuilding* 340.

118 Ibid.

5 The Women's Court in Sarajevo

Challenges and reflections

Introduction: people's and women's tribunals

In response to some of the shortcomings of more conventional justice mechanisms, such as local and international courts and tribunals, civil society actors have sought to find alternative and innovative ways to seek justice, on behalf of, and together with, survivors of mass human rights violations.[1] One of these innovative ways of seeking justice is people's tribunals or courts, which operate independently of state authorities. Since the 1960s there have been at least 80 'people's tribunals,' 'citizens' tribunals' or similar commissions of inquiry, established outside formal state and international structures.[2] Over the past 50 years, as Dianne Otto noted, such tribunals have been 'a recurring form of popular protest'.[3]

A number of international tribunals on crimes against women have been established to respond to past atrocities, and in consequence, problematise past impunity for gender-based violence. These are non-institutionalised, non-judicial bodies that have sprung up since the 1970s.[4] Although they differ in their size and format, they are modelled on international war crimes courts that function more as truth commissions, where victim witnesses speak about their personal experiences of various forms of gender-based violence. The key difference is that the people's tribunals lack judicial and institutional power to enforce their verdicts, and to make transformative and tangible changes. They do, however, represent alternative modes of justice, which raise awareness about state responsibility for

1 Nicola Henry, 'Civil Society and Gender-Based Violence: Expanding the Horizons of Transitional Justice' (2016) 42(1) *Australian Feminist Law Journal* 119.

2 See Andrew Byrnes and Gabrielle Simm, 'People's Tribunals, International Law and the Use of Force' (2013) 36(2) *University of New South Wales Law Journal* 711; Gabrielle Simm and Andrew Byrnes, 'International Peoples' Tribunals in Asia: Political Theatre, Juridical Farce, or Meaningful Intervention' (2014) 4(1) *Asia Journal of International Law* 103.

3 Dianne Otto, 'Beyond Legal Justice: Some Personal Reflections on People's Tribunals, Listening and Responsibility' (2017) 5/2 *London Review of International Law* 225.

4 The first one was held in Brussels from 4–8 March 1976. See Russell, Diana E. H. and Nicole Van de Ven, *Crimes Against Women: Proceedings of the International Tribunal* (Femmes Publications, 1976)

the harms inflicted on its people, and serve as symbolic reparation to survivors. As Otto argues: 'people's tribunals give life to imaginings of a more hopeful future than the individualised justice of the criminal law'.[5]

These informal courts and tribunals aim to right the 'wrongs' of the formal judicial proceedings, that have often been criticised as not treating victims and witnesses as central, but rather peripheral to the process.[6] The other reason for establishing these mechanisms is the recognition that the vast majority of crimes have gone unchallenged and perpetrators have enjoyed immunity; and even where local and international courts had been established, there was largely a failure to prosecute – either due to lack of political willingness or jurisdictional limitations.[7] War crimes trials have been largely critiqued for being biased, political rather than legal, and becoming mere show trials.[8] Although they remain an important avenue for dealing with a legacy of human rights abuses, they should not preclude from obtaining diverse complementary forms of justice – such as reparative, restorative and socio-economic. Dealing with past atrocities requires a continuation of innovation and creativity that goes beyond criminal trials and formalised criminal justice.[9]

What is common to both women's and people's tribunals, is that they have been initiated due to the desire to bring unheard voices into the public arena. Nancy Fraser puts forward the idea of 'subaltern counterpublics', which she defines as 'parallel discursive arenas where members of subordinated social groups invent and circulate counterdiscourses, which in turn permit them to formulate oppositional interpretations of their identities, interests and needs'.[10] Fraser argues that these 'counterpublics' play a vital role in critiquing hegemonic domination in the bourgeois public sphere, and in redefining the problematic boundaries that exist between public and private spheres.[11] The format of people's tribunals, enables 'the protest movements to symbolically harness [the] power to create an archive that gives credibility to dissenting perspectives and recognise subjects whose experiences have been ignored or dismissed by law as irrelevant'.[12]

5 Ibid.

6 Kirsten Campbell, 'The Gender of Transitional Justice: Law, Sexual Violence and the International Criminal Tribunal for the Former Yugoslavia' (2007) 1(3) *International Journal of Transitional Justice* 411; Michelle Staggs Kelsall and Shanee Stepakoff, '"When We Wanted to Talk About Rape": Silencing Sexual Violence at the Special Court for Sierra Leone' 2007 1(3) *International Journal of Transitional Justice* 355; Marie-Bénédicte Dembour and Haslam Emily, 'Silencing Hearings? Victim-Witnesses at War Crimes Trials' (2004) 15(1) *European Journal of International Law* 151; Nicola Henry, *War and Rape: Law, Memory and Justice* (Routledge, 2011).

7 Louise Chappell, 'The Role of the ICC in Transitional Gender Justice: Capacity and Limitations' in Susanne Buckely-Zistel and Stanley Ruth (eds), *Gender in Transitional Justice* (Palgrave Macmillan, 2012) 37.

8 Gerry Simpson, *Law, War and Crime: War Crimes Trials and the Reinvention of International Law* (Polity Press, 2007) 11, 107.

9 Janine Natalya Clark, 'Transitional Justice as Recognition: An Analysis of the Women's Court in Sarajevo' (2016) 10(1) *International Journal of Transitional Justice* 67, 68.

10 Nancy Fraser, 'Rethinking the Public Sphere: A Contribution to the Critique of Actually Existing Democracy' (1990) 25 *Social Text* 56.

11 Ibid.

12 Otto, above n 3, 244, 245.

People's tribunals have been largely praised for 'building solidarity and networks, and recording and memorialising otherwise unacknowledged experiences'.[13] The Permanent People's Tribunal (PPT), for example, an international body and a grassroots initiative founded in Bologna, Italy in 1979, goes beyond the recognition of criminal responsibility in order to produce truth, memory and moral reparation. In 1995 the PPT held two sessions on the former Yugoslavia.[14] The first session, held in Bern, heard oral evidence from around 35 witnesses, including that on CRSV, especially against Bosniak women.[15] The PPT identified 'the massive and systemic sexual violence exerted by the Serbian troops on Muslim women as a form of war and as an element of the policy of "ethnic purge"'.[16] The second session of the Barcelona Tribunal went even further and applied the international definition of genocide, set out in the United Nations' *Genocide Convention*, to the rapes of Bosniak women by Serbs, and 'recommended that the Hague Tribunal [the International Criminal Tribunal for the Former Yugoslavia (ICTY)] qualify as a crime against humanity the acts of ethnic rape . . . and also as genocidal deeds'.[17]

The first of the world's women's courts was established in Lahore, Pakistan in 1992, and to date, close to 40 tribunals have been held around the world, mostly in Asia and Africa. Women's courts are a global movement that seek to bring 'other notions of justice from the lives and life visions of women – particularly from the Global South'.[18] Over the last two decades these courts have crystallised some core principles, such as that they are not convened by official institutions but by women's groups. Further, central to the process is listening to women, since their testimonies are at the heart of the courts' operations. One of the trademarks of the women's courts, is that immense care is taken to ensure the process is inclusive, meaning that 'a great effort is made to give a voice to *all those voices which have not yet been heard* and, if it were not for these courts, would not be heard'.[19]

13 Simm and Byrnes, above n 2, 103.

14 See The Permanent Peoples' Tribunal, *Crimes Against Humanity in the Former Yugoslavia*, held in Bern, Switzerland, 17–20 February 1995 (Judgment only available in Italian), http://permanentpeoplestribunal.org/23-crimes-against-humanity-in-the-former-yugoslavia-i-bern-17-20-february-1995/?lang=en; The Permanent Peoples' Tribunal, *Crimes Against Humanity in the Former Yugoslavia II*, held in Barcelona, Spain, 7–11 December 1995 (Judgment only available in Italian), http://permanentpeoplestribunal.org/25-crimes-against-humanity-in-the-former-yugoslavia-ii-barcelona-7-11-december-1995/?lang=en.

15 See Gabrielle Simm, 'Peoples' Tribunals, Women's Courts and International Crimes of Sexual Violence' in Andrew Byrnes and Gabrielle Simm (eds), *Peoples' Tribunals and International Law* (Cambridge University Press, forthcoming). Draft chapter on file with author.

16 Barcelona [19] cited in Simm above n 15.

17 Barcelona [40] cited in Simm above n 15.

18 Women Living Under Muslim Laws, 'India Court of Women on Dowry and Related Forms of Violence Against Women: Daughters of Fire' (Bangalore, India, 27–29 July 2009), www.wluml.org/fr/node/5387, 5

19 Dasa Gordana Duhacek, '"The Women's Court" A Feminist Approach to In/Justice' (2015) 22(2) *European Journal of Women's Studies* 159, 160–161 (emphasis in original).

One of the most recent women's tribunals, the Cambodian Tribunal, wanted, for example, to draw attention to the 'inability or unwillingness' of the judicial transitional justice mechanisms in the region to apply the law in the way that would provide justice for survivors of gender-based violence.[20] Three women's hearings were held in Phnom Penh in 2011, 2012 and 2013 with the aim of addressing CRSV. Probably the most well-known international women's tribunal is the Women's International War Crimes Tribunal for the Trial of Japan's Military Sexual Slavery (the Tokyo Tribunal). The negotiations for the establishment of the International Criminal Court (ICC) provided impetus for the transnational networking that led to the establishment of the Tribunal.[21]

The Tokyo Tribunal took place on 7 December 2000 to address charges of rape and sexual slavery that had not been prosecuted at the International Military Tribunal for the Far East, held from 1946–1948[22] (despite evidence being available on which indictments could have been based).[23] In its judgement, the Tokyo Tribunal stated that

> this Tribunal steps into the lacuna left by states and does not purport to replace their role in the legal proceedings . . . the power of the Tribunal . . . lies in its capacity to examine the evidence, develop an accurate historical record, and apply principles of international law to the facts as found.[24]

The Tokyo Tribunal sought to fill a vacuum by providing justice to elderly survivors of the sex camps – the so-called 'comfort women'.[25] The Tribunal saw itself as restoring dignity to victims in place of the shame, fear and regret that they had continued to experience decades after the events of sexual abuse took place.[26] Gabrielle Simm and Andrew Byrnes suggested that rampant sexual violence in the war in Yugoslavia prompted elderly survivors to break their long decades of silence.[27] Although the ICTY was lauded for delivering groundbreaking judgements in relation to CRSV, feminist activists from the former Yugoslavia were not convinced that the ICTY brought justice to women victims who testified before the court, let alone to all female victims. Feminist scholars and activists have criticised the ICTY by observing that 'many victims of sexual violence who

20 Cambodian Defenders Project, 'Concept Note', in *Material Package for International Guests* (Asia-Pacific Regional Women's Hearing on Gender-Based Violence in Conflict, 2012) 31–32, cited in Otto, above n 3, 231.

21 Tina Dolgopol, 'The Judgment of the Tokyo Women's Tribunal' (2003) 28(5) *Alternative Law Journal* 242, 243.

22 Transcript of Oral Judgment delivered on 4 December 2001 by the Judges of the Women's International War Crimes Tribunal on Japan's Military Sexual Slavery, www.iccwomen.org/wigjdraft1/Archives/oldWCGJ/tokyo/summary.html, [4].

23 Neil Boister and Robert Cryer (eds), *Documents on the Tokyo International Military Tribunal: Charter, Indictments and Judgments* (Oxford University Press, 2008) 540.

24 Tokyo's Women Tribunal Judgement, above n 22, [8].

25 For a detailed account of this Tribunal, please see Henry, above n 2.

26 Dolgopol, above n 21, 247.

27 Simm and Byrnes, above n 2, 111.

testified before the ICTY have found their experiences as witnesses humiliating and disrespectful'.[28]

They felt that there is a necessity to deliver justice outside the official and formal justice structures and create a space in which they will not be seen only as 'a source of information, but agents and interpreters of history'.[29] Breaking away from the tradition of most women's courts, the Court established in the ex-Yugoslavia, covered not only the CRSV crimes, but also the socio-economic and political crimes committed against women; so the conception of rape 'as a weapon of war' is not the only lens through which courts and many policy makers see women's experiences of armed conflict.[30]

Despite the proliferation of scholarship on 'official' transitional justice mechanisms, far less attention has been paid to unofficial local practices of seeking justice and responding to the mass violence.[31] In particular, little is known about the impact of women's tribunals on victims, feminist activists and other participants. More empirical research into the experiences of participants may be needed in order to yield important insights into the challenges and limitations of such alternative, informal justice mechanisms.[32] In the remainder of this chapter, I draw on interviews with feminist activists about the Women's Court held in Sarajevo and its work in order to bolster the dearth of empirical research into this topic so far.

The Women's Court in Sarajevo

The first of the world's women's courts in Europe was held for three days in Sarajevo from May 7–10 in 2015. Officially named the Women's Court – a Feminist Approach to Justice, the Court gathered around 500 local and international participants who listened to 35 female witnesses. The Court itself had been in the making for several years before feminist activists started to translate an idea into action. The initial idea for organising the Women's Court for the former Yugoslavia was articulated in 2000 by Žarana Papić, a feminist philosopher and activist. A few years later, in 2006, the idea was picked up again after the death of Slobodan Milošević who died without being sentenced for the crimes he had committed.[33] In 2007 the Regional Commission for the Establishment of Facts about War Crimes and Other Serious Violations of Human Rights

28 Katherine M. Franke, 'Gendered Subjects of Transitional Justice' (2006) 15 *Columbia Journal of Gender and Law* 813, 818; see also Nicola Henry, 'Witness to Rape: The Limits and Potential of International War Crimes Trials for Victims of Wartime Sexual Violence' (2009) 3(1) *International Journal of Transitional Justice* 114.

29 Staša Zajović (ed.), *Women's Court: About the Process* (2015) Women in Black, www.helsinki.org.rs/doc/Womens%20Court%20About%20the%20Process.pdf, 40.

30 Doris Buss, 'International Criminal Courts' in Jill Steans and Daniela Tepe-Belfrage (eds), *Handbook on Gender in World Politics* (Edward Elgar, 2016) 162, 166.

31 Lia Kent, 'Local Memory Practices in East Timor: Disrupting Transitional Justice Narratives' (2011) 5(3) *International Journal of Transitional Justice* 434, 435.

32 Henry, above n 1, 135.

33 See Nevenka Tromp, *Prosecuting Slobodan Milošević: The Unfinished Trial* (Routledge 2016).

Committed in the Former Yugoslavia from 1 January 1991 until 31 December 2001 (RECOM)[34] was established, and Women in Black, Belgrade (WiB), along with other local non-government organisations (NGOs) were initially actively engaged with its activities.

While RECOM was an important initiative, WiB and other women's groups were not convinced that it would have a feminist perspective, so the idea of establishing the Women's Court was revived. Between 2008 and 2010 Staša Zajović from Serbia (WiB), Memnuna Zvizdić, (Žene Ženama) from Bosnia and Herzegovina (BiH), and Biljana Kašić from Croatia started to have meetings and talk more intensively about this idea, and decided to include activists from other states in their meetings. Since the beginning of 2010 to the Women's Court's eventuation in May 2015, the leader of the Organisational Committee, WiB organised a series of workshops, lectures, screenings of documentary movies, performances, regional educational seminars, public educational workshops and presentations about women's and people's tribunals, to raise awareness of their significance and introduce the idea of the women's tribunal to the people in in the former Yugoslavia. A total of 136 public presentations were held in around 100 cities and towns in the region,[35] organised and coordinated by more than 200 local NGOs.

From its very beginning, the Court attempted to reflect what Brinton Lykes and Alison Crosby describe as transformative, embodied and creative methodologies of justice[36] by using art and theatre, exhibitions and film screenings to raise awareness about the plethora of harms that women suffered during the war and in its aftermath. As one participant told me:

> The very best part of the Women's Court was the women's energy and solidarity. I really appreciated the fact that we all came together – women survivors and activists from all over the world – and that we had a chance to talk and listen to each other. I felt inspired and motivated to continue with my own work on social justice.[37]

As for their geographical distribution, a large majority of workshops and other activities in preparation for the Court were held in Sarajevo, the capital of the Federation of BiH (FBiH). In Republika Srpska (RS) presentations were organised only in two towns: Bratunac and Višegrad. This lack of attention that RS received may explain why many Serb women victims who I talked to in the Banjaluka region, had never heard of the Court. There were no organised presentations or activities in the Posavina region either, which perhaps has the largest number of Serb

34 Coalition for RECOM, *Women's Court: Preliminary Decisions and Recommendations* (2015), www.recom.link/womens-court-preliminary-decisions-and-recommendations/.

35 Zajović, above n 29, 18.

36 Lykes M. Brinton and Crosby Alison, 'Creative Methodologies as a Resource for Mayan Women's Protagonism' in Brendon Hamber and Gallagher Elizabeth (eds), *Psychosocial Perspectives on Peacebuilding* (Springer, 2014) 147.

37 Email from activist from FBiH to author, 9 February 2017.

female victims of CRSV.[38] Organisers invited all relevant governmental institutions, embassies and other diplomatic institutions to come as participants and listen to women's testimonies.[39] The representatives of the Gender Centre office based in Sarajevo, FBiH, were invited too and participated in the daily events of the Court.[40] While the organisers told me that the representatives of the Gender Centre based in Banjaluka, RS, had also been invited, their representative disagreed:

> We were not contacted nor in any way informed about the Women's Court, neither during its proceedings, nor later. We did not receive any information about its activities or results either directly or indirectly. Because we know nothing about it, we cannot give any view on the Court and whether it was useful for women or not.[41]

The idea of the Court was to provide 'a space for women's voices about the daily injustices suffered during the war and now, in peace'.[42] Women have traditionally been marginalised from transitional justice processes, and the Court was intended to make such women's contributions valuable and visible.[43] The different forms of violence were the subject matter of the five sessions of the hearing: *ethnic violence*, *gender-based violence* (including sexual and domestic violence), *military violence*, *political violence* and *socio-economic violence*.[44] With this plethora of forms of violence, the Court focused its attention on not only individual, but also structural forms of violence and inequality that often stay neglected, not only by the courts and tribunals, but also by transitional justice research.[45]

The aim of the Court was to 'write an alternative history', collect women's experiences of violence, and 'strengthen global feminist-pacifists' alliances and coalitions' by taking a 'feminist approach to justice',[46] which WiB defines as:

38 The first trials before the local courts for rapes of Serb women 1992 committed in the Posavina region by the Croatian Army started only in 2014.

39 Email from the organisers to the author, 8 February 2017.

40 Ibid.

41 Email from Gender Center RS to author, 8 February 2017.

42 Zajović, above n 29.

43 Women's Court – Feminist Approach to Justice, *Women's Court – Feminist Approach to Justice, Rules of the Women's Court* (n.d.), www.zenskisud.org/en/pdf/RULES_Womens_Court.pdf, 5.

44 Women's experience of sexual violence has been privileged over other experiences of women's victimhood or harms, such as socioeconomic. For feminist critique of international criminal law, see Catherine O'Rourke, 'International Law and Domestic Gender Justice, or Why Case Studies Matter' in Martha Albertson Fineman and Estelle Zinnstag (eds), *Feminist perspectives on Transitional Justice: From International and Criminal to Alternative Forms of Justice* (Intersentia, 2013).

45 Rosemary Nagy, 'Transitional Justice as Global Project: Critical Reflections' (2008) 29(2) *Third World Quarterly* 275; Fionnuala Ni Aolain, 'Advancing Feminist Positioning in the Field of Transitional Justice' (2012) 6(2) *International Journal of Transitional Justice*, 227; Padraig McAuliffe, *Transformative Transitional Justice and the Malleability of Post-Conflict States* (Edward Elgar, 2017).

46 Women's Court – Feminist Approach to Justice, *Methodology of Work* (2012), www.zenskisud.org/en/Metodologija.html, 5.

> an act of feminist responsibility which is motivated by the invisibility of women's contributions to transitional justice processes – women are marginalised and reduced to objects of violence. [It] is a correction of the injustice done to a significant number of women who participated in nonviolent resistance to war; in processes of rebuilding trust/reconciliation and peace.[47]

The Court aimed to 'deliver public condemnations'[48] at the end of its proceedings, but so far, the Judicial Council has published only preliminary decisions and recommendations.[49] Although people's and women's tribunals vary in their methodologies and forms of delivering judgements,[50] they often deliver them soon after the proceedings are over.[51] In general, the verdict should include 'pronouncements on how the evidence demonstrates that specific actors have violated international human rights standards, international and domestic law, and treaty obligations'.[52] The Women's Court in its *Rules of the Court, Article 8* specifically proclaimed:

> Based on the testimonies made by witnesses and expert witnesses, the Women's Court shall give a public verdict on the political and civic responsibility of perpetrators, appealing to judicial institutions with its requests and proposals, and monitoring the response of the said institutions.[53]

The Court, however, has not yet released its public verdict. The WiB representative told me that they do not expect any other decisions to be published by the Judiciary Council and that they were not aware that 'the judgment is in preparation'.[54] Two members of the Judicial Council, however, reported that the 'Judicial Council agreed to write a verdict, but we still have not received the necessary materials from [the Court's] Organising Committee in order to proceed with the writing'.[55] It remains unclear when or whether the verdict will be issued.

One of the central tenants of the Court was to have open discussions about how to mitigate expectations, since some potential female witnesses demanded certain actions with respect to specific states. For example, there were expectations that Serbia and Montenegro should be under pressure to be punished (with criminal and non-criminal sanctions) because of their 'responsibility and accountability for state-organised crimes'.[56] As Priscilla Hayner argues, it is not unusual

47 Zajović, above n 29, 12.

48 Women's Court, above n 43.

49 Coalition for RECOM, above n 34. Preliminary decisions and recommendations represent some key points and conclusions achieved immediately after the Court has finished its work.

50 For a general overview of people's tribunals, see Byrnes and Simm, above n 2.

51 For example, the Tokyo Women's Tribunal delivered 265 pages of judgments one year after finishing its procedures.

52 Grace Harbour, *Speak and Be Heard: APWLD Guide to Women's Tribunals* (2016), http://apwld.org/apwld-launches-speak-and-be-heard-apwld-guide-to-womens-tribunals/, 53.

53 Women's Court, above n 43.

54 Email communication with author, 3 February 2017.

55 Email communication with author, 7 February 2017.

56 Zajović, above n 29.

that the expectations of survivors from truth-seeking bodies are often much greater than what these bodies can achieve, and that some level of disappointment and disillusion will arise with the end of the processes.[57] The Organising Committee had to explain that it is not in a position to sanction anyone, and that any justice the women will get, would be symbolic.

WiB reported that one major significance of the initiative for the Court, was that it 'gathers women from all states from former Yugoslavia: Bosnia and Herzegovina, Montenegro, Croatia, Kosovo, Macedonia and Slovenia'.[58] BiH, although one state, is more complex than the others born out from the dissolution of Yugoslavia, due to its ethnically separated administrative, political and economic structures. This inherited complexity, I argue, has been reflected in the organisation, process and delivery of the Court itself.

In the WiB report about the process of creating the Court, only half a page was dedicated to its 'Challenges and Difficulties'. According to WiB, in the course of preparing the Court, a large number of NGOs participated in some way in public presentations and other activities. There were expectations, however, that NGOs' participation would be much higher, but that did not happen due to a

> lack of critical perspectives, NGOs are too much focused on states; international foundations and donors impose themes and networking from above; competition and struggle for survival among civil society organisations; NGOs are predominantly pro-governmental [and] not interested in questions of transitional justice.[59]

According to one of my interviewees, such critique of civil society by WiB will be particularly directed at the BiH NGO scene, which was reportedly 'the most difficult to work with',[60] and the ones who 'were not as professional and organized as they should have been in finding potential witnesses'.[61] WiB also reported that in some regions they could see that it will be more challenging to have female witnesses to testify because many women were 'already drained by giving their testimonies which put them in the role of objects'.[62]

In deciding where the Court should take place, a few cities were suggested. The two main options were 'Belgrade – as a symbol of accountability for war crimes'[63]

57 Priscilla B. Hayner, 'Introduction: In Pursuit of Justice and Reconciliation: Contributions of Truth Telling' in Priscilla B. Hayner (ed.), *Unspeakable Truths: Facing the Challenge of Truth Commissions* (Routledge, 2010) 1, 5–6.

58 Zajović, above n 29, 10–11.

59 Ibid., 21.

60 Interview with author, 16 November 2016.

61 Staša Zajović, leader of WiB, cited in Clark, above n 9.

62 Zajović, above n 29, 24.

63 Žene u Crnom [Women in Black], *Ženski Sud Feministički Pristup Pravdi: Izveštaj januar 2014–decembar 2014* [Trans: *Women's Court Feminist Approach to Justice: Report January 2014–December 2014*] (2015), www.zenskisud.org/pdf/Izvestaj_ZS_jan_2014_dec_2014.pdf, 9.

and for being seen as the 'belly of the beast',[64] and Sarajevo – 'as a symbol of suffering'.[65] The identification of Belgrade with Serbia's collective culpability for war crimes is a well-known position of WiB and anti-nationalist feminists from Serbia. Their own denial of national and ethnic identities has created a starting point in communication: refusal of their own ethnic identities came to symbolise their refusal of nationalism[66] and embracing collective Serb responsibility for the crimes committed on the territory of the former Yugoslavia. As Zarkov argues: 'if ethnicity was introduced into the rhetoric it was only to declare the Serb government, Serb people and especially Serb men, as the ultimate war villains'.[67] This standpoint was also embraced by some Court observers who praised the WiB as organisers coming from 'the land of [the] aggressor'.[68] The standpoint of WiB as the leader of the Organising Committee would become one of the key obstacles to progressing the conversation with Bosnian Serb feminist activists, and for survivors to engage in meaningful participation and collaboration.

A (lack of) critique of civil society

In transitional justice scholarship there is an overarching agreement that civil society organisations have played an important role in 'promoting and supporting transitional justice experiments around the world'.[69] While civil society actors are important transitional actors that develop innovative and alternative methods that contest institutionalised forms of transitional justice, 'few attempts have been made to develop analytical frameworks that may be useful for approaching a wider set of civil society encounters and engagements with transitional justice'.[70] Similarly, Lucy Hovil and Chrispus Okello argue that there is a 'dearth of strong civil society critiques' in transitional justice analysis, and that future analysis of civil society should consider 'the dynamics in the relationship between civil society actors and those they claim to represent; between civil society and those who fund it'.[71] Nicola Henry also suggests that the people's tribunals 'have rarely been examined within the growing field of transitional justice'.[72]

64 Zajović, above n 29, 28.
65 Žene u Crnom [Women in Black], above n 63.
66 Dubravka Žarkov, 'Feminism and the Disintegration of Yugoslavia: On the Politics of Gender and Ethnicity' (2002) 24(3) *Social Development Issues* 59.
67 Ibid., 68.
68 Marieme Helie Lucas, 'Bosna-Sarajevo: Ženski sud u bivšoj Jugoslaviji' [Trans: 'Bosnia-Sarajevo: Women's Court in the Former Yugoslavia'] (2015), www.zenskisud.org/pdf/Marieme_Helie_Lucas_bhs.pdf.
69 Eric Brahm, 'Transitional Justice, Civil Society, and the Development of the Rule of Law in Post-Conflict Societies' (2007) 9(4) *International Journal of Not-for-Profit Law* 62.
70 Iavor Rangelov, 'Civil Society and Transitional Justice in the Balkans: Three Models of Interactions' (2015) *Security in Transition*, www.securityintransition.org/publications/civil-society-and-transitional-justice-in-the-balkans-three-models-of-interaction/, 3–4.
71 Lucy Hovil and Chrispus Okello, 'Editorial Note' (2011) 5(3) *International Journal of Transitional Justice* 333, 334.
72 Henry, above n 1, 120.

Henry wonders whether the lack of critique and far less public attention that is given to international or national unofficial justice mechanisms, is due to 'the benevolence in which civil society initiatives are attributed'.[73] Likewise, Hovil and Okello argue that civil society often escapes scrutiny because it is perceived as a mechanism that keeps in check the power of the state and as such 'works an overwhelming faith in its benefit to society simply by virtue of its existence'.[74]

Perhaps due to such reasons, there has been little critique about whether civil society actors were 'genuinely inclusive' and whether they delivered 'the goods in practice'.[75] Yet such scrutiny is vital given that 'transitional justice civil society activity has proliferated and remains relatively unmonitored'.[76] Susanne Buckley-Zistel and Magdalena Zolkos specifically encourage a critical gender perspective to examining 'exclusions and inclusions' and the ideological constructs of gender within transitional justice:

> [C]ritical gender analysis traces the processes whereby gendered subjectivity is constructed in social and political life, and how this subjectivity is formed and perpetuated through diverse systems of knowledge . . . it . . . draws attention to the subjects at the margins of political communities – those that on the basis of gender, class, ethnicity, or other categories of social differentiation tend to be regarded as 'invisible' or 'silent', or unable to exert political participatory agency.[77]

Transitional justice scholars have critiqued the uncertain impacts of civil society by problematising the effects relating to demand for, or promise of, catharsis and closure that transitional justice mechanisms offer.[78] They argued that approaches to addressing mass harm may serve to consolidate the notion of perpetual victimhood, and that victims' narratives of suffering may be co-opted for other agendas (for example, to serve nationalist goals).[79] Regardless of the forum, transitional justice measures may promote a false universalism and generate problematic representations of suffering.[80] All of this runs a risk of creating a spectacle of pain and suffering.[81] Ruti Teitel writes that while transitional justice promises a kind of closure it does so at a cost:

73 Ibid., 129.

74 Hovil and Okello, above n 71, 334.

75 Ibid., 333.

76 Ibid., 336.

77 Susanne Buckely-Zistel and Magdalena Zolkos, 'Gender in Transitional Justice' in Susanne Buckley-Zistel and Ruth Stanley (eds), *Gender in Transitional Justice* (Palgrave Macmillan, 2012) 1, 19.

78 Anne Orford, 'Commissioning the Truth' (2006) 15(3) *Columbia Journal of Gender and Law* 851; Ruti G. Teitel, 'Transitional Justice Genealogy' (2003) 16 *Harvard Human Rights Journal* 69.

79 Franke, above n 28, 813.

80 Sarah C. Soh, *The Comfort Women: Sexual Violence and Postcolonial Memory in Korea and Japan* (The University of Chicago Press, 2008).

81 Brinton and Alison, above n 36.

> By these practices, a line is drawn delineating the parameters of that collective memory to be preserved: what is to be remembered and what repressed; what is to be abandoned and what validated; what is to be rendered incontestable and what will remain controverted.[82]

So far, there has been little critical analysis and research into women's tribunals as a global movement and, in particular, on their impact. While the Women's Court in Sarajevo has been described as 'transcending nationalists' divisions',[83] and the one that 'successfully delivered justice as recognition at a symbolic level',[84] a closer look at its organisation, preparation processes and delivery may, I argue, suggest that it potentially further deepened ethnic divisions between and among both female survivors and female activists. As Sarah C. White argues, while the notion of 'participation' by women has the potential to challenge patterns of dominance and empowerment, it may also be 'the means through which existing power relations are entrenched and reproduced'.[85]

Some of the greatest contributions attributed to women's tribunals have been that they seek to promote redistribution, recognition and representation.[86] In Nancy Fraser's view, recognition entails acknowledgement of the identity and the status of the 'other' and the cultural injustices against groups that are 'rooted in social patterns of representation, interpretation, and communication'.[87] Whether all groups have been represented is here under scrutiny: '[w]ho are the "locals" whose voices need to be heard and heeded and how does the local-empowering process overcome hierarchical differences within a local community that could otherwise preclude giving agency to the most marginalised?'[88] As Patricia Lundy and Mark McGovern argue, it is important that advocates of participatory approaches, in the discipline of transitional justice, seek and address participatory methods as early as possible; ideally in the design and development of such strategies.[89] In the next section of this chapter, I examine if and how the Court in Sarajevo succeeded in doing this, and thereby contributed to two important

82 Ruti G. Teitel *Transitional Justice* (Oxford University Press 2000) 229–230.

83 Lucas, above n 68.

84 Clark, above n 9, 67.

85 Sarah C. White, 'Depoliticising Development: The Uses and Abuses of Participation' (1996) 6(1) *Development in Practice* 6; Institute of Development Studies (IDS), *Participation* (n.d.), www.ids.ac.uk/ids/particip, 6.

86 Here, Nancy Fraser's three-dimensional model of justice is particularly helpful; justice as recognition (acknowledging the status of others), representation (symbolic representation through language) and redistribution (fair distribution of burdens and benefits). See Nancy Fraser, 'Reframing Justice in Globalizing World' in Held David and Ayse Kaya (eds), *Global Inequality: Patterns and Explanations* (Polity Press, 2007) 252.

87 Ibid.

88 Eirin Mobekk, 'Conference Report' in Anja E. Ebnöther and Philipp H. Fluri (eds), *After Intervention: Public Security Management in Post-Conflict Societies: From Intervention to Sustainable Local Ownership* (2005) 377, www.dcaf.ch/content/download/35127/525471/file/complet.pdf, 384.

89 Patricia Lundy and Mark McGovern, 'Whose Justice? Rethinking Transitional Justice from the Bottom Up' (2008) 35(2) *Journal of Law and Society* 265, 283.

justice goals – recognition and representation. Or, whether it fell into the same trap as criminal tribunals, namely 'misrecognition'[90] of certain groups and victims.[91]

My intention here is not to dismiss the enormous effort and diligence of hundreds of women activists working towards delivering alternative justice to women victims, but to critically evaluate the Court so that lessons may be learned, and the transitional-justice field strengthened.[92] I am particularly interested in contributing to Hovil and Okello's suggestion that future transitional-justice analysis considers 'the dynamics in the relationship between civil society actors and those they claim to represent'.[93] This is because such 'practices have their own power dynamics, exclusions and silences'.[94] In the remainder of this chapter, I draw on interviews I have conducted with 13 feminist activists from BiH (both entities) and Serbia, who participated to various degrees in the preparation processes for the Court and later on as participants at the event.

'My pain is lesser than the pain of others': reflecting at the Women's Court, work and results

In 2010 WiB invited the association Mothers of Srebrenica, which represents survivors of the Srebrenica genocide and which is based in FBiH, to become a member of the BiH Court's Organising Committee. Between 2010 and 2012 none of the women NGOs from RS were part of the Committee. In 2012 Lara, (Bijeljina), Budućnost (Modriča), and in 2013 Forum Žena Bratunac, joined the Committee. Lara withdrew in 2013 followed by Forum Žena two years later. Forum Žena brought an official decision to withdraw from the Committee on 25 March 2015, less than six weeks before the Court was about to start.[95] The main reason for this decision, which was reached by consensus among its members, was 'solidarity and support' for Spasenija, the only Serb female survivor of CRSV from RS who was in the process of preparing to testify before the Court.

In December 2014, Spasenija sent a letter to Forum Žena, which was then forwarded to all women's NGOs involved in the Committee, about her disappointment with the preparatory process. In her letter, Spasenija reflected on a conference that had been held in Tivat, Montenegro in November 2014, in which she had participated with a number of other women survivors and women activists. She reported:

90 Fraser, above n 86.

91 Doris Buss, 'Rethinking Rape as a Weapon of War' (2009) 17 *Feminist Legal Studies* 145.

92 Henry, above n 1, 135.

93 Hovil and Okello, above n 71, 334.

94 Kent, above n 31, 443.

95 Forum Žena Bratunac, 'Odluka o istupanju Udruženja Forum žena Bratunac iz regionalne inicijative Ženski sud za bivšu Jugoslaviju' [Trans: 'Decision about Withdrawal of Forum žena Bratunac from the Regional Initiative Women's Court for Ex-Yugoslavia'], 25 March 2015. Document on file with author.

> It became very clear to me that I do not belong there. I felt that the pain I carry within me I have to continue to keep only for myself; that my pain belongs only to me . . . I understood that my pain was much lesser than pain from women from Srebrenica, Goražde, Foča, Višegrad, Đulića, Klise . . . I could see that there is a care only for these victims because they were enabled to talk about everything without interruptions . . . there is lots of care only for these victims . . .You, I, we do not exist, we are not victims, we are just symbolic numbers of those who are less important because our pain, my pain is lesser than the pain of others . . . there is nothing honest about this; about so-called care for all victims, only victims from Srebrenica and these other places are considered victims.[96]

According to Forum Žena, 'no one from the Organising Committee has ever replied to Spasenija's letter' that was sent to all women activists across the former Yugoslavia involved in the process. In January 2015, a few weeks after sending the letter, Spasenija was simply removed from the list of potential women witnesses 'without being informed or consulted about removal'.[97] Due to these circumstances, Forum Žena decided to withdraw from the process, and in its decision to withdraw stated that they believed that further participation of their organisation in 'this process will not contribute to achieving individual peace to which the initiative [the Court] was supposed to bring to all survivors'.[98] In an interview with Cana Tešić, a representative of Forum Žena, she told me that their vision of the Court has changed over time from the initiative that started in 2010, and that they joined in 2013 and left in 2015. According to Tešić, her association has seen 'some problems' with the process, but they believed these will be addressed over time:

> The decision to pull out altogether was not just my own, but of all our members. We noticed that after Spasenija sent that letter, she was simply removed from the list of potential witnesses that was circulated to all of us. After that, we closely monitored the process. We concluded that the whole initiative has become problematic and that it was not clear how, as such, it can contribute to peace building in BiH and improve the status of survivors. For the past 15 years we have been meeting women who were many times disappointed and hurt by the governmental institutions, but for us it is unacceptable that they feel insulted by women activists and feminists. After everything that happened to Spasenija, we did not trust to bring other Serb women into the process.[99]
>
> We are sad that solidarity, empathy and care have been lost and that on our decision to pull out, not one women's NGO has reacted . . . Women in

96 These towns are all the hotspots of the Serb Army's crimes during the war. Letter from Spasenija dated 9 December 2014 on file with author.

97 Email to author, 26 March 2015.

98 Article 3 of the Decision, above n 94.

99 Forum Žena Bratunac, above n 95.

> Black sent us a message to thank us for our cooperation, but without one word of compassion towards Spasenija or any signs that this organisation will do something to change the process . . . The Women's Court should be about all women feeling safe and not hurt again, that all traumatic experiences of all women are equally important . . . all of this shows to us that our decision is our choice and that our concerns are not important to activists in BiH and the region.[100]

With the pulling out of Spasenija and Forum Žena, the Court lost an NGO from RS on its Committee board, and the only Serb female witness from RS who could testify. After this, the representatives of a few RS women's NGOs came to attend the Court, but 'only as observers to support women who testified'.[101] The relationship between the Committee, led by WiB and women's NGOs in RS, was difficult from the beginning. According to Stanojka Tešić , there was an overall lack of support for the Court's initiative since 'the civil society organisations from RS were not very interested in this topic [CRSV] because this topic is not welcomed by the political institutions in RS'.[102] The lack of interest in taking full part in the initiative, comes from the fact that some women's NGOs have been partially funded from the RS budget and were afraid to lose the funds that are vital for their work and survival. Other RS feminist activists perceived the Court to be biased even during its preparatory phases:

> There were problems early on in the Court's preparation phases. The organisers did not take care of Serb female victims. We left the Organising Committee because we did not agree on many things. In the end, the Court was organised with no women's NGO from RS and no Serb female victims to testify. We were just formally invited to come and participate at the Court's events as everyone else. My impression of the whole thing is poor. We just listened to testimonies from *their* [emphasis added] victims. Our victims [Serb] were not there to tell their stories. It was all one way. I think that the Court brought more division then unification amongst women's groups.[103]
>
> The whole process was not done properly. We first needed to work out our own internal questions and pull out some issues that we had buried under the carpet and discuss them openly. We need to break down some prejudices that we have about each other . . . the whole process was developing badly. We do not have the same views and perspectives on some issues, such as the character of the war in Bosnia – about who was the aggressor, who the victim. I think we were not ripe for that process. We needed to resolve some of the core issues amongst us before going into the whole process, and that did not happen. I think that women from BiH needed

100 Email communication with author, 1 April 2015.
101 Telephone interview with RS activist, 11 February 2016.
102 Email communication with author, 6 April 2015.
103 Telephone interview with RS activist, 8 February 2017.

> more space to talk. There is a need that women from BiH who come from different ethnic backgrounds have a platform to listen to each other, and unfortunately that did not happen. The unequal status that female victims have in RS and FBiH, due to politics, has been mirrored in the civil society sector and the Court was not immune to that.[104]

A few women told me that they did not agree, and felt frustrated that WiB had used the language of 'aggressor' to describe Serbia, and to collectively blame Serbs for the war and crimes that had happened. They felt that from the beginning of the Court's preparations, the dichotomy of victim–perpetrator was maintained and reinforced. Also, the fact that Mothers of Srebrenica were part of the Committee from its establishment, was met with resistance by two women's organisations from RS, since Mothers has never been a feminist organisation, but an association of genocide survivors.[105] As soon as Forum Žena stepped into the Committee, they expressed their disagreements with Mothers being part of it, and suggested that it will 'only be fair if NGOs representing other victims – of other ethnic groups, not just Bosniak – are also invited to join'.[106]

While it was expected that the Mothers of Srebrenica should testify at the Court, three other feminist activists from RS told me:

> These voices [the Mothers'] have been heard many times in public and while I feel empathy, I felt that there were perhaps too many women from Srebrenica who were telling the stories all of us have heard before. Women's courts should be about bringing those women who have not received any justice so far and have never been heard speaking up. This was an opportunity for them to be listened to . . . Mothers could occupy less time and space since we have had prosecutions for crimes in Srebrenica and they told their stories many times . . . I just felt that it would be better that some of that time was given to women who never spoke about their experiences.[107]
>
> In my opinion, the Women's Court failed. We do not have the same strategy; we do not have the same opinions about war, its causes and consequences, its victims and perpetrators. If Mothers of Srebrenica were the core of the Organising Committee, why did they not invite the associations of mothers from other ethnic communities? We were invited to the Organising Committee as feminist activists, and Mothers are the association of civilian victims of war, not feminist activists. If you invite them then you have to

104 Telephone interview with RS activist, 3 February 2017.

105 The main aims of the Mothers of Srebrenica association are finding the truth about those people who disappeared in July 1995; participation in the process of postmortem exhumation, and the identification and burials of victims. See Movement of Mothers of Srebrenica (Mothers) and Žepa Encalves (n.d.), http://enklave-srebrenica-zepa.org/english.onama.php.

106 Skype interview, 3 February 2016. Suggestion by Forum Žena, however, was never taken on board, and WiB remained closely connected to Munira Subašić, the president of Mothers. WiB has a long history of collaboration with Mothers and every year marks the genocide anniversary.

107 Interview with RS activist, 8 June 2015.

> invite the representatives of other victims' associations. We could not win these arguments and we withdrew.[108]
>
> We really had an issue and dilemma whether Mothers of Srebrenica, as an association of victims, needed to be part of the process. We had a problem with the Women in Black coordinator who, although we were against it, invited Mothers, but did not want to include other victims' associations. None of the victims' organisations from RS was included.[109]

One feminist activist specifically referred to the ICTY and said that Mothers had had the opportunity to speak and be heard in the 'world court of justice', so 'the whole world knows their story'.[110] A few local activists from RS shared a similar opinion.

While the WiB strongly believes in alternative models of justice, and hence decided to organise the Court, the main point of their departure and reference was the ICTY. In WiB's documents and reports they, for example, have not articulated the findings of the PPT hearings held in Bern and Barcelona, where Bosniak women testified. It is not clear why these hearings were not part of WiB's analysis, but instead the ICTY's, that received a substantial amount of feminist critique.

According to Janine Natalya Clark, when she asked about the ethnic composition of the panels, all interviewees involved in the organisation of the Court told her that 'the process was never about equalising ethnic victimhood'.[111] In my interviews with members of the Committee, not all felt comfortable with the fact that Serb women victims of CRSV from RS missed the opportunity to be listened to:

> The women from RS were in the audience, but no one testified. We have tried but did not succeed. It was the responsibility of the Bosnian NGOs to prepare female witnesses. The most difficult situation to work in was in Bosnia and then Kosovo. The same goes for Kosovo – there was not one non-Albanian woman. We know that in Kosovo it was not just violence against Albanians, but Serbs and other ethnic groups too. But women's NGOs had to think about it. We could not organise it all. We split the work. We could not influence these processes; our agreement was that we would not interfere in the work of the other nation-state female organisers.[112]
>
> I feel bad that after 20 years of direct investment with female survivors, we don't have at least three women from RS to testify. We should not allow an absence of women from RS in the Women's Court.[113]

108 Interview with RS activist, 24 November 2015.
109 Interview with RS activist, 13 October 2016.
110 Interview with RS activist, 18 November 2016.
111 Clark, above n 9, 82.
112 Interview with M. N., 16 June 2015.
113 Email communication with author, 16 March 2015.

A long-term anti-nationalist feminist activist from Serbia who attended the Court told me:

> If you ask me, it was a total fiasco that there were no Serb women representatives from RS at the Women's Court. There is no doubt about it; all those who organised the Court knew that, there was no justification for that. It was not done carefully. Full stop. In fact, that is a shame.[114]

So far, there has been a scarcity of scholarly analysis written about the Court. Clark has recently published her reflections on the Court and while enthusiastic about it, arguing that the Court 'successfully delivered justice as recognition',[115] towards the end of her paper, Clark raises questions of 'the ethnic balance of this recognition'.[116] She asked one of the organisers, Vesna Teršelič, a member of the Court's Judicial Council to reflect on the ethnic imbalance:

> Yes, the Women's Court could have been more ethnically balanced, but how would you achieve this? You work with those women who are prepared to tell their stories. If the organizers had waited until they had a balanced witness set, the Women's Court might never have happened.[117]

Another two members of the Committee agreed with Teršelič:

> The process itself lasted too long and one of the reasons we pushed for May 2015 was the 20-year anniversary of the Srebrenica genocide that year and we wanted this to happen before July when the anniversary takes place. Another one was 20 years of the World Women's Conference in Beijing. It was a symbolic recognition of the genocide in Srebrenica as the biggest crime and the Women's Court worked with issues of war crimes, including genocide. The Court had already been rescheduled twice and we did not want to reschedule it again.[118]
>
> I do not think there is a right or wrong moment for the Women's Court in BiH. The process has to start somewhere and at some point. We have some kind of agreed practice not to talk about what women survived here, and women victims have been an object of work for many of us. I think that the time has come that they become subjects as well, and that a new generation has to find a new model of conversation about painful subjects.[119]

Two female-activist attendees thought, however, that the Court was premature and that 'we should have waited for more time' and that after all, 'the Tokyo

114 Email communication with author, 1 February 2016.
115 Clark, above n 9, 68.
116 Clark, above n 9, 81.
117 Clark, above n 9, 82.
118 Interview with S. Z., 15 June 2016.
119 Ibid.

Tribunal happened 70 years later'.[120] Both agreed that the exclusion of some women should not have happened and that it would be better had the organisers waited to ensure that women from all ethnic groups are equally represented. A few scholars who reported on the Court noted that the Court 'had the potential to challenge the deeply entrenched ethnic narratives'.[121] The lack of women from some ethnic groups before the Court, according to Clark: 'gave the impression that certain ethnic groups suffered from wartime violence more than others'.[122] According to Maria O'Reilly, the panel on CRSV was the smallest of all panels and was composed of a narrow range of witnesses (Kosovo and eastern BiH), 'whose narratives highlighted experiences of being targeted as Muslim/Bosniak women by Serb men'.[123] As a consequence, the Court 'failed to seize this opportunity to fully challenge ethno-nationalist narratives and related narratives of victimhood that dominate discussions of wartime rape within BiH'.[124] Di Otto, the judicial member of the Court, in her reflections on the Court, writes that despite organisers' efforts to stay alert to complexities and specificities of their own identities and political choices, 'some women's experiences were still excluded'.[125]

Two long-term feminist activists from RS said that to them it was not surprising that there were no Serb women witnesses: 'There were no Serb women from RS to testify at any of the panels. This fact just mirrors the situation in Bosnia which is totally ethnically divided.'[126]

> We did not want to participate in that circus. You probably know that the project ended with quarrels between women's groups. We were asked a few times to become part of it, but we did not want to. We avoided being involved with the Organising Committee because we knew how that would look and what would happen at the end. We gave our support, but we are much more pragmatic: you cannot do something when you know that there is no political will around that topic here [in RS]. We would only make problems for ourselves, while achieving nothing. There is no chance to change anything with respect to this topic [CRSV] here for now. Women in RS do not have the status of victim. We know that none of the Serb women from RS testified and that just mirrors the situation in our entity and the country. It reflects divisions. None of the women from RS would go there anyway.[127]

To my question as to why women from RS did not testify, a long-term feminist activist from FBiH who attended the Court told me:

120 Interview with activists from Serbia, 18 December 2016.

121 Clark, above n 9, 82.

122 Clark, above n 9, 81.

123 Maria O'Reilly, 'Peace and Justice through a Feminist Lens: Gender Justice and the Women's Court for the Former Yugoslavia' (2016) 10(3) *Journal of Intervention and State Building* 419, 431.

124 Ibid.

125 Otto, above n 3, 247.

126 Interview with R. S., 16 June 2016.

127 Telephone interview 3 February 2017.

> To me it speaks that there is no freedom of speech in RS, and that those who survived fear retribution from both sides – from their 'own' side, for taking part in events that involve 'others', and from the 'others' if they state that the 'others' committed crimes as well. I was very sorry that women of Serb nationality in RS were not ready to speak at the Women's Court as witnesses. In my opinion, the fact that they did not participate equally and addressed their identities and problems together with us, shows that we are still far away from a joint platform that will represent all victims and survivors of war.[128]

It seems that all interviewees are in agreement, albeit to various levels, that despite the enormous positive energy and solidarity that the Court brought to female participants, it could not overcome ethnic divisions. The feminist activists who I talked to may have disagreed about the reasons why this didn't happen, but they all drew the conclusion that the Court, if not failed, then certainly 'mirrored' the complexities of the political situation in the country. It did not, nor could not, stay immune from the wider political context in which the processes were happening. After the Court took place, the chief organisers of the Court continue to organise workshops and meetings to which they invite the female witnesses who testified. There have been few such meetings so far[129] and it is unclear whether, at any point in the future, Serb female victims of CRSV from RS will ever be invited to join them.

Conclusion

The Women's Court in Sarajevo was the first of the worlds' women's courts to be held in Europe. The Court brought together hundreds of activists and civil society groups to organise and deliver justice to women survivors of armed conflicts across former Yugoslavia. Lots of work, vision and hope was put into its work. However, as discussed in this chapter, the Women's Court in Sarajevo failed to bring feminist activists and female witnesses belonging to different ethnic groups together. As some feminist activists have suggested, it was necessary to discuss openly the 'prejudices and assumptions' they perhaps had against each other before even discussing other aspects of the Court.

Rather than silencing difficult conversations, the Court could be used as a platform to transparently discuss the wounds that have not healed and the differences in views on the war itself; its causes and consequences, its victims and perpetrators. These issues should have been discussed before the Court commenced its work, or maybe one of the panels of the Court could have been left open for such conversations to take place. By not having an open forum that would allow disagreements to be heard and challenged in a respectful and considerate way,

128 Email communication with author, 9 February 2017.

129 Žene u Crnom [Women in Black], *Ženski sud – feministički pristup pravdi, Izveštaj januar–august 2016* [Trans: *Women's Court – Feminist Approach to Justice: Report January–August 2016*], http://zenskisud.org/pdf/2016/Zenski_sud_janaur_avgust_2016_izvestaj_sh.pdf.

my impression is that the Court left a bitter taste for many feminist activists and female victims from RS who could have been potential witnesses.

The politics of inclusion and exclusion – who is to be listened to, who is to be left out – and the kinds of implications that would have on the Court's legacy, needed to be discussed early on. While many long-term anti-nationalist feminists in ex-Yugoslavia, who were part of the Organising Committee, have been tirelessly struggling against the forces of nationalism over the past two decades, they perhaps unintentionally trapped themselves into the nationalist politics of victimhood. Rather than breaking through nationalism and ethnicism, they instead have been co-opted into the men's nationalist agendas and projects that have successfully and persistently constructed, maintained and reinforced the victim–perpetrator dichotomy. Time will tell if and when the space will come to bring different women's voices in inclusive representation and mutual recognition.

6 The role of civil society in assisting women victims of conflict-related sexual violence

The role of women's non-government organisations

The role of non-government organisations (NGOs) varies from offering support to a specific group of individuals, to lobbying and raising public awareness about issues of particular concern to their agendas. The NGOs may have an important role in relation to reporting to international agencies, since they take over the role of service delivery from the government. They do so due to the lack of state programs or because the NGOs are more closely affiliated with the target group than are the state institutions. In the case of Bosnia and Herzegovina (BiH), both these reasons, as well as donors' support, have influenced NGOs in assuming responsibilities from the state.

In order to provide the necessary assistance to women survivors of CRSV, the NGO sector in BiH has been playing a significant role. The first women's NGOs in Federation of Bosnia and Herzegovina (FBiH) had already been established in the midst of war. Medica Zenica was founded in 1993 to provide support to women victims of wartime violence, in particular rape, regardless of the women's ethnic backgrounds. Due to a large absence of state programs for women survivors, NGOs such as Medica Zenica still play a vital role in providing psychosocial support, vocational training and other assistance to women. They have established themselves as an alternative support mechanism by resolving a number of problems women survivors face, which the state cannot resolve by itself or does not care enough about.[1] While there are dozens of NGOs in FBiH that systematically provide psychological, social or economic support to women survivors of CRSV and torture, even after 20 years since the war ended, there have been no government organisations or NGOs formed to do this work in RS entity.

Besides providing services to women, one of the key women's NGO advocacy activities is the preparation of so-called 'shadow reports', which represent alternative and additional information to governmental periodical reports for the United Nations (UN) bodies. The women's NGOs play a vital role in delivering relevant and independent analysis of women's human rights to the UN committees about

1 For a detailed analysis of the role and importance of NGOs see UNDP, *Priručnik za nevladine organizacije u Bosni i Hercegovini* [Trans: *Handbook for Non-Governmental Organizations in Bosnia and Herzegovina*], Report, UNDP (2006), www.omladina-bih.net/download/Prirucnik.pdf.

issues that may be neglected by governments, such as violence against women. Shadow reports are submitted to treaty monitoring bodies at the UN and other international institutions as an alternative to a government's official report regarding the human rights situation in its respective country.

In 2013 representatives of the most prominent BiH women's NGOs jointly prepared periodical shadow reports for the Committee on the Elimination of Discrimination against Women, which emphasised the difficult status of women victims of CRSV. The report underlined the unequal treatment of women victims in Republika Srpska (RS) and FBiH:

> Victims of rape and other forms of sexual violence do not have the same opportunities in both entities to exercise their rights on the status of civilian victim of war. This status they can receive only in Federation BiH. Women victims of rape and other forms of sexual violence are not recognised in Republika Srpska as a special category of civilian victims of war and cannot exercise their rights since deadlines have passed a long time ago.[2]

Similarly, the report on reparations for victims in the former Yugoslavia, recognised 'a need to avoid differential treatment of victims who have suffered similar violations during the same conflict, as this is likely to further increase ethnic polarization'.[3] Scholarly literature on BiH women's NGOs that work with women survivors often leaves an impression that these NGOs are equally established across the entire geographical territory of BiH. In reality, such NGOs exist and operate only in FBiH. Due to the popular image of Bosniak women as the predominant victims of CRSV, from 1993 onwards, women's NGOs flourished in this entity with the support of foreign donors. Conversely, due to strong perceptions of Serbs as the main villains in the war, women's NGOs in RS were less attractive to international donors. In RS, the first NGO established to gather women survivors of CRSV was founded only in 2012. This NGO, however, does not provide any psychosocial or other type of services to women victims nor does it have any donor-driven funds and long-term projects.

Although international donors have turned their attention and support to FBiH, in the course of my fieldwork I discovered that at least one international women's NGO was willing to support projects in RS that would be amenable to assisting women survivors of CRSV. Still, they could not find partner women's NGOs willing to take on the offer.

2 Sabiha Husic, '*Women Victims of War*', *Annex to the Shadow Report on the Implementation of the CEDAW Convention and on Women's Human Rights in Bosnia and Herzegovina* (2013), www.ecoi.net/file_upload/1930_1375090959_jointngosubmission-forthesession-bih-cedaw55.pdf, 10 (document on file with author).

3 Peter Van der Auweraert and Igor Cvetkovski, *Reparations for Wartime Victims in the Former Yugoslavia: In Search of the Way Forward*, Report, International Organization for Migration (2013), www.iom.int/files/live/sites/iom/files/What-We-Do/docs/Reparations-for-Wartime-Victimes-in-the-Former-Yugoslavia-In-Search-of-the-Way-Forward.pdf, 26.

In summer 2013, I met with the long-term feminist activist in city X[4] who told me that an NGO – AMICA – from Italy approached NGO Y, which she was affiliated with, and offered them financial support to work on this issue. To my surprise, she said: 'We rejected their offer and told them that this [CRSV] is a political issue and we do not have experience working with such victims. I took them to NGO Z but they rejected them too.'[5] The representative of NGO Y told me that they were reluctant to work on 'such a politically sensitive issue that the RS government continuously ignores'.[6] The NGO Y enjoys some benefits from the government (such as free office space) and, as they told me: 'sees no point in working on something that is not only ignored by the government but repressed and silenced'.[7] NGO Z also rejected AMICA's offer to fund projects that would support women victims of CRSV based in RS. Although Z was the only women's NGO in RS that provided support and assistance to women survivors of CRSV during the war, they told AMICA and me that 'they were not interested in working with women survivors of CRSV anymore'.[8]

During my fieldwork, some Serb activists based in RS were sceptical about my research into Serb women's experiences with CRSV. An activist from NGO Z told me bitterly that she believed 'no matter what one publishes about Serb women, it is all irrelevant because who cares if you find out a few Serb women were victims of rape when there were apparently 20,000 Bosniak women raped'.[9] Another activist had a similar opinion:

> We helped these women, but we have had no contact with them anymore for the last 15 years . . . We know nothing about them, where they are, how they are . . . They did not want to talk publically about their ordeal, so we did not talk either. There are some documents and reports published about their experiences, but only with their initials because they did not want their full identity to be revealed. These are not Bosniak women who came out and publically spoke about their ordeal. You know there is a thesis about mass rape of Bosniak women that has been widely accepted and which automatically disqualifies any experience of women who did not survive mass rape. They [Bosniaks] talk about tens of thousands of raped women, so if we have three, tens or hundreds that somehow is considered as not relevant experience. What is hundreds in comparison to thousands? That's why we did not write anything and did not talk about it . . . it was them [Serb women] who did not want to talk primarily so we respected that. Most of these women came from the Posavina region.[10]

4 In order to protect the identity of my interlocutor I have anonymised her name, location and the organisation that she works for. X, Y and Z are pseudonyms for NGOs.

5 Interview with R.O., 15 May 2013.

6 Ibid.

7 Interview with a long-term feminist, 18 May 2015.

8 I asked AMICA to confirm that two women's NGOs from city X rejected their offer, and it did so. Email from AMICA employee to author, 15 September 2014.

9 Interview with M. A., 15 May 2013.

10 Interview with K. L., 13 June 2015.

I asked NGO Z representatives whether I could have a look at some of their archival material from the wartime period when they worked with the women victims, but I was denied. They made it clear to me they do not want to talk about their activities during the war because they do not believe that would contribute to anything. I felt heavy after meeting these activists who had done a great deal of work for women survivors during the war, but who now refuse to talk about it at all. In RS there are only two women's victims associations that gather female survivors of CRSV and torture. The Association of Women Victims of War from the Republic of Srpska (the Association) was established in December 2012 and is based in Gradiška. In 2013, the Association of the Former Camp Inmates of Republika Srpska established the Section for the Protection of Women Victims of Torture and Rape (the Section), which is based in Trebinje. These two NGOs are the first and only associations that aim to register all women who have been raped and tortured in concentration camps, established by the Army of the Republic of Bosnia and Herzegovina, and Croatian Defence Forces. Even though these associations have been the only ones working on registering and identifying women who survived war crimes, their work is voluntary.

Other women's NGOs that work with women victims of violence (mainly domestic violence) do not have specific programs and services to offer women survivors of CRSV. However, some women's NGOs that provide support and have developed programs for victims of domestic violence, regularly encounter survivors of CRSV as their clients. The fact is that women victims of CRSV often become domestic violence victims in the aftermath of war[11] and experience a 'continuum of violence'.[12] A woman who was sexually abused while she was a teenage prisoner during the war reported recently to local media: 'I spent 20 days in a detention camp, where I survived rape. The abuse during the marriage, both physical and psychological, lasted longer.'[13] The local women's organisation that supports female victims of domestic violence, reported that 90 per cent of women who seek help were once victims of CRSV.[14]

A few women's NGOs in RS – such as 'Budućnost' in Modriča, 'Izvor' in Prijedor and 'Forum žena' in Bratunac – have worked for years tirelessly and

11 The continuity of violence towards women is seen not just in relation to women victims of war but also in other post-dictatorial states, such as the post-apartheid regime in South Africa where violence against women has continued and even worsened since the end of apartheid. See Romi Sigsworth and Nahla Valji, 'Continuities of Violence Against Women in South Africa: The Limitations of Transitional Justice' in Susanne Buckley-Zistel and Ruth Stanley (eds), *Gender in Transitional Justice* (Palgrave Macmillan, 2011) 115.

12 Cynthia Cockburn, 'The Continuum of Violence: A Gender Perspective on War and Peace' in Wenona Giles and Jennifer Hyndman (eds), *Sites of Violence: Gender and Conflict Zones* (University of California Press, 2004) 24; Lia Kent, 'After the Truth Commission: Gender and Citizenship in Timor Leste' (2016) 17(1) *Human Rights Review* 51.

13 Albina Sorguc, 'Domestic Violence Revives Bosnian Women Nightmares', *BIRN*, 19 February 2015, www.balkaninsight.com/en/article/domestic-violence-revives-ex-prisoners-wartime-nightmares/1440/3.

14 Ibid.

without any financial support to provide ad hoc support to these women. Stanojka Tešić from 'Forum žena', Bratunac stated:

> We do not work specifically with women victims of wartime rape . . . we occasionally meet and talk to them . . . the biggest thing would be if the government of Republika Srpska would show an interest in these women . . . the issue of sexual violence in war and its victims is a political issue and many shy away from this topic . . . these women (victims) cannot get a public platform. They are marginalised and discriminated against on many levels . . . these women need a permanent and long-term, systematic solution to their concerns which only the government can deliver.[15]

Gordana Vidović from 'Budućnost', Modriča reports:

> We don't have a special program to help women victims of war from 1996, but we have free legal, welfare and psychological support. Our clients are mainly victims of domestic violence, but many of them have also been victims of wartime violence. Many suffer from domestic violence as a consequence of sexual abuse in war and some have divorced after speaking up about it publically, due to our conservative tradition. These women are dying. One woman who publically spoke about her experience of rape died 2–3 years ago . . . There is another woman who does not want to talk about it anymore because when she did, her story was misused. These women are constantly faced with barriers and difficulties from their own people and government. They need to have a special program of rehabilitation and re-socialisation.[16]

According to Edin Ramulić, an activist with the Association of Prijedor 'Izvor', women victims are facing mainly basic existential problems:

> Some of them are literally starving because they don't have any permanent income. Because of their poor health and due to their age, women have no chance of finding work. Furthermore, in this part of the state [RS] there isn't any specialized centre where they can get professional psychological support. The rapists are in the most cases free and victims often meet them on the streets. Women in the Republika Srpska are exposed to discrimination compared with women who are from the Federation because they can't exercise any of their rights and don't have equal access to medical help. All of them [from RS and FBiH] are equally stigmatised though, and the stigmatisation goes to the level of blaming women for being victims of rape. *In the local society rape is acceptable if it's done against women of another ethnicity and people do not condemn rape done by members of their own ethnic group towards women from the other group* [emphasis added].[17]

15 Skype conversation with Stanojka Tešić, 23 December 2013.
16 Skype conversation with Gordana Vidović, 23 December 2013.
17 Email from Ramulić to author, 3 December 2013.

Ramulić's observation about denying 'other' women's experiences of the same crime is important and goes to the essence of the political situation in a country in which ethnic division, even among women survivors, is entrenched. Minimising the suffering of 'others' and maximising the suffering of its 'own' ethnic group is something that is common to all ethnic groups and genders in BiH.

According to interviewees, while some women do want to seek justice, the majority of women who I met were not interested in pursuing any form of legal justice. In June 2016, I met with a group of seven women survivors now residing in a small town in eastern Bosnia. I spent two hours talking with them about their past and the current situation they live in. The youngest woman in the group was only 11 when the war started and spent four years in captivity with her mother. The women in the group claimed that she was the youngest girl child survivor of CRSV who has seen no justice. She is now 36 with two young children. She married when she was 16 and never finished primary school, but taught herself to read and write.

Although she has been married to, according to her, 'a good man' and they have 'a good marriage' she said she 'will never tell him what she survived because he could never understand it'.[18] The group of women interviewees I spent that day with all have serious illnesses, such as cardiovascular diseases, high blood pressure and/or high sugar levels. They are dealing with cumulative stress and suffer to varying degrees from post-traumatic stress disorder. After two hours of chatting over a coffee that was organised by a local women's NGO, they told me how they would love to have more opportunity just to meet 'over coffee' and talk to each other; to get out from their houses and socialise.[19]

All of these women have been internally displaced persons (IDPs). Some had been living for years in public IDP spaces, such as schools and sports halls. One of them, Mira, still lives in a space that is not meant to house people; she lives in the attic of a residential building. When it rains, the roof leaks and things get wet. This was intended as temporary accommodation, but she has been living there for the past 10 years, since the local government is unwilling to provide her with decent accommodation. During the summer it is hot and during the winter, cold.

Mira told me that she never returned to her property and that she decided to sell her land to some Saudi Arabian businessmen who are buying land cheaply from the Serbs who lived in that area.[20] Only three women out of

18 Conversation with A. M., Bratunac, 14 June 2016.

19 On the importance of the ritual of coffee drinking in Bosnia, see, e.g., Tone Bringa, *Being Muslim the Bosnian Way: Identity and Community in a Central Bosnian Village* (Princeton University Press, 1995); Tone Bringa, 'Reconciliation in Bosnia-Herzegovina' in Elin Skaar, Siri Gloppen and Astri Suhrke (eds), *Roads to Reconciliation* (Lexington Books, 2005) 187, 194; Elissa Helms, *Innocence and Victimhood: Gender, Nation, and Women's Activism in Postwar Bosnia-Herzegovina* (University of Wisconsin Press, 2013).

20 On buying a land in Sarajevo and FBiH by Gulf Arabs, see Matthew Brunwasser, 'Bosnia's Biggest Foreign Investment: Bonanza or Threat?', *BBC News Online*, 26 September 2016, www.bbc.com/news/business-37429682.

the seven that I talked to on that day obtained the status of civilian victim of war and receive a BAM110 (EUR55) monthly pension. They were all preoccupied with the struggles of surviving day-to-day life, and finding something to occupy themselves so they think less about the war and the difficulties of survival. Indeed, they do not want to think about it since, as the youngest woman in the group explained, from 'too much thinking nothing good can come'.[21] She was angry that her psychologist was constantly trying to prompt her to speak about her war ordeal: 'she does not want to do me good but wants me to feel terrible. I thought you go to a psychologist to relax not to make you more anxious'.[22] For all these women this was the first time they had received psychological support.

There is a need for systematic and ongoing support for women survivors – financial, medical and psychological – which must be provided by the government and, if possible, NGOs. But a few NGOs in RS, as I have shown, have not been open to international donor support in running the programs for survivors. In the following section, I briefly outline the work of two NGOs from RS that have attempted to gather women victims of CRSV and torture.

The Section for the Protection of Women Victims of Torture and Rape in BiH

The Section for the Protection of Women Victims of Torture and Rape in BiH (the Section) was founded in January 2013. Dr Olga Draško, who is a survivor of the notorious Dretelj camp, is the leader of the Section.[23] Dr Draško was the first to testify about the ill-famed Dretelj camp in which hundreds of Serb males and females were tortured and killed by Bosniak army members. During her detention, Dr Draško survived sexual abuse and torture,[24] and suffers lifelong health consequences from this maltreatment:

> I was imprisoned for three months in Dretelj camp near Čapljina where more than 80 women were rounded up and many more men. All the women survived physical abuse and rape. I survived the most horrific torture which damaged my health and life forever.[25]

21 Conversation with A. M., 14 June 2016.

22 Ibid.

23 From May to August 1992 there were 211 Serbs detained in Dretelj camp (129 males and 82 women): Goran Maunaga, 'Edib Buljubašić: Repak mi dao 1.000 maraka za ubistvo' [Trans: 'Edib Buljubašić: Repak Gave Me 1,000 Marks for Murder'], *Vijesti Dana*, 14 September 2008, www.glassrpske.com/novosti/vijesti_dana/Edib-Buljubasic Repak mi dao 1000 maraka za ubistvo/lat/11352.html.

24 On 14 April 2011, the Supreme Court of Norway sentenced Mirsad Repak to eight years in prison for illegal deprivation of liberty and detention of civilians. However, he was not prosecuted for rape: TRIAL, *Mirsad Repak*, TRIAL (2016), https://trialinternational.org/latest-post/mirsad-repak/.

25 Telephone interview with Dr Draško, 23 May 2015.

Dr Draško was also a key witness in a case before the Norwegian and Swedish courts against Mirsad Repak and others,[26] and she told me how difficult it was for her to testify since she had no legal support either from the government or NGOs in the preparation of her case, and she did not know who to ask for help.[27] According to Dr Draško, despite these challenges, women survivors want to be listened to, to have their experiences acknowledged and the perpetrators of the crimes committed against them punished. It is, however, important for women to withhold their identities as they do not want their families to find out what has happened to them: 'in our society, rape is still considered to be shameful for the family'.[28] Speaking up about their experiences is, however, 'already 80 per cent of their healing',[29] for fear of the stigma attached to CRSV, women will often come forward after their husbands die. Gordana Tadić from the BiH Prosecutor's Office recently reported:

> Some women need time to speak up. In one case, an older woman testified that she was raped in a camp. Although she had given a testimony earlier in the same case on another matter she did not confess that fact then – she was waiting for her husband to die.[30]

Jasminka Džumhur, Ombudsman for BiH, cautions that it is important to ask ourselves which women would benefit from speaking up

> [i]f they have not been recognised by law or not been able to exercise the rights stipulated by law. The second question is to whom they have to talk about their experiences if BiH institutions did not adopt adequate measures to regulate issue of all victims, including victims of sexual abuse. Third, if they apply for the status of civilian victims of war and in some cantons the right to seek status has been denied to them, then we have to question why they would speak about it because that means another layer of trauma for them.[31]

26 She has recently lost her claim for reparation from the Federation of BiH for the mental and physical suffering she survived. The original judgement from Okružni Sud Trebinje, on file with the author, 23 September 2013. Mirsad Repak was sentenced to eight years of prison in Norway and Ahmet Mekitan to five years in Sweden; Banja Luka, 'Forminarana sekcija žena žrtava torture i silovanja' [Trans: 'Formed Section of Women Victims of Torture and Rape'], *SRNA*, 16 January 2013, www.srna.rs/novosti1/70486/formirana-sekcija-zena-zrtava-torture-i-silovanja-.htm.

27 This lack of legal support is something I have heard from other women too. One female interviewee told me that one of her former fellow camp inmates who now lives in Germany was ready to come to testify before the BiH courts, but she could not afford to pay the travel and other expenses. She has not received any financial support from the RS institutions and finally gave up the idea of testifying.

28 Telephone interview with Dr Draško, 23 May 2015.

29 Marijana Senjak, 'Kontekst: Žene žrtve silovanja u ratu' [Trans: 'Context: Women Victims of Rape in War'], *Al Jazeera Balkans TV*, 25 June 2012, http://balkans.aljazeera.net/video/kontekst-zene-zrtve-silovanja-u-ratu?page=1.

30 Aida Đugum, 'Ukorijenjena stigmatizacija žrtava ratnog silovanja' [Trans: 'Stigmatization of Victims of Rape'], *Radio Slobodna Evropa*, 4 April 2014, www.slobodnaevropa.org/content/ukorijenjena-stigmatizacija-zrtava-ratnog-silovanja/25321741.html.

31 Al Jazeera Balkans TV, 'Jasminka Džumhur o silovanjima u ratu u BiH', 29 March 2012, www.youtube.com/watch?v=TieGZx7Jp0g.

Still, according to Dr Draško, women will speak but:

> You have to find the right way to approach them and explain to them that investigations will start against their perpetrators; that personal details won't be publicised; that they will have the status of protected witness; that they will see their perpetrators punished. So we need to go for physical security and to process crimes and not allow the situation where a woman sees her torturer on the street and cannot do anything about it.[32]

Some women, such as Anđelka Bratić, a survivor of CRSV, called women victims to speak up:

> All these years there has been a silence about Serb women victims of rape and it is a well-known fact that many of them were raped in Tarčin, Bradina, Osenik, and Doljani . . . I call on all Serb women not to be silenced because silence is complicit in crime.[33]

Because women feel helpless and do not trust the justice system, they tend not to speak up about their experiences of CRSV. One of my interviewees, a psychologist who works with victim witness protection units in one of the courts in RS, told me that women who come (often from abroad) to testify, do so for other matters such as robbery or property damage done during the war. While they do not press charges for CRSV, women would often confess in private conversations with the counsellors, such as her, that they were sexually abused. However, they do not want to press charges for that crime, either for fear of being stigmatised or they simply lack the will to go through a lengthy and unpleasant court procedure. According to my interlocutor, women do not want any risk of stigma and ostracism. As Megan Mackenzie argues, women often suffer a 'double-assault' in states affected by war. They are not only victims of CRSV during war, but are stigmatised in their communities in the aftermath of war.[34] According to Mackenzie, women would often say: 'I started a new life. No one among my family or friends knows about this. I don't want to risk being ostracised. Why would I do so? I will get nothing in return except misery.'[35] These women do not trust the local justice system and do not believe anything good would come out from their testimonies.

32 Telephone interview with Dr Draško, 24 May 2014.

33 Anđelka Bratić, from the village Dub near Hadžići, was first beaten and then gang raped on 8 September 1992 by eight members of the Bosnian army in her own house. The ordeal happened before her 5-year-old daughter Vedrana and 2-year-old son Goran. Not long after this event, members of the Croatian paramilitary army *Crnokošuljaši*, entered their home. One of the soldiers attempted to rape her and another beat her son terribly with his rubber military boots. Her 2-year-old son Goran has remained disabled since witnessing this attack. Perica Vasović, 'Molila sam da me zakolju' [Trans: 'I Beg Them to Kill Me'], *Večernje Novosti*, 27 March 2006, www.novosti.rs/vesti/naslovna/reportaze/aktuelno.293.html:181409-Molila-sam-Boga-da-me-zakolju.

34 Megan Mackenzie, 'Securitizing Sex? Towards a Theory of the Utility of Wartime Sexual Violence' 12 (2010) *International Feminist Journal of Politics* 202–220.

35 Ibid.

Dr Draško argues that it is important that women organise themselves so they can seek justice together and that their experiences are not being used only for political purposes. She hopes that by establishing the Section, women survivors will, in future, receive some financial, legal and health assistance:

> These are all older women and they want to have some security. They need a monthly compensation and not to live from one short-term project to another. They need something more sustainable and long term. They are not capable any more to be in the work force and earn income but they have to because they have nothing to live from. A woman who was with me in a camp and who was 45 is now 65, and lives off her husband's pension (BAM300). She is ill and has to survive only on his tiny pension. She has nothing else.[36]

While many survivors preferred not to talk about their past in order to start a new life, others wanted to tell their stories and confront the public. They have expected that their courageous act of speaking up will lead to action: acknowledgement of the crimes they survived, investigations, prosecutions, material and symbolic reparations. However, even those few women who did speak up have not received even symbolic acknowledgement from the RS government for their public act of bravery. On the contrary, they exposed themselves to the risk of being stigmatised in the community and even losing their family members. They were not supported and encouraged, embraced by their community and family; rather their words have been met with a wall of silence. One woman who was among the first to speak up, after many years, about her personal experience of rape, decided not to talk ever again to the media or indeed anyone else about her experience. She told a long-term activist who has supported and known her for a great deal of time:

> [D]on't call me to ask me to speak up, don't ask me ever again about my experience any more . . . my husband has left me, I have stayed alone without a pension or any financial means to survive . . . and those women who stayed silent are still married, have a pension and some security. I have a grandson who is in his fifth grade of elementary school. Could you imagine if he found out what had happened to me? Please, don't make trouble in my family; don't ever ask me to speak up again.[37]

Another woman also said she will never speak to the media again because 'all they want to know are the details of sexual abuse', while they 'have no interest in women as such'.[38] She told me that the media, according to her opinion, just want to publish the text so they get a sensational story that will sell their paper.

36 Telephone interview with Dr Draško, 24 May 2014.

37 Interview with G. M., Banjaluka, 14 June 2015.

38 Interview with S. A., Banjaluka, 10 June 2015.

The women survivors of CRSV need support and social acceptance, a space where there is a sufficient sense of safety to be able to move out of the dark, to speak up.

Dr Draško reported that there are also many women in the Section who never registered and never gave their testimonies because 'no one has ever asked them to do so'.[39] She mentioned the town of Trnovo as one of these places where many women, despite surviving some form of CRSV, have not had their stories documented and made available to the public. All women victims who registered with the Section need medical assistance and psychological support. The large majority of them have never had any psychological support so far. 'No one cares about these women: not the government, not society, no one,' an activist from Bratunac told me.[40]

Dr Draško emphasised that most of the women are unemployed, without adequate health care and the necessary funds for living. Not treating trauma and ignoring women's experiences has brought devastation to their psychological and physical health. According to Dr Draško, women who register with the Section are mainly from Herzegovina, where camps, such as Čelebići, Heliodrom and Dretelj run by the Croat and Bosniak armies, were established and Serb women raped. She has also received calls from women who reside in Sarajevo and its surroundings. Women can call Dr Draško to register and once she receives a call, Dr Draško asks them whether they want to give a statement about the crime they survived so police can start an investigation. The main objective is to gather the evidence and encourage women to report the crimes. The Section has no funds, programs or office – the work is voluntary and the collection of data and registrations is done via telephone conversations between Dr Draško and women survivors. Despite all these efforts to archive women's experiences, the RS government has not yet supported the work of the Section in any way.

The Association of Women Victims of War from the Republic of Srpska

> I don't talk about Serb women because I want to downplay the experiences of other women. But when someone says 'women suffered here' [in BiH] everyone thinks about Bosniak women only. No one thinks about us . . . as if Serbs do not have women too. Everyone knows about Bosniak women all the way up to the UN. They are an *authentic* symbol of suffering in BiH. Until now, only one story has been told. Serb women have always faced 'a wall' of silence even when we wanted to talk.[41]

The recently established Association of Women Victims of War from the Republic of Srpska (the Association) is the first association established in RS with an aim

39 Telephone interview with Dr Draško, 24 May 2014.

40 Conversation with D. P., 18 June 2016.

41 Email from Božica Živkovic Rajilić, the Director of the Association, 6 February 2014 (emphasis added).

of gathering and registering primarily Serb women victims of CRSV and torture. The director of the Association, Božica Živković Rajilić, a victim of torture herself, works on collecting information and data about women who survived some form of torture during the war. The Association was established in Brod in December 2012. At the time of its establishment, the Association had around 40 members and today, according to Živković Rajilić, it has more than 300 women registered. One of its aims is to establish an intensive media campaign to inform domestic and international audiences about the suffering of Serb women:

> We want to draw attention to the fact that Serb women were wartime victims of torture and rape too, and to see what we can do to help them to get reparation for the injustice that has been done to them.[42]

To support this advocacy project, in October 2016 the Association published the book called *Our Testimony: Women Victims of War from Republika Srpska 1992–1995*, that gathered stories of 15 women survivors of CRSV and torture from RS.[43] The stories are testimonies of women who were detained in the Bosniak and Croatian detention centres during the war. These are stories from Serb, but also from Croat and Bosniak women, who were at the time married to Serbs and as such, were raped and tortured as a part of a retaliation strategy. Since its inception, Živković Rajilić has been against any hierarchy of crimes, according to which CRSV should be treated differently from other forms of bodily harm:

> Wartime rape is only a fraction of other types of torture we experienced . . . it is to serve a particular media campaign when you use the word 'rape' all the time. Why do you want to separate and highlight this type of torture in comparison to beatings or long-term psychological abuse? That's what Bosniak NGOs and foreign mercenaries across Bosnia do with bad intentions, because such stories attract attention. Foreign actors, such as Angelina Jolie, ask that only female survivors of sexual abuse be protected. That is an effrontery . . . that is humiliating for women and treats them as sexual objects. There is no one torture that is worse than any other. Each of us carries her own pain and deals with it however they can and know best. These things are not to be compared.[44]

42 Ibid.

43 *Naša ispovjest – žene žrtve rata iz Republike Srpske 1992–1995* [Trans: *Our Confessions – Women Victims of War in Republika Srpska 1992–1995*], Udruženje žena žrtava rata Republike Srpske, Republički Centra za istraživanje rata, ratnih zločina i traženje nestalih lica Republike Srpske i Predstavništva Republike Serbije u Srbiji, 2016.

44 Božica Živković Rajilić, '*Promocija monografije Naša ispovijest – žene žrtve rata iz Republike Srpske 1992–1995* [*Promotion of Monograph Our Story – Women Victims of War from Republika Srpska 1992–1995*], Media center Belgrade, 12 September 2016, www.webtv.rs/play/86914/promocija-monografije-nasa-ispovijest---zene-zrtve-rata-iz-republike-srpske-1992---1995.

Nicola Henry argues that the unprecedented attention to wartime sexual violence within international criminal law has had wide-ranging and unintended consequences. Živković Rajilić has been bringing these unintended consequences to the fore by giving a practical example of such unintended consequences on the lives of women survivors on the ground. International criminal law is one that decides which harms are 'extraordinary' and who can speak about them[45] and such hierarchisation of crime and victims raised internal competitions among those women who survived CRSV and those who did not. As Engle argues, the dominant narrative of international criminal law is of women solely as victims of rape.[46] According to Henry, contemporary feminist scholarship on rape has identified a number of interconnected problems associated with fixating on sexual violence as the universal source of women's oppression.[47]

Postmodern feminists, such as Carol Smart and Sharon Marcus, have argued that Western feminists have often fixated on rape as the universal experience of women and have failed to acknowledge or capture the diversity of victims or the intersections of marginalisation. Such focus in turn isolated women's sexuality as the basis of oppression that serves to reinforce the sexed body as an inevitable target of sexual violence and also reduced women to passive, vulnerable objects of law, whose identities have become defined rather than challenged by this subjection.[48] Henry notes that a fixation on whether or not rape is the 'worst' of crimes is at best a distraction to the real issues at stake; that is, whether or not international criminal law provides requisite recognition of the gendered harms of sexual violence in wartime.[49] At worst, and as we see in case of Serb women experiences with CRSV, this fixation contributed to problematic ethnic and crime hierarchies of victimisation that have served to marginalise certain categories of victims further in their pursuit of justice after mass atrocity.

The book published by the Association has been financially supported by the governments of RS and Serbia and used to raise awareness about the Serb people's victimhood rather than about specific crimes and the women who survived it. At their recent book launch in Belgrade, the director of the Representative body of RS in Serbia reportedly stated:

> For us [Serbs] it is very important to create and sustain the culture of memory of victims, because the world has created a wrong picture, and that is: that only one [group of] people in BiH suffered, and that Serbs were people

45 Doris Buss 'Rethinking Rape as a Weapon of War' (2009) 17 *Feminist Legal Studies* 145–163.

46 Karen Engle, 'Feminism and its (Dis)contents: Criminalizing Wartime Rape in Bosnia and Herzegovina' (2005) 99(4) *American Journal of International Law* 778–816.

47 Nicola Henry, 'The Fixation on Wartime Rape: Feminist Critique and International Criminal Law' (2014) 23(1) *Social and Legal Studies* 93–111.

48 Sharon Marcus, 'Fighting Bodies, Fighting Words: A Theory and Politics of Rape Prevention' in J. Butler and J. Scott (eds), *Feminists Theorize the Political* (Routledge, 1992) 385–403; Carol Smart, *Feminism and the Power of the Law* (Routledge, 1989).

49 Henry, above n 47.

> who tortured and committed aggression against other people. It is extremely important to have such books, which aim to show the real truth about what had happened in the war in Bosnia.[50]

According to Živković Rajilić, the majority of women who approached the Association live in the region of Posavina, Brod and its surroundings, in Prijedor, East Sarajevo, Trnovo, Bratunac, Han Pijesak, Gornji Vakuf-Uskoplje, Brčko and Tuzla and its surroundings. Women who have registered with the Association are primarily between 60 and 80 years old, although there are some younger women too. The Association also strives to support and advise women as how they should initiate criminal proceedings. According to Živkovic Rajilić: 'The Association cannot provide any rights, but only support women in the process of achieving their rights.'[51] The women's victims' priority is to receive the status of civilian victim of war and subsequent reparation. Thus, aside from registering women victims, the Association encourages women to come forward and testify. According to Živković Rajilić:

> The Prosecutor in BiH is going through the lists of dozens of former members of the Bosniak and Croatian army who committed war crimes of torture and rape against Serb women. The Association, in cooperation with the Center for War Crimes, actively gathers data and relevant information and testimonies of victims and witnesses, and sends them to the RS police and the BiH prosecutor's office. The problem is that some women victims and witnesses face threats for speaking up.[52]

The Association also gathers women who are Bosniaks and Croats, but were raped in Croatian and Bosniak camps as a punishment for having Serb husbands or partners. Several women survivors who were detained in different rape camps have confirmed that women from 'other' ethnic groups were detained and raped with them by their 'own' men. Rape of one's 'own' women occurs when women are seen to be political traitors[53] (by refusing to go along with prevailing ethnic chauvinism, for example), social traitors (in romantic relationships with members of the 'other'), or are victims of the spill over violence that

50 Director of Representation of Republike Srpske in Belgrade, Serbia Mlađen Cicović, *Naša ispovjest – žene žrtve rata iz Republike Srpske 1992-1995* [Trans: *Our Confessions – Women Victims of War of the Republic of Serbia 1992–1995*], 8 July 2016, http://predstavnistvorsbg.rs/predstavnistvo_rs/index.php/sr/aktuelnosti/prethodni-dogadjaji/1838-nasa-ispovijest-zene-zrtve-rata-iz-republike-srpske-1992-1995.html.

51 Email from Božica Živkovic Rajilić, 6 February 2014.

52 Blic, 'Provera podataka o silovanim srpkinjama' [Trans: 'Proof of Data on Raped Serbs'], *Blic*, 13 August 2014, 2.

53 Vesna Kesić, 'From Reverence to Rape: An Anthropology of Ethnic and Genderized Violence', in Marguerite R. Waller and Jennifer Rycenga (eds), *Frontline Feminisms: Women, War, and Resistance* (Routledge, 2001) 25, 32.

occurs when a society becomes highly militarised.[54] Zarkov notes that male power defines the women of the 'other' through rape, thus 'defining the female body as the ethnic female body'.[55]

Huzba Nukić, a 69-year-old Bosniak woman and member of the Section, was one such woman. She was detained together with Serb women and a few Croatian women, and repeatedly raped by the Croatian military forces in Bosanski Brod:

> I was raped first at the football stadium in Bosanski Brod before the group of women by a Croatian soldier, named Lepar. Later, they took us in groups to Croatian soldiers who would rape us during the night . . . I remember a woman Kaća, a Croatian woman married to a Serb, who had two brothers in the Croatian army . . . One night, nine Croatian soldiers raped Kaća in the warehouse of the Belgrade department store in Bosanski Brod. She could not stand on her feet for three days.[56]

The Croatian military forces in Odžak detained another survivor, also a member of the Section – Nusreta Milošević, a Bosniak woman married to a Serb. She was 33 years old at that time, held for three months and repeatedly raped. She reported, 'I was *chetnik* [member of the paramilitary Serb unit] for them because I was with a Serb man.'[57] As a consequence, she had a stroke. Today she is disabled and lives in poverty. She lives in RS, has not received the status of civilian victim of war and does not receive any financial assistance. In 2014 she was a witness in the first case to be prosecuted before the Court of BiH for the wartime rapes in Odžak and Posavina region. She reported on her experience of being a witness: 'It was terrible and humiliating. I, as a witness and victim, have no protection, and he was sentenced to ten years because he is a family man. I don't know if I could go through this again.'[58]

54 The links between wartime violence and domestic violence are also significant here. See, e.g., Liz Kelly, 'Wars Against Women: Sexual Violence, Sexual Politics and the Militarised State', in Susie Jacobs, Ruth Jacobson and Jennifer Marchbank (eds), *States of Conflict: Gender, Violence and Resistance* (Zed Books, 2000) 45; Vanessa Farr et al., *Gender Perspectives on Small Arms and Light Weapons: Regional and International Concerns* (Bonn International Center for Conversion, 2002), www.bicc.de/publications/publicationpage/publication/gender-perspectives-on-small-arms-and-light-weapons-regional-and-international-concerns-128/.

55 Dubravka Žarkov, 'Gender, Orientalism and the History of Ethnic Hatred in the Former Yugoslavia' in Helma Lutz, Ann Phoenix and Nira Yuval-Davis (eds), *Crossfires: Nationalism, Racism and Gender in Europe* (Pluto Press for the European Forum of Left Feminists, 1995) 105.

56 Dragan Čolić, 'Tukli su me i silovanli' [Trans: 'They Beat and Raped Me'] *Blic* (online), 24 May 2002, www.blic.rs/stara_arhiva/reportaze/27076/Tukli-su-me-i-silovali.

57 Boris Knežević, 'Stravični zločini nad Srbima: devojčica dozivala mamu dok su je silovali muslimanski vojnici' [Trans: 'Terrible Crimes Against Serbs: A Girl Called her Mother While She was Raped by Bosniak Soldiers'], *Večernje Novosti*, 15 July 2016,, www.blic.rs/vesti/republika-srpska/stravicni-zlocini-nad-srbima-devojcica-dozivala-mamu-dok-su-je-muslimanski-vojnici/sppgmzy.

58 Alexander Slavnić, 'Zaboravljene žrtve silovanja u BiH' [Trans: 'Forgotten Victims of Rape in Bosnia and Herzegovina'], *DW*, 7 March 2015, www.dw.com/bs/zaboravljene-%C5%BErtve-silovanja-u-bih/a-18560219.

Many women died without seeing justice. In December 2015 two Serb women victims, one from Sarajevo and the other from the Posavina region, committed suicide.[59] They were both members of the Association. Many women were accompanied by their children in detention camps. Commonly they witnessed rape and torture themselves. In 2014, just before she was supposed to go Sarajevo to give testimony as a witness, Lj. L. died. She had a heart attack after many years living in poverty and with poor health. Her sister – M. Đ. – told me that the deceased witness's son decided to testify instead. He was 15 years old at the time the incidents occurred and detained with his mother and brother. 'He recounts everything very well . . . knows the dates and times when they were taking her.'[60] M. Đ. was concerned about his mental health and whether he will be able to testify. She told him not to do so but he was determined. Children who witnessed rape have been of no concern to either the RS government or NGOs and they have had no psychological or any other support. Being neglected may not only increase the pain, but also inflate anger and bitterness and a sense of denigration.

The Association operates on a voluntary basis since they have neither properly developed projects, nor financial assistance for their activities. They have occasionally received small donations from the RS government, enough to cover some basic costs of the yearly Association meeting. Due to the obvious financial constraints that the Association has, I asked Živkovic Rajilić whether the Association has plans to develop cross-ethnic cooperation with women victims NGOs from FBiH:

> [W]e are totally different in our principles and programs. We respect each other, personally, but what they ask for Bosniak and Croat women, I ask for Serb women. They seek to condemn Serb crimes but don't want to condemn crimes of Bosniaks and Croats. I seek condemnation of Bosniak and Croat crimes, and don't believe that Serbs are perpetrators in the majority of cases. Then we disagree about other issues: who started the war, who cleansed the country from whom, who is a traitor, who wanted to destroy Yugoslavia . . . We cannot talk about these topics, let alone cooperate with each other.[61]

As discussed in Chapter 5, an open and meaningful cross-ethnic conversation about perspectives on wartime rape has so far been avoided. The Association does not want to receive any funds apart from the RS budget. They have been offered assistance from several international organisations, but Živković Rajilić refused them:

59 Email from Božica Živkovic Rajilić, 21 January 2016. On file with author.
60 Interview with M. Đ. (Banjaluka, 12 May 2016).
61 Email from Božica Živković Rajilić, 10 September 2014.

> I told them I don't want some sort of international assistance. I don't want funds that would force me to cooperate with Croatians and Bosniaks and build some joint state. For me, that would be an erasure of my suffering and as if RS does not exist. We want that our problems are resolved by the government of Republika Srpska. They cannot ask us to build a future with our war enemies.[62]

While such reluctance for cooperation was also reported to me by other Serb women victims, it is also possible that there is fear that by cooperating with NGOs from FBiH, the government of RS and other Serb associations of victims would close a door to them for good. They fear that they will be treated as 'traitors' for cooperating with 'enemies'.[63]

On 27 November 2013, Judge Theodor Meron, the former President of the International Criminal Tribunal for the Former Yugoslavia (ICTY), organised a conference for Bosnian NGOs to mark the twentieth anniversary of the Tribunal. Živković Rajilić and two male representatives of the former detention camp survivors' associations from RS were, according to her, the only Serb survivors present in the conference hall. Živković Rajilić told me although this was her first meeting with the NGOs from FBiH and the first visit to Sarajevo after the war, she summoned the courage to raise a hand and pose a question to Judge Meron and ask him why no one in the ICTY cares about Serb victims. According to her, she had hardly finished her question when a dozen Bosniak women victims, primarily, the Mothers of Srebrenica, jumped from their seats and verbally attacked her, by reportedly saying, 'You genocidal Serb, what do you want? You deserved what you got. Serbs are genocidal people who committed terrible things. Shame on you.'[64] Živković Rajilić told me that she felt shocked and shaken. Once these verbal abuses were translated to Judge Meron, he raised his hand to quieten the women and he gave the word to Živković Rajilić who told him:

> Mister, I am just an ordinary woman peasant, but if someone from the international community sent me to some state in Africa and made the protocol according to which I have a duty to pay respect only to victims in one location,[65]

62 Email from Božica Živković Rajilić, 11 September 2014.

63 The refusal to receive international funding for their projects fits with the overwhelming Bosnian Serb feelings of animosity towards international community. From very early on Bosnian Serbs believed that international community works against them and this view has been cemented over years following the end of the war. According to Christopher Bennett, the Serb Bosnian Presidency led by Radovan Karadžić had obstructed implementation of the peace accord and refused international reconstruction assistance. The first $1,7 billion, which was pledged in 1996, had gone almost entirely to the Federation of BiH, since none of the representatives of Republika Srpska had even attend the donor's conference. Christopher Bennett, *Bosnia's Paralysed Peace* (Hurst & Company, 2016), 110–111.

64 Email from Božica Živković Rajilić, 14 March 2014.

65 The conference was organised in in the same year and only a few months after one of the largest primary mass gravesites in the region was discovered, and that is Tomašica near Prijedor. The

> I would reject that. Why? Even I, a woman from a village knows that for war at least two opposite sides are needed, and since you are the president of the Hague Tribunal, you know that here we had three regular armies and at least 30 paramilitary units. How is it then possible that victims are just on one side, and there are no Serb and Croat victims? Why did you not also visit the Serb graveyards? Do you think that the other sides do not have victims? Do you think there are no Bosniak war crime perpetrators? Why do you respect only one group of victims and not comment upon others?[66]

According to Živković Rajilić, Judge Meron tried to explain how impartial he was and he apologised by saying that he did not think about 'all of this' before. In this public performance of victimhood, Živković Rajilić wanted to gain recognition and empathy for non-recognised victims of BiH war; to appropriate victim narratives, evoke empathy and garner international support. However, as Sissel Rosland argues, the construction of victimhood 'involves [a] mechanism of inclusion and exclusion, creating "we" – "them" dichotomies, producing collectives of victimhood', which in many cases serve as a platform from which political agency could be voiced.[67] Živković Rajilić, as a Serb woman survivor, lacks such agency and the moral integrity of a victim who can produce 'political truths'.[68] Some victims are seen as more legitimate than others and only certain individuals are unambiguously recognised as victims in BiH. Those victims define themselves and/or are defined by others as (ideal) victims regardless of whether or not the law grants them this status.[69] According to Kieran McEvoy and Kirsten McConnachie, it is common that 'those who consider themselves or are considered by others to be "innocent" victims dispute the "deservingness" of other "bad" or "impure" victims to recognition'.[70]

As the Special Rapporteur on the promotion of truth, justice, reparation and guarantees of non-recurrence argues, asymmetrical treatment and perception of the victims has politicised the debate and has tended to assimilate victims' complaints with political and party affiliations, to the detriment of any concern for

discovery sent shock waves across the region and the world. According to expert reports, up to 1,000 Bosniak and Croat victims were killed and dumped into the mass grave by Bosnian Serb forces. BBC News, 'Huge Bosnian Mass Grave Excavated at Tomašica', *BBC News*, 1 November 2013, www.bbc.com/news/world-europe-24778713; more on mass gravesites including Tomašica, see also, Howard Ball, *Working in the Killing Fields: Forensic Science in Bosnia* (University of Nebraska, 2015).

66 Email from Božica Živkovic Rajilić, 11 September 2014.

67 Sissel Rosland, 'Victimhood, Identity, and Agency in the Early Phase of the Troubles in Northern Ireland' (2009) 16(3) *Identities: Global Studies in Culture and Power* 295.

68 Ibid.

69 Vincent Druliolle, 'Recovering Historical Memory: A Struggle Against Silence and Forgetting? The Politics of Victimhood in Spain' (2015) 9(2) *International Journal of Transitional Justice* 323.

70 Kieran McEvoy and Kirsten McConnachie, 'Victims and Transitional Justice: Voice, Agency and Blame' (2013) 22(4) *Social & Legal Studies* 500.

their human rights.[71] Although within transitional justice literature there now exists a 'near unanimity among most scholars, as well as practitioners, that societies coming out of periods of violence must in some way examine, acknowledge, and account for violence committed by various groups in order to move forward',[72] there is still long way to go for this rhetoric to turn into practice. Pablo de Greiff argues that all transitional justice mechanisms 'seek to provide recognition to victims',[73] so the law, but also other mechanisms must grant *all* victims moral standing as individual human beings. Victims must receive acknowledgement that they have been harmed.

They need to be recognised as 'victims and right bearers'[74] and ultimately as citizens.[75] Still, to try to cast Serbs as also victims/survivors, and Bosniak/Croat as perpetrators, would mean deviating from the constructed narrative and risk of being labelled and attacked as a denier. Such an embedded victim/perpetrator binary is detrimental to post-conflict transitional justice project. It is necessary to shift away from an 'ethnic victim' discourse and unlock the binary of 'doer and done to' in order to transcend this split and bring all survivors together to pursue justice and reparation. Feminist scholars and activists and the law have a role to play in ensuring that *all* women are included in transitional justice processes.

Conclusion

There is a need for systematic and ongoing support of women survivors of CRSV in BiH, but in particular in RS. The two associations I discussed in this chapter – the Association of Women Victims of War from the Republic of Srpska and the Section for the Protection of Women Victims of Torture and Rape – have access to women survivors and have gained their trust. It is important for the RS governmental institutions to cooperate with these and other NGOs that have data that can be of importance, while developing strategies

71 United Nations General Assembly, *Report of the Special Rapporteur on the Promotion of Truth, Justice, Reparation and Guarantees of Non-Recurrence, Pablo de Greiff*, 27th sess., Human Rights Session A/HRC/27/56/Add.1 (22 July 2014), para. 9.

72 Tristan Anne Borer, 'Truth Telling as a Peacebuilding Activity: A Theoretical Overview' in Tristan Anne Borer (ed.), *Telling the Truths: Truth Telling and Peace Building in Post-Conflict Societies* (University of Notre Dame Press, 2006), 4.

73 Pablo de Greiff, 'Normative Conceptions of Transitional Justice' (2010) 50(3) *Politorbis* 17, 22.

74 Ibid.

75 Victims also enjoy the right to be recognised as victims under international human rights law. For example, *International Covenant on Civil and Political Rights*, open for signature 16 December 1966, General Assembly Resolution 220A (XXI) (entered into force 23 March 1976) in its 2(1) article promulgates that each state party: 'undertakes to respect and to ensure to all individuals within its territory and subject to its jurisdiction the rights recognized in the present Covenant, without distinction of any kind, such as race, colour, sex, language, religion, political or other opinion, national or social origin, property, birth or other status'. See also article 2(2) of the *International Covenant on Economic, Social and Cultural Rights*, opened for signature 16 December 1966, 993 UNTS 3 (entered into force 3 January 1976).

and mechanisms for assistance to women. An overall ignorance and lack of recognition of women survivors' basic human rights and freedoms has resulted in discriminatory treatment of women survivors geographically, according to the region in which they live. BiH, unfortunately, remains 'Ethnopolis',[76] where ethno-nationalist identities count more than being a human; being a victim.

Almost 20 years after the war, one of the biggest obstacles to reconciliation and long-lasting peace in BiH is the ignorance of the experiences of thousands of women victims of CRSV and the discriminatory status these women have in respect to exercising their rights to material and symbolic reparation. Serb women survivors still struggle to be recognised as legitimate victims and political actors. Their struggle has remained marginalised politically, academically and socially. They simply have not yet been acknowledged as deserving to be recognised as genuine, 'ideal' victims. As discussed in this chapter, anti-victim discourse against Serb victims is local and global and reinforced by scholars, but also feminist activists and victims who are affiliated with other ethnic groups and who consider themselves as the only victims of CRSV. Such anti-victim discourse that disqualifies some victims from victimhood needs to be integrated into the theoretical framework and discussion.[77]

The Special Rapporteur on the promotion of truth, justice, reparation and guarantees of non-recurrence insists on the importance of initiatives by the state and by civil society that cover the claims of *all* human rights and humanitarian law victims, regardless of their political affiliation, or that of the perpetrators.[78] Although knowledge about the suffering of Serb women exists and cannot be denied, there is a need 'to move from knowledge to acknowledgment . . . Knowledge is just knowing the facts . . . but it's abstract . . . [A]cknowledgment means it enters into your emotional world, your world of responsibility.'[79] The Serb women are still struggling to gain that recognition and validation of their harm not only in a legal but communal sense too.

While Serb women were silenced by others, they also in some ways contributed to their own silencing and invisibility. As I discussed in this chapter, international organisations have offered some assistance to women's NGOs to work with women survivors in RS territory, but the funds for developing specific programs were rejected; either due to fear of retribution by the RS government, or resentment towards women's NGOs based in FBiH. So, while it is true that Serb women did not receive foreign attention, the women's NGOs in RS also bear responsibility, to some extent, for a lack of interest in reaching for the funding that may have been available to them.

76 Asim Mujkić, *Mi Građani Etnopolisa* [Trans: *We, the Citizens of Ethnopolis*] (Šahinpašić, 2007).

77 See Alyson M. Cole, *The Cult of True Victimhood: From the War on Welfare to the War on Terror* (Stanford University Press, 2007).

78 United Nations General Assembly, n 71, para. 9.

79 Merryl Lawry-White, 'The Reparative Effect of Truth Seeking in Transitional Justice' (2015) 64(1) *International and Comparative Law Quarterly* 151

7 The politics of writing/researching the 'silenced' women

'Is it possible, do you think, to write a book such as yours and not produce a nationalistic text?'[1]

Reflexivity in feminist writing

A key tenet of standpoint feminism is that the self-reflective researcher acknowledges their own position and experiences within society, which frame a particular perspective on the chosen topic.[2] It requires the researcher to be open about their social standing and background, both in order to be aware of the impact of their own perspective on their research, and to systematically and consciously view data from different angles.[3] Reflexivity in qualitative research has a long history, as a means of 'examining how the researcher and intersubjective elements impinge on, and even transform, research'.[4]

Standpoint feminism requests reflective research in order to enhance the validity of the research. It also takes an approach that gives particular weight to women's perspectives and experiences as being more insightful, as compared to men's, which are seen to be distorted by their interests in maintaining their position of power.[5] Following the approach of standpoint feminism, it is important to identify myself and the particular context that I come from. My own work has grown out of a commitment to feminist politics and recognition of the value and significance of transitional justice as a discipline. My interest is in women's histories, which far too often have stayed untold and undocumented. I was born in the Socialist Federative Republic of Yugoslavia (the former Yugoslavia) in the 1970s in Banjaluka, the second biggest city in Bosnia and Herzegovina (BiH).

1 A long-term feminist activist from Serbia asked me this question via email, 12 January 2017. On file with author.

2 Alessandra Tanesini, *An Introduction to Feminist Epistemologies* (Blackwell, 1999) 139.

3 Mats Alvesson, *Postmodernism and Social Research* (Open University Press, 2002) 171.

4 Linda Finlay, 'Negotiating the Swamp: The Opportunity and Challenge of Reflexivity in Research Practice' (2002) 2(2) *Qualitative Research* 209, 210.

5 Tanesini, above n 2, 139.

My parents identify themselves as Orthodox Serbs and they were members of the Communist Party before the 1990s. My brother participated in the war after being drafted in 1992 into the Bosnian Serb Army. I was to be drafted into the Bosnian Serb civilian protection unit and received a uniform, after which my parents decided that I should leave the country as soon as possible.[6] During the war, I was a refugee. Afterwards, I became a feminist activist and later an academic.

This background has placed me in a particular position while undertaking this research, presenting opportunities and obstacles. As a woman who was born in the former Yugoslavia, I am familiar with the region, traditions and cultures of my former country. I speak what used to be called Serbo-Croatian, now divided into Serbian, Croatian and Bosnian,[7] and have a wide social network of friends, feminist activists and former colleagues – many of whom are active in the non-governmental sector established by women in their efforts to foster peace and help women to recover from conflict-related sexual, and other types of, violence. This helped me to get access to and meet women survivors, as well as governmental and non-governmental representatives, all of whom were my interviewees.

My background and these connections also helped in building an atmosphere of trust, familiarity and friendliness with my interviewees. However, the familiarity and other advantages I have had because of my background did at times present challenges and even disadvantages. In post-war BiH, ethnic identity has become the most important individual and collective attribute: one that can open a door or close it for good. Ethnic nationalism has often reduced me to my ethnic identity. Being perceived first and foremost as a Serb, has often been prioritised over my gender identity. In contemporary BiH I am no longer simply a Bosnian woman. I am a Serb woman. With my previous research – which focused on Serbs as perpetrators of war violence – I was largely perceived among those who identify as Serbs as a 'traitor of my own ethnic group' and as 'anti-Serb'. By Bosniaks, my research has been seen as empathetic to the Bosniak cause. My study on Serb women as victims of war, however, turned these labels around and re-positioned

6 It is unknown how many Bosnian women were fighters in the 1990s conflict, and how many provided support as cooks, nurses or served in other support service roles. During the war, women who had trained as nurses were drafted into the army, and were sent to the front lines, where a number of them died. Other women were not compelled to join the army by draft, although they were readily accepted as volunteers, and were also publically invited to join the ranks. However, women were formally drafted into the civilian protection sector, and were expected to take care of their local communities and undertake humanitarian work. There is scant information on the experiences of any of these women. No official data was maintained, and only a few scattered references or stories about them can be found within local media or grassroots articles. See Lejla Hadžiahmić, 'Women-Combatants in Defense of Sarajevo: Agents or Victims' (2011) 6(19) WBSO; Sunita Dautbegović-Bošnjaković, 'Zaboravljena Dimenzija Ratu u BiH – Vojnikinje' in Damir Arsenijević and Tobias Flessenkamper, *Kojeg Je Roda Sigurnost?* (Sarajevski Otvoreni Centar, Sarajevo 2013).

7 For more about the splitting of the Serbo-Croatian language into Croatian, Serbian and Bosnian see e.g. Tomasz Kamusella, *The Politics of Language and Nationalism in Modern Central Europe* (Palgrave Macmillan, 2009); Nick Miller, *The Nonconformists: Culture, Politics, and Nationalism in a Serbian Intellectual Circle, 1994–1991* (Central European University Press, 2007) 26.

my status within different ethnic communities: within Serb communities it propelled me from a 'traitor' and 'anti-Serb', to 'the Serb' who has 'finally become openly compassionate to the Serb people's suffering'; within Bosniak and Croat communities I became 'Serb nationalist'.

I, however, do not recognise myself in any of those qualifications. Rather, I see myself as a feminist whose work challenges homogenous views of Bosnian woman as victims of rape, highlighting a need to complicate the notions of 'victim' and 'perpetrator' beyond the dominant ethnic divides that have marked both regional and international politics and scholarship. There have been other feminist scholars, however, not many of them, who did that before me, such as Dubravka Zarkov, Cynthia Cockburn, Vesna Nikolic-Ristanovic and Rhonda Copelon, whose work I have referred to throughout this book. My work builds on this existing scholarship, which adopted a critical angle that links the identity politics in feminist debates around wars in the former Yugoslavia, to the ethnicisation of the armed conflict and its victims in feminist and popular discourse. With this book I went one step further, by exploring how ethnicisation has affected 'non-ideal' victims – Serb women – more than two decades after the war ended. Such a challenge remains a contentious political and academic issue, because various aspects of the victimisation of the Serb population have been disputed, as I have discussed throughout this book, as either exaggerated or wholly fabricated for propaganda purposes. As such, researching the rape of Serb women is not only a 'sensitive' research topic; it is a highly political one.

My engagement in research from a feminist perspective means not intentionally drawing boundaries between those doing the research and those being researched.[8] In feminist research, women are considered to be experts regarding their own lives, who communicate and reveal the narratives about the events that have taken place in their lives, and their feelings about and interpretation of those events.[9] As someone born in BiH – as an 'insider' – I have a strong understanding of the dynamics and the interplay of social relationships that inform the situations in my home country. As someone who has lived outside the country for more than a decade now – thus as a relative 'outsider' – I have been critically and extensively engaged with the scholarly literature concerned with war crimes, ethnicity and gender in the Balkan region.

Being in this ambiguous position calls for self-reflection on experiences and conditions that frame, explicitly or obliquely, my particular perspective on the chosen topic,[10] in order to be aware of the impact of my perspective on the research, and in order to systematically and consciously view the data from different angles.[11]

8 See Betty-Ann Lloyd, Frances Ennis and Tannis Atkinson, *The Power of Woman-Positive Literacy Work: Program Based Action Research* (Fernwood, 1994).

9 See Karen A. Foss and Sonja K. Foss, 'Personal Experience as Evidence in Feminist Scholarship' (1994) 58 *Western Journal of Communication* 39.

10 Tanesini, above n 2, 139.

11 Alvesson, above n 3, 171.

Researching the invisible 'Other'

It is perhaps one of the greatest powers of feminism that it makes women's experiences and lives intelligible.[12] Feminist research is concerned with individual experiences of women, particularly those of marginalised groups. Since women have, for the most part, remained theoretically and philosophically 'mute', feminist epistemology became 'a vehicle through which women can come to find their own voices'.[13] Still, the voices of many women remain muted. The Gayatri Chakravorty Spivak seminal 1998 essay, 'Can the Subaltern Speak?', has had groundbreaking implications in diverse fields of scholarship; from politics and literature to feminist legal studies.[14] It transformed the analysis of colonialism and enabled minority discourses by 'clearing a theoretical minefield that lay buried beneath certain Eurocentric discourses'.[15] Krupa Shandilya argues that scholars in postcolonial studies 'have attempted to resuscitate the subaltern, and imbue her with voice'.[16] She notes, that while the subaltern studies have been momentous 'in (re)writing history from below', their analyses, however, have focused primarily 'on the subaltern consciousness that is being re-presented'.[17] Shandilya asks:

> Who is being re-presented (in terms of the subject as a narrative construction) is closely tied to who purports to represent her (in terms of the subject as a political being), the interconnection between the two is largely obscured . . . [and] focused . . . on the representation of the subaltern alone without taking into account the narrative voice that structures subalternity.[18]

Wendy Brown raises a similar question by asking, 'What kind of subject, produced by what kind of politics is led to seek what kind of rights, in the context of what kind of legal, cultural and state discourses with what kind of effects?'[19] The question of representation brings forth the issue of intersectionality. As Eilish Rooney argues, intersectionality functions 'as a conceptual framework or heuristic device for posing critical questions otherwise not asked or for seeing women

12 Marilyn Frye, *The Politics of Reality: Essays in Feminist Theory* (Crossing Press, 1983) xi–xii.

13 Alice Crary, 'A Question of Silence: Feminist Theory and Women's Voices' (2001) 76 *Philosophy* 371, 375.

14 Gayatri Chakravorty Spivak, 'Can the Subaltern Speak?' in Cary Nelson and Lawrence Grossberg (eds) *Marxism and the Interpretation of Culture* (University of Illinois Press, 1998) 271–313.

15 Abdul JanMohamed, 'Between Speaking and Dying: Some Imperative in Emergence of the Subaltern in the Context of U.S. Slavery' in Rosalind Morris (ed.), *Can the Subaltern Speak? Reflections on the History of an Idea* (Columbia University Press, 2010) 139.

16 Krupa Shandilya, 'Writing/Reading the Subaltern Woman: Narrative Voice and Subaltern Agency in Upamanyu Chatterjee's *English, August*' (2014) 9(3) *Postcolonial Text* 1.

17 Ibid., 1.

18 Ibid., 2.

19 Wendy Brown, 'Revealing Critique: A Response to Kenneth Baynes' (2000) 28(4) *Political Theory* 469, 477.

otherwise hidden from view (or seen only within a certain frame)'.[20] The scholarship on the importance of intersectionality in feminist theory has increased our understanding of relevance of class and race, in relations between Western white women *versus* black women. As Daniela Nadj argues, post-colonial feminists have largely focused on the condition of the 'Third World Woman', while not paying much attention to women located 'in the between', such as Yugoslav women, who are neither seen as Western European, nor as 'Third World Women', due to their geographical location in South Eastern Europe.[21]

Intersectionality has failed to account for the complex interplay of ethnicity, gender, the nation and armed conflict when it comes to sexual violence.[22] Similarly, what comes under the category of a 'woman' and who are the 'women victims' within transitional justice feminist scholarship, who represents them and gives voice to them, has hardly been scrutinised. Feminist activism too, while contributing to the development and expansion of international frameworks for justice and recognition of women's rights as human rights, 'has yet to adequately address racial, ethnic, and/or cultural differences *among* women'.[23]

With this book I open and challenge the unified category of 'female victims' in the field of transitional justice theory and practice, stressing that in feminist transitional justice scholarship not all women victims have been represented, but rather, such representation privileges particular ethnic and racial groups of women. Importantly, over-representation of certain groups of women has often been translated into under- or no representation of the other groups, resulting in particular groups of women not being given feminists' attention. This may be so because transitional justice is still 'pursued in a very specific way: through dealing with past wrongs that were committed by particular perpetrators against particular victims'.[24]

Intersectionality and anchored ethnic identity is one of the issues that have been neglected in this academic field. What intersectionality is trying to do in feminism is to correct the portrayal of one particular perspective – often of white, heterosexual, able-bodied and middle-class women – as dominant and universal to all women. It points to the relevance of different contexts and social locations of women for the ways they represent themselves and are represented by others. In transitional justice scholarship on the Bosnian war, the context and social locations also matter: only certain groups of women victims are represented – those

20 Eilish Rooney, 'Intersentionality: A Feminist Theory for Transitional Justice' in Martha Albertson Fineman and Estelle Zinnstag (eds), *Feminist Perspectives on Transitional Justice: From International and Criminal to Alternative Forms of Justice* (Intersentia, 2013), 91.

21 Daniela Nadj, *ICTY Wartimes Sexual Violence Jurisprudence and the Surrounding Debate: A Critical Feminist Analysis* (PhD Thesis, University of Westminster, 2011) 166.

22 Ibid.

23 Pascha Bueno-Hansen, *Feminist and Human Rights Struggles in Peru: Decolonizing Transitional Justice* (University of Illinois Press, 2015), 139.

24 Colleen Murphy, *The Conceptual Foundations of Transitional Justice* (Cambridge University Press, 2017) 112.

seen to belong to the same ethnic group as the men who have been regarded as the largest victims, i.e. Bosniak women. Women who are seen to belong to the ethnic group regarded as the main 'perpetrator' – seen as the ethnic 'other' – are largely absent from feminist analysis, leaving the ethnicism of the victim–perpetrator dichotomy intact. This dynamic is created through 'subjects that are constituted through exclusion, that is, through the creation of a domain of deauthorized subjects, presubjects, figures of abjection, populations erased from view'.[25] As Jana Cattien argues, intersectional feminism produces 'certain ideal subjectivities that speak to some more than to others'.[26]

In BiH, Bosniak women victims of war have obtained a status of privileged victimhood; a status that gives them a voice not because they were the only victims, but because of their identity and membership of a certain ethnic group. Here, intersectionality was not taken into account, and as a result, 'other' female victims and their unique experiences stayed invisible and unsought after. My research indicates that the experiences of these invisible, 'other' women are profoundly different and manifest themselves in diverse cultural, social and political contexts and practices that need to be studied. I argue that such studies could produce counter discourses to the currently dominant narratives of women victimhood that could disrupt the workings of patriarchy and male-nationalist projects, which often thrive on politicising female victims. The 'other' women's experiences need to be moved from the margins in order to disrupt the centre.[27] If such intersectionality is not employed in each context, then Serb women – defined by belonging to the same ethnic group as the perpetrator – will remain subaltern and subordinated. An inclusive feminism here needs to be practised; one that will incorporate an intersectional ethics of feminist praxis that brings together critical theory with self-reflectiveness. As Fionnuala Ni Aoláin argues:

> In looking forward and learning from the genealogy of decades of transitional justice theorising and practice, there is much reflective learning to follow and a need to be focused on the actual harms and needs of women in these particular sites to better understand what a feminist theorisation and practice of transitional justice would look like.[28]

In this respect, this book has been a feminist reflective exercise by using a particular case study – BiH – to explore actual but neglected harms of particular groups of women.

25 Judith Butler, 'Contingent Foundations: Feminism and the Question of "Postmodernism"' in Linda Nicholson (ed.), *Feminist Contentions: A Philosophical Exchange* (Routledge, 1995) 47.

26 Jana Cattien, 'Feminist Epistemology and the Question of Difference Reconfigured: What can Wittgenstein Tell Us About "Women"? (2017) 18(3) *Journal of International Women Studies* 11.

27 Homi K. Bhabha, 'DissemiNation: Time, Narrative, and The Margins of the Modern Nation' in Homi K. Bhabha (ed.), *Nation and Narration* (Routledge, 1990) 291.

28 Fionnuala Ni Aoláin, 'Advancing Feminist Analysis of Transitional Justice' in Martha Albertson Fineman and Estelle Zinnstag (eds), above n 20, 43, 62.

Researching silences and silencing

Researching silences is a sensitive project that has political and social implications. Sieber and Stanley define socially sensitive research as

> [s]tudies in which there are potential consequences or implications, either directly for the participants in research or for the class of individuals represented by the research. Such studies may lead to a shift in public policy and it might also affect people's attitude towards a particular group.[29]

Claire Renzetti and Raymond Lee define a 'sensitive' research topic as one that is 'intimate, discreditable or incriminating'.[30] Lee puts forward another definition of sensitive research, which encompasses the topic, the consequences, the situation and any number of other issues that may arise, by saying that sensitive research is 'research which potentially poses a substantial threat to those who are or have been involved in it'.[31] This definition suggests that sensitive research has the potential to impact on all of the people who are involved in it. Sensitive methodologies are particularly important when research involves violence against women, and even more so when the women have experienced violence of a sexual nature.[32] Researching topics that are linked to violence against women can pose risks to participants, their families and also the fieldworkers involved in a research project.[33]

Sensitive research can be seen as threatening in three broad areas. The first of these areas is *intrusive threat*, which deals with areas that are 'private, stressful or sacred'.[34] As Campbell writes, 'our emotions influence our research, and our research can affect us emotionally'.[35] It is important to examine our feelings and the emotional impact that research has on us since it can provide us with a deeper intellectual understanding of the social phenomenon we analyse.[36] The second type of threat is a *threat of sanction*, which relates to studies of deviance

29 Joan E. Sieber and Barbara Stanley, 'Ethical and Professional Dimensions of Socially Sensitive Research' (1988) 43(1) *American Psychologists* 49; Rob Kitchin and Nick J. Tate, *Conducting Research in Human Geography: Theory, Methodology and Practice* (Routledge, 1999) 37.

30 Claire M. Renzetti and Raymond M. Lee (eds), *Researching Sensitive Topics* (Sage, 1993) ix.

31 Raymond M. Lee and Claire M. Renzetti, 'The Problems of Researching Sensitive Topics: An Overview and Introduction' (1990) 33(5) *American Behavioral Scientist* 512.

32 Chein Reis, 'Ethical, Safety and Methodological Issues Related to the Collection and Use of Data on Sexual Violence in Conflict' in Anne Marie de Brouwe, Charlote Ku, Renee Romkens, Larissa van der Herik (eds), *Sexual Violence as an International Crime: Interdisciplinary Approaches* (Intersentia, 2013), 189; Charlotte Watts et al., *Putting Women First: Ethical and Safety Recommendations for Research on Domestic Violence Against Women* (World Health Organization Report, 2007), 6.

33 Henrica A. F. M. Jansen, 'Swimming Against the Tide: Lessons from Field Research on Violence Against Women in the Solomon Islands and Kiribati' (United Nations Population Fund Report, 2010), 27.

34 Renzetti and Lee, above n 30, 519.

35 Rebecca Campbell, *Emotionally Involved: The Impact of Researching Rape* (Routledge, 2001) 15.

36 Ibid.

and involves the possibility that research may reveal information that is stigmatising or incriminating in some way. The third type of threat that may be imposed by sensitive research is a *political threat*.[37] This refers to the 'vested interests' of the powerful in society, and in these situations researchers may trespass into areas that involve some sort of social conflict. My study into Serb female war victims seems to meet all three criteria, since it is politically and socially contentious and it is of a potentially problematic nature for the researcher as well as the researched.

Since I belong ethnically to what has been perceived in the context of the Bosnian war as the 'perpetrator' nation, I have always been driven by feelings of personal and academic responsibility to account for the crimes committed by what is consistently perceived from the outside as 'my own' group of people. I have been vocal against the Serb crimes committed during the war in BiH ever since I entered academia and, as noted earlier, my work has been received by many of the Serb population, including my family, as a 'traitorous' act. It has often been judged by ethnic rather than scholarly standards. On the other hand, my work has been largely positively received among the Bosniak community, which has been constructed – internationally and within the Federation of BiH (FBiH) – as the exclusive victim of the Bosnian war.

The Serb women I interviewed for the purpose of this study, often wanted to talk to me, because in their eyes I was primarily a Serb woman, and only secondarily, an academic. My Serb name and my status as a researcher were enough to build the trust necessary for women I approached, and who approached me with their stories. Paradoxically, my Serb ethnic identity – that I have tried so hard to denounce – made the encounters with the women survivors of conflict-related sexual violence (CRSV) possible. Although I have invested lot of energy in stripping myself of ethnic identity, I have come to realise that it is better to reconcile with the fact that I cannot change other people's assumptions and ethnic labelling.[38] As Subotic writes:

> Try as I might to de-ethnify myself, to cloak myself in the robes of an academic scholar, ethnicity comes back to define both me and my work. While I may assume that scholarship provides neutrality, objectivity, and standing that would overcome ethnicity – it does not.[39]

Similarly to Subotic, my research has been conditioned by my own ethnicity and how I appear to others. Upon this realisation, I decided to actively and strategically use my perceived ethnic identity for academic benefit. In April 2015 I finalised a report on the situation of Serb women victims of CRSV (in further text: the Report), commissioned by the Gender Centre of Republika Srpska (RS)

37 Renzetti and Lee, above n 30, 519.

38 I describe these struggles in more detail in my book, Olivera Simić, *Surviving Peace* (Spinifex Press, 2014).

39 Jelena Subotic, 'No Escape From Ethnicity? Confessions of an Accidental CNN Pundit' (2010) 43(1) *PS: Political Science & Politics* 115, 119.

with the objective of assessing their situation and recommending institutional measures in their support. The aim of the Report was to make Serb women victims in particular visible, and to lobby the RS government to bring laws that would recognise the victimhood of women victims living in its territory. Some 20 years after the war, there was still no serious public discussion about CRSV in RS, let alone comprehensive information about the lives of these women; nor were there any institutional instruments in RS to provide assistance (for example, reparations, medical and psychosocial assistance, and alike). In contrast, as I discussed in detail in Chapter 4, women survivors in FBiH have been legally recognised as a special category of victims and as such enjoy certain privileges and benefits.

By the time this book went into production the Gender Center of RS has not yet published the Report. However, the document titled the *Information, Analysis and Recommendations of the Study about the Status of Serb Female Victims of Wartime Rape in Bosnia and Herzegovina* (in further text: the *Information*), based on my Report, was produced and made public in local languages on the Gender Center website.[40] The *Information* has been drafted by the Gender Centre and summarised some of the Report's key findings and recommendations. The *Information* was presented in May 2015 at one of the government parliamentary sessions of RS.

I did not know about the publication of the *Information*, nor its delivery before the RS parliament until I received an email from a female lawyer from FBiH, who informed me that 'the Report had been published' on the Internet. Since the full draft version of the Report had never been published, yet Bosnian feminist activists knew I was working on it, they assumed that the document titled the *Information* was in fact the Report. Some 24 hours after the *Information* was uploaded on the Gender Center's website, a few feminist activists based in FBiH gathered under the initiative 'Women's Peace Activism' and drafted an *Open Letter to the National Assembly of Republika Srpska with Respect to Recommendations Laid Out in the Information about the Study on the Status of Serb Female Victims of Wartime Sexual Violence in BiH* (henceforth, the *Open Letter*) in which they noted:

> We welcome the awakened interest of the RS government and in particular the National Assembly of RS, to start solving the problem and to offer female victims of sexual violence a respectful and productive life, but at the same time we express our concern about the discussion that occurred on the 3rd meeting of the National Assembly RS, with respect to the *Information about Serb Victims* [the *Information*] . . . and which was restricted to women of one nationality only, and not all women who live in the territory of RS.

40 Gender Center, 'Informacija o nalazima i preporukama studije o položaju srpskih žena žrtava ratnog zločina seksualnog nasilja u Bosni i Hercegovini' [Trans: 'Information on the Findings and Recommendations of the Study on the Situation of Serbian Women Victims of War Crimes of Sexual Violence in Bosnia and Herzgovina'] *Republika Srpska, Vlada, Gender Centar – Centar za jednakost i Ravnorpavnost Polova* 2015, www.vladars.net/sr-SP-Cyrl/Vlada/centri/gendercentarrs/Documents/Informacija%20%20latinica_204855676.pdf.

> We call on the National Assembly RS not to make solutions for one group of women only but that the law protects women from all ethnic groups who live in the territory of RS so as to avoid further discrimination against these women, which is against international standards, the constitution and the law on the prohibition of discrimination in BiH.[41]

While I understand concerns expressed in this letter, namely that it may invite possible discrimination against non-Serb women in RS, I was surprised by the reaction of signatories to the very first discussion about the Serb women victims before the parliament of RS. In the 20 years since the Dayton Peace Accord (1995) this was the first time ever that the RS parliament had discussed CRSV. The *Open Letter* was drafted although there was nothing in the Report or the *Information* about lobbying for Serb women only.

Rather, in the light of the fact that hardly anything is known about CRSV of Serb women, and while ample information exists about such crimes committed against Bosniak and Croat women, the Report was meant to broaden the scope of knowledge about until then (regionally and internationally) invisible victims. This was explicitly stated in the Report[42] as well as in the *Information.*[43]. In addition, unlike Bosniak and Croat women in FBiH, Serb women in RS raped in war have received neither legal recognition nor reparations. This is not to say that the FBiH measures for Bosniak and Croat victims are considered sufficient, but rather to note that the Report was supposed to offer an assessment of the situation of Serb women who were totally invisible, in order to pressure the RS government agencies into action.[44]

But clearly, it was not perceived as such. I was perplexed by the strong reaction to the document and believe that – due to the dominant discourses on victims and perpetrators of CRSV in the Bosnian war – it was not carefully read by feminist activists. There was a warning in the *Open Letter* that only Serb women may receive justice and that this needed to be halted. While the majority of those who

41 Inicijativa Ženski Mirovni Aktivizam, 'Otvoreno pismo Narodnoj Skupštini Republike Srpske povodom rasprave o Informaciji o nalazima i preporukama studije o polozaju srspkih zena zrtava ratnog zlocina seksualnog nasilja u BiH', [Trans: 'Open Letter to the People's Assembly of the Republic of Serbia on the Occasion of the Debate on the Information on the Findings and Recommendations of the Study on the Situation of Srpskih, Women Victims of War Crimes of Sexual Violence in Bosnia and Herzegovina'] *Women Organising for Change*, 24 April 2015, http://womenorganizingforchange.org/izjave/otvoreno-pismo-narodnoj-skupstini-republike-srpske-povodom-rasprave-ns-rs-o-informaciji-o-nalazima-i-preporukama-studije-o-polozaju-srpskih-zena-zrtava-ratnog-zlocina-seksualnog-nasilja-u-bih/, 93 individuals and NGOs signed this letter, majority of them situated in FBiH.

42 Ibid., 3.

43 Ibid., 5.

44 The Gender Center RS with *Information* succeeded in lobbying the RS National Assembly to acknowledge the findings of the study and adopt wide-ranging recommendations including to initiate the legislative changes to remove current restrictive criteria and recognise a special status for all, not just Serb, victims of CRSV.

signed the *Open Letter* were representatives from FBiH non-government organisations (NGOs), one Bosniak feminist told me in private conversations that she did not want to sign the protest letter and commented: 'So, what if only Serb women get something? They have nothing. Let them get something.'[45]

Similarly, one long-term feminist activist from RS told me that the issue of the Report (i.e. the *Information*) about Serb female victims came up at an international conference that gathered feminist activists from BiH. One of them commented how it is not acceptable that someone writes 'about Serb women only'. A female activist from RS responded to her: 'Why is it a problem that we have at least one study on Serb women? There has been none so far in the past 20 years. Let the woman [me] finish that study, once and for all.'[46]

In the course of my field work I have been discouraged to do a study that does not provide, as I have been told numerous times by a few local activists: 'a balanced view of women from all ethnic groups' raped during the war in BiH. This discouragement confirms how difficult and contested the topic of researching Serb women victims' experiences has been. I have, however, found the warnings to 'balance' the stories somewhat hypocritical since in the mass production of BiH wartime rape literature there have been hardly any attempts to 'balance' the stories by bringing experiences of women from all three major ethnic groups, as the focus of writing has predominantly been on one group of women, Bosniaks.

I have also been asked: 'How I have been paid to do such research and by whom?'; have been warned to think about 'my responsibility for writing something that may have long lasting consequences on the feminist movement in ex-Yugoslavia'; and asked to 'share' the findings with the 'feminist movement' in ex-Yugoslavia before I publish it. Most recently, I received an email from a senior female academic originally from Croatia who, after reading my first ever published paper on Serb female victims of CRSV, told me how disappointed she was, and 'warned me' that I should never reproduce narratives from 'Nazi *fela* [Nazi-like] women'.[47]

The written or verbal disagreements with my project, received over the past few years, have come from all quarters: international feminist scholars and activists, feminists from the ex-Yugoslav region living abroad, feminist activists based in Serbia and women working with survivors of CRSV based in FBiH and RS. The fact that all of them see this study as problematic demonstrates the complexities and paradoxes of the socio-political situation in which Serb women survivors of CRSV have found themselves.

However, I have not been the only researcher in ex-Yugoslavia exposed to unpleasant comments and ostracism. Ana Miškovska Kajevska has recently faced similar challenges while conducting research that critically analysed the positioning of feminist activists from Serbia and Croatia towards the post-Yugoslav wars

45 Interview with an activist, 24 July 2015.

46 Interview with an activist, 14 July 2015.

47 Email from senior female academic, 21 February 2016.

and towards each other. Disseminating research results is an important part of the research process and researchers are increasingly expected to share their research with others, beyond the research community.[48] However, sharing research findings is not a simple process and its reception and utilisation is diverse and complex.[49] As Miškovska Kajevska wrote to me:

> I was hoping that with my work I would break the silences among activists. Instead, my work has been embraced with the same silence full of unspoken emotions. That raises a question – when after the war comes the moment when the war is really over? In the context where we still search for the missing, in which there is entrenched institutionalised hate speech and denial of crimes and responsibilities; in which victim still have to fight to be recognised and receive reparation for the harm they suffered and for punishment of their perpetrators – when will activists find a moment to critically examine their positions and roles in relation to wars and nationalism, including categories such as "victim", "perpetrator", "nationalism"? When will they be able to do so and not think of such critical re-examination of their work as ethically irresponsible towards victims, as losing their own legitimacy and throwing in the garbage bin all they have done so far?[50]

Tsai argues that political sensitivity is always a challenge for the scholar doing fieldwork in non-democratic and transitional systems, especially when doing surveys and quantitative research.[51] She notes that not only are more research topics likely to be politically sensitive in these systems, but in trying to collect precise and unbiased data, researchers are often doing what the government, and sometimes certain members of that population, would like to prevent.[52]

Indeed, doing sensitive research may leave the researcher, as Melrose contends: 'feeling methodologically vulnerable . . . because of emotional and anxiety challenges . . . that may arise in this context'.[53] During the course of writing this book, I have been feeling anxious and threatened, not physically but emotionally and

48 Kay Tisdall, John M. Davis and Michael Gallagher, *Researching with Children and Young People: Research Design, Methods and Analysis* (Sage, 2008) 519.

49 Hurriyet Babacan and Alperhan Babacan, 'Difficult Research Conversations: Sharing Socially Sensitive Research in the Public Domain' (2013) 21(1) *eTropic* 52.

50 Personal email communication, 1 February 2015. Full name disclosed with consent of Ana Miškovska Kajevska 13 March 2017. For more on intra-feminist dynamics and the feminist activists tensions and disagreements in the region, see Ana Miškovska Kajevska, *Feminist Activism at War: Belgrade and Zagreb Feminists in the 1990s* (Routledge, 2017).

51 Lily Tsai, 'Quantitative Research and Issue of Political Sensitivity in Rural China' in Allen Carlson, Mary E. Gallagher, Kenneth Lieberthal and Melanie Manion (eds), *Contemporary Chinese Politics: New Sources, Methods, and Field Strategies* (Cambridge University Press, 2010) 246, 252.

52 Ibid. For more on challenges of researching in post-conflict societies, see Olivera Simić, '"Doing the Research I Do Has Left Scars": Challenges of Researching in the Transitional Justice Field' (2018 forthcoming) 1(5) *Transitional Justice Review*.

53 Margaret Melrose, 'Labor Pains: Some Considerations on the Difficulties Researching Juvenile Prostitution' (2002) 5(4) *International Journal of Social Research and Methodology, Theory and Practice* 331, 338.

mentally, as I received many indications that my study is not welcome and that I have no support from many feminists who do not want to disturb the dominant narratives and who strongly feel that feminists from Serbia and RS, and all those seen as Serb feminists, should talk about – if not only, but certainly primarily and publically – crimes committed 'by their own people'; this, even if none of them actually consider war criminals as 'their own people'.

During the research process, I have also encountered difficulties in the process of collecting and translating Serb women's testimonies scattered in various documents. In the first year of my work, I received research assistance from a woman, a long-term feminist and activist residing in Serbia. I asked her to translate some original testimonies of Serb women survivors of CRSV that have never been translated in English before. She initially agreed to do so, but after translating one story, she told me she did not want to work on translations anymore:

> It is not appropriate for me to transcribe or translate these texts [testimonies of rape] because they are ideologically and politically loaded, and that is something that bothers me a lot. I do not want to participate in anything that has to do with Republika Srpska. I am sorry but that is against my political views. Please, do not send me such texts anymore.[54]

The decision of my research assistant not to translate Serb women's experiences has symbolically attempted to silence these women once again. And although I have received many negative reactions, discouragements and warnings about my research, this rejection still came completely unexpectedly. After careful reading of the reasons for her rejection on working with Serb women victims' testimonies, I have come to realise that this feminist activist perhaps adopted a specific understanding of justice, which is, according to her 'ideological and political' and treats women who seemingly belong to 'perpetrators' as those who do not have the right to complain if abused.

Serb women victims' testimonies have not been welcomed but instead reinterpreted as political texts rather than as women's authentic experiences of CRSV. The key problem of listening to, writing about and researching these texts, as I have discussed in this book, is that they have been embraced and perceived not as women's experiences of crime, but as loaded political and ideological tools for Serb nationalist propaganda. Conversely, non-Serb women's testimonies have not necessarily been viewed or interpreted as such, but produced and reproduced in feminist scholarship and analysis.

Epilogue: on the politics of writing

A series of obstacles imposed by feminist activists and scholars in the course of writing this book, have raised a number of questions that need attention: what do they mean for feminist struggles for justice, for regional divisive politics and for

54 Email communication with author, 26 August 2014.

the politics of reconciliation that *some* women's experiences are not only recognised, but continuously reinforced, supported and cherished, while others remain ignored and downplayed? What do they mean for many feminists in Serbia and RS to deliberately choose not to talk about some experiences for fear of falling prey to nationalists in their own regions? Why do these same feminists have no fear that the silencing of women of one ethnic group will encourage the nationalism of 'the other' politicians who claim that only 'their women' were the victims of wartime rape?[55]

Hence, instead of discouraging me from continuing this research, these obstacles have strengthened my determination to analyse why this topic has been difficult to research, and was avoided by many, for such a long time. This decision brought home all the complexities of the entrenched ethnic and national politics still in play in BiH, the region, and internationally. As feminist scholars and activists sort through and engage with women's experiences, they necessarily link personal experiences to larger contexts of geo-politics, feminist politics and the politics of writing they live in.[56] Due to the complex politics of victimhood, researchers' attention to some victims in BiH has contributed to increasing social visibility and recognition of some categories of victims, while others have stayed largely 'invisible and unrecognised'.[57]

If the goal of feminist research is to discern and discover the actual facts of women's lives and experiences, the facts that 'have been hidden, inaccessible, suppressed, distorted'[58] or ignored, then the research on Serb women victims of CRSV needs to be undertaken. If we don't take into account experiences of women who are seen to belong to 'perpetrator' – we leave out an important part of female victims' experiences and offer only a modicum of understanding of and remedy for female victims. As Fionnuala Ni Aoláin argues, in many contexts the harm that is 'legally captured' may be only one piece of overall 'macro-structure of harm, exclusion and discrimination' that captures the woman's interplay with the state and broader civilian context in which she lives.[59]

As Marsha Henry notes, feminist researchers need to be 'inclusive of all women's experiences', both as participants and researchers, in order to contribute to, reconceptualise and continuously challenge the qualitative research literature.[60] The researcher's identity, as well as that of the researched, have multilayered consequences to the process of undertaking research. As demonstrated, due to

55 Thanks to Dubravka Zarkov for sharing with me her ideas expressed in these questions.

56 Foss and Foss, above n 9, 40.

57 Magnus Lindgren and Vesna Nikolić-Ristanović, 'Crime Victims: International and Serbian Perspective', *OSCE Report*, 2011, www.osce.org/serbia/85268?download=true, 46.

58 DuBois 1985 as cited in Raquel Kennedy Bergen, 'Interviewing Survivors of Martial Rape: Doing Feminist Research on Sensitive Topics' in Claire M. Renzetti and Raymond M. Lee (eds), *Researching Sensitive Topics* (Sage, 1993) 152, 200.

59 Ni Aoláin, above n 28, 57.

60 Marsha Giselle Henry, 'Where Are You Really From': Representations, Identity and Power in the Fieldwork Experiences of a South Asian Diasporic' (2003) 3(2) *Qualitative Research* 229, 230.

my perceived ethnic belonging, but also due to the sensitivity of the issue, I have chosen to critically engage with, I encountered obstacles that I would, perhaps, have not otherwise. At the same time, my ethnic identity has also opened the space to reach the Serb female victims who otherwise, possibly, would not be willing to confide in me such personal issues. As a researcher who is both an insider and outsider of the context I research, I found myself in this paradoxical situation: my ethnic identity worked both ways – detrimentally, but also fruitfully in reaching a group of women who I would not otherwise have been able to reach. I feel, however, that I am neither an insider nor outsider, but what Acker calls 'somewhere in between'.[61]

Finally, I would like to go back to the question with which I opened this chapter and that I received from a long-term feminist from Serbia. She too struggled with all the complexities and dilemmas that are inevitably raised when writing a book such as this. In one of our email communications she asked me: 'Is it possible, do you think, to write a book such as yours and not produce a nationalistic text?' My answer to her is, 'No, probably it is not.' I accepted the fact that my words could be interpreted and used for boosting the Serb nationalist project. However, by refusing to write I would be co-opted in the discourse of silence. I decided to write as cautiously as I could and take the risk. I owe it to the women who trusted me with their stories.

61 Sandra Acker, 'In/Out/Side: Positioning The Researcher in Feminist Qualitative Research' (2000) 28(1/2) *Resources for Feminist Research* 189.

Bibliography

Cases

Čolić and Others v Bosnia and Herzegovina, Judgment, Strasbourg, European Court of Human Rights, 19 November 2009.

Delalić et al. v Prosecutor, Trial Judgment, International Criminal Tribunal for the former Yugoslavia, Trial Chamber, Case No. IT-96-21-T, 16 November 1998.

Đurić and Others v Bosnia and Herzegovina, Judgment, Strasbourg, European Court of Human Rights, 20 January 2015.

Iwane Matsui, International Military Tribunal for the Far East, 12 November 1948.

Ivan Zelenika and Others v Prosecutor, Court BiH, Case No. S1 1 K 009124 12 KrI, 14 April 2015.

Prosecutor v Anto Furundžija, Judgment, Case No. IT-95-17/1-T, 10 December 1998.

Prosecutor v Anto Furundžija, Order of the President on the Application for the Early Release of Anto Furundžija, Case No. IT-95-17/1, 29 July 2004.

Prosecutor v Jean-Paul Akayesu, International Criminal Tribunal for Rwanda, Case No. ICTR-96-4-T, 2 September 1998.

Prosecutor v Kunarac, Trial Judgment, International Criminal Tribunal for the Former Yugoslavia, Trial Chamber, Case No. IT-96-23-T and IT-96-23/1-T, 22 February 2001.

Prosecutor v Kunarac et al., Judgment, Case No. IT-96-23, 12 June 2002.

Prosecutor v Kunarac, Transcript of Proceedings, International Criminal Tribunal for the Former Yugoslavia, Trial Chamber, Case Nos IT-96-23-T and IT-96-23/1-T. 6273–6274.

Prosecutor v Naser Orić, Judgment, Case No. IT-03-68, 3 July 2008.

Prosecutor v Rasim Delić, Amended Indictment, International Criminal Tribunal for the Former Yugoslavia, Case No. IT-04-83-PT, 14 July 2006.

Prosecutor v Rasim Delić, Judgment, International Tribunal for the Prosecution of Persons Responsible for Serious Violations of International Humanitarian Law Committed in the Territory of the Former Yugoslavia since 1999, Trial Chamber I, Case No. IT-04-83-T, 15 September 2008.

Prosecutor v Simsic Boban Trial Judgment, The Court of Bosnia and Herzegovina, Case No. X-KR-05/04, 11 July 2006.

Prosecutor v Zdravko Mucić et al. (Celebici case) ICTY Judgment, International Criminal Tribunal for the Former Yugoslavia, Case No. IT-96-21-A, 20 February 2001.

Skočić (Indictee Sima Bogdanović and others) Issuing of Verdict, Higher Court in Belgrade, Case No. Kžl Po2 6/2013, 22 February 2013.

Soemu Toyoda, US Military Tribunal sitting in Tokyo, 6 September 1949, *Official Transcript of Record of Trial*, 4998–5007.

In re Yamashita (1946) 327 U.S. 1.

Books/articles/reports/webpages

Acker, Sandra, 'In/Out/Side: Positioning The Researcher in Feminist Qualitative Research' (2000) 28(1/2) *Resources for Feminist Research* 189.

African Union, *Rwanda – The Preventable Genocide: The Report of the International Panel of Eminent Personalities to Investigate the 1994 Genocide in Rwanda and the Surrounding Events*, Report, African Union (2000), www.refworld.org/pdfid/4d1da8752.pdf.

Ajanović, Irfan (ed.), *I Begged Them to Kill Me: The Crimes Against Women in Bosnia and Herzegovina* (Center for Investigation and Documentation, 2007).

Al Jazeera Balkans TV, 'Jasminka Džumhur o silovanjima u ratu u BiH', 29 March 2012, www.youtube.com/watch?v=TieGZx7Jp0g.

Alvesson, Mats, *Postmodernism and Social Research* (Open University Press, 2002).

Amnesty International, *Bosnia and Herzegovina: Rape and Sexual Abuse by Armed Forces*, Report (1993), www.amnesty.org/en/documents/eur63/001/1993/en/.

Amnesty International, *Whose Justice? The Women of Bosnia and Herzegovina are Still Waiting*, Report (2009), www.amnesty.org/en/documents/EUR63/006/2009/en/.

Amnesty International, *Bosnia and Herzegovina: Old Crimes Same Suffering: No Justice for Survivors of Wartime Rape in North-East Bosnia and Herzegovina*, Campaign for International Justice, Paper (2012), www.amnesty.org/en/documents/EUR63/002/2012/en/.

Amnesty International, *When Everyone Is Silent: Reparations for Survivors of Wartime Rape in Republika Srpska in Bosnia and Herzegovina*, Report (2012), www.amnesty.org/en/documents/EUR63/012/2012/en/.

Amnesty International, *Bosnia and Herzegovina: Submission to the United Nations Human Rights Committee*, 119th Session, 6–29 March 2017, www.amnesty.org/en/documents/eur63/5554/2017/en/.

Andreas, Peter, *Blue Helmets and Black Markets: The Business of Survival in the Siege of Sarajevo* (Cornell University Press, 2008).

Andric Ruzicic, Duska, 'War Rape and Political Manipulation of Survivors' in Wenona Gils, Malathi de Alwsi, Edith Klein, Kuluka Siva and Maja Korac (eds), *Feminists Under Fire: Exchanges Across War Zones* (Between the Lines Press, 2003) 103.

Anti-ratni bilten SOS-a (SOS telefon za žene i decu žrtve nasilja, 1993).

Arnstein, Mimi, 'Consciousness Raising: Self-Defining Feminism and the Problem of Postmodern Politics' in Gail Currie and Celia Rothenberg (eds), *Feminist (Re)visions of the Subject: Landscapes, Ethnoscapes, and Theoryscapes* (Lexington Books, 2001) 159.

Arslanagic, Sabina, 'Justice for Wartime Rape Victims in Bosnia "Painfully Slow"', *Balkan Insight* (online), 29 November 2010, www.balkaninsight.com/en/article/justice-for-victims-of-war-time-rapes-in-bosnia-painfully-slow.

Askin, Kelly Dawn, *War Crimes Against Women: Prosecution in International War Crimes Tribunals* (Martinus Nijhoff, 1997).

Askin, Kelly Dawn, 'Prosecuting Wartime Rape and Other Gender-Related Crimes Under International Law: Extraordinary Advances, Enduring Obstacles' (2003) 21(2) *Berkeley Journal of International Law* 288.

Association for Women's Rights in Development, 'Intersectionality: A Tool for Gender and Economic Justice' (2004) *9 Women's Rights and Economic Change: Facts & Issues* 1, https://lgbtq.unc.edu/sites/lgbtq.unc.edu/files/documents/intersectionality_en.pdf.

Attitude, 'Sabiha Husić, '"Žena svijeta" i direktorica "Medice" Zenica: Mnogima je teret i slušati o žrtvama silovanja' [Trans: 'Sabiha Husić, "The Women of the World" and director of "Medica" Zenica: Many Burden and Listen on Rape Victims'], *Attitude*, 3 September 2015, http://zenskamreza.ba/sabiha-husic-zena-svijeta-i-direktorica-medice-zenica-mnogima-je-teret-i-slusati-o-zrtvama-silovanja/.

Avdukić, Nermina, 'Osuđene za ratni zločine otkupili kazne za 18.300 eura' [Trans: 'Convicted of War Crimes Bought Penalties for 18,300 euros'], *Aljazeera Balkans* (online), n.d., http://balkans.aljazeera.net/vijesti/osudeni-za-ratne-zlocine-otkupili-kazne-za-18300-eura.

Babacan, Hurriyet and Alperhan Babacan, 'Difficult Research Conversations: Sharing Socially Sensitive Research in the Public Domain' (2013) 21(1) *eTropic* 52.

Bakić-Hayden, Milica, 'National Memory as Narrative Memory: The Case of Kosovo' in Maria Todorova (ed.), *Balkan Identities: Nation and Memory* (Hurst & Company, 2004) 25.

Ball, Howard, *Working in the Killing Fields: Forensic Science in Bosnia* (University of Nebraska, 2015).

Banjaluka.net, 'Završeno prvo rociste' [Trans: 'Finished First Hearing Oric: Mothers of Srebrenica Want to Testify'], *Banjaluka.net* (online), 26 January 2015, http://banjaluka.net/zavrseno-prvo-rociste-oricu-majke-srebrenice-zele-da-svjedoce/.

Banjeglav, Tamara, *Gender, Nation, Rape: Intersections of Gender and Ethnic Violence During the War in Bosnia and Herzegovina* (MA Thesis, Central European University, 2009).

Barkan Elzar, *The Guilt of Nations: Restitution and Negotiating of Historical Injustices* (W. W. Norton & Company, 2000).

Barkan, Elazar and Belma Bećirbasić, 'The Politics of Memory, Victimization, and Activism in Postconflict Bosnia and Herzegovina' in Klaus Neumann and Janna Thompson (eds), *Historical Justice and Memory* (University of Wisconsin Press, 2015) 95.

Bartal, Daniel, Lily Chernyak-Hai, Noa Schori and Ayelet Gundar, 'A Sense of Self-Perceived Collective Victimhood in Intractable Conflicts' (2009) 91(874) *International Review of the Red Cross 229.*

Bassiouni, M. Cherif and Marcia McCormick, *Sexual Violence: An Invisible Weapon of War in the Former Yugoslavia, Occasional Paper no. 1* (International Human Rights Law Institute, DePaul University College of Law, 1996).

Batinic, Jelena, 'Feminism, Nationalism, and War: The "Yugoslav Case" in Feminist Texts' (2001) 3(1) *Journal of International Women Studies* 1.

Baverly, Allen, *Rape Warfare: The Hidden Genocide in Bosnia-Herzegovina and Croatia* (University of Minnesota Press, 1996).

BBC News, 'Huge Bosnian Mass Grave Excavated at Tomašica', *BBC News*, 1 November 2013, www.bbc.com/news/world-europe-24778713.

Beevor, Antony, *The Fall of Berlin 1945* (Viking, 2002).

Benderly, Jill, 'Rape, Feminism, and Nationalism in the War in Yugoslav Successor States' in Lois A. West (ed.), *Feminist Nationalism* (Routledge, 1997) 59.

Bennett, Christopher, *Bosnia's Paraylsed Peace* (Hurst & Company, 2016).

Bergen, Raquel Kennedy, 'Interviewing Survivors of Martial Rape: Doing Feminist Research on Sensitive Topics' in Claire M. Renzetti and Raymond M. Lee (eds), *Researching Sensitive Topics* (Sage, 1993) 152.

Bergsmo, Morten, Kjetil Helvig, Ilia Utmelidze and Gorana Žagovec, *The Backlog of Core International Crimes Case Files in Bosnia and Herzegovina* (Torkel Opsahl Academic EPublisher, 2008), www.fichl.org/fileadmin/fichl/documents/FICHL_3_Second_Edition_web.pdf.

Bernstein, J. M., 'Suffering Injustice: Misrecognition as Moral Injury in Critical Theory' (2005) 13(3) *International Journal Philosophy Studies* 303.

Bessel, Richard and Dirk Schumann (eds), *Life After Death: Approaches to a Cultural and Social History of Europe During the 1940s and 1950s* (Cambridge University Press, 2003).

Bhabha, Homi K., 'DissemiNation: Time, Narrative, and the Margins of the Modern Nation' in Homi K. Bhabha (ed.), *Nation and Narration* (Routledge, 1990) 291.

Bideleux, Robert and Ian Jeffries, *The Balkans: A Post-Communist History* (Routledge, 2007).

Binetti, Ashley, *Gender-Sensitive and Transformative Reparations in Bosnia*, Georgetown Institutte for Women, Peace & Security (2015), https://giwps.georgetown.edu/sites/giwps/files/I2A%20-%20Gender-Sensitive%20and%20Transformative%20Reparations%20in%20Bosnia.pdf.

Balkan Investigative Reporting Network,'Katalog ratnih zločina' [Trans: 'The Catalogue of War Crimes'] 5 June 2008.

Björkdahl, Annika and Selma Mannergren Selimovic, 'Gender Justice Gaps in Bosnia-Herzegovina' (2014) 15(2) *Human Rights Review* 201.

Blic, 'Provera podataka o silovanim srpkinjama' [Trans: 'Proof of Data on Raped Serbs'], *Blic*, 13 August 2014.

Boas, Gideon, James L. Bischoff, Natalie L. Reid and B. Don Taylor, *International Criminal Law Practitioner Library Volume III* (Cambridge University Press, 2011).

Boesten, Jelke, *Sexual Violence During War and Peace: Gender, Power, and Post-Conflict Justice in Peru* (Palgrave Macmillan, 2014).

Boister, Neil and Robert Cryer (eds), *Documents on the Tokyo International Military Tribunal: Charter, Indictments and Judgments* (Oxford University Press, 2008).

Bojić, Dušica, 'The War in Bosnia with a Description of Events in the Tuzla Region (1992–1995)' (2003) 17(2) *Journal of the North American Society for Serbian* Studies 225.

Bonacker, Thorsten, 'Global Victimhood: On the Charisma of the Victim in Transitional Justice Processes' (2013) 9(1) *World Political Science Review* 97.

Borer, Tristan Anne, 'Truth Telling as a Peacebuilding Activity: A Theoretical Overview' in Tristan Anne Borer (ed.), *Telling the Truths: Truth Telling and Peace Building in Post-Conflict Societies* (University of Notre Dame Press, 2006) 1.

Borger, Julian, 'Bosnia Rape Victims May Claim Compensation for First Time', *Guardian* (online), 30 June 2015, www.theguardian.com/world/2015/jun/30/bosnia-victims-compensation-landmark-ruling.

Botić, Nedim, '*Silovane žene – pucanj* u *dušu savjesti čovječanstva*' [Trans: 'Raped Women – Shot in the Soul of Humanity's Conscience'], *Aljazeera Balkans* (online), 12 December 2015, http://balkans.aljazeera.net/blog/silovane-zene-pucanj-u-dusu-savjesti-covjecanstva.

Bouris, Erica, *Complex Political Victims* (Kumarian Press, 2007).

Brahm, Eric, 'Transitional Justice, Civil Society, and the Development of the Rule of Law in Post-Conflict Societies' (2007) 9(4) *International Journal of Not-for-Profit Law* 62.

Bringa, Tone, *Being Muslim the Bosnian Way: Identity and Community in a Central Bosnian Village* (Princeton University Press, 1995).

Bringa, Tone, 'Reconciliation in Bosnia-Herzegovina' in Elin Skaar, Siri Gloppen and Astri Suhrke (eds), *Roads to Reconciliation* (Lexington Books, 2005) 187.

Brinton, Lykes M. and Crosby Alison, 'Creative Methodology as a Resource for Mayan Women's Protagonism' in Brendon Hamber and Gallagher Elizabeth (eds), *Psychosocial Perspectives on Peacebuilding* (Palgrave Macmillan, 2014) 147.

British Embassy Sarajevo, *Legacy of Wartime Sexual Violence in Bosnia Still Far From Addressed* (2013) GOV.UK, www.gov.uk/government/world-location-news/legacy-of-wartime-sexual-violence-in-bosnia-still-far-from-addressed.

Brown, Wendy, 'Revealing Critique: A Response to Kenneth Baynes' (2000) 28(4) *Political Theory* 469.

Brownmiller, Susan, *Against Our Will: Men, Women, and Rape* (Bantam Books, 1975).

Brunwasser, Matthew, 'Bosnia's Biggest Foreign Investment: Bonanza or Threat?', *BBC News Online*, 26 September 2016, www.bbc.com/news/business-37429682.

Buckely-Zistel, Susanne and Magdalena Zolkos, 'Gender in Transitional Justice' in Susanne Buckley-Zistel and Ruth Stanley (eds), *Gender in Transitional Justice* (Springer, 2012) 1.

Bueno-Hansen, Pascha, *Feminist and Human Rights Struggles in Peru: Decolonizing Transitional Justice* (University of Illinois Press, 2015).

Burnet, Jennie, *Genocide Lives in Us: Women, Memory, and Silence in Rwanda* (University of Wisconsin Press, 2012).

Burnet, Jennie E., 'Situation Sexual Violence in Rwanda (1990–2011): Sexual Agency, Sexual Consent, and the Political Economy of War' (2012) 4 *Anthropology Faculty Publications* 1.

Buss, Doris, 'Rethinking Rape as a Weapon of War' (2009) 17 *Feminist Legal Studies* 145.

Buss, Doris, 'International Criminal Courts' in Jill Steans and Daniela Tepe-Belfrage (eds), *Handbook on Gender in World Politics* (Edward Elgar, 2016) 162.

Butler, Judith, 'Contingent Foundations: Feminism and the Question of "Postmodernism"' in Linda Nicholson (ed.), *Feminist Contentions: A Philosophical Exchange* (Routledge, 1995) 3.

Butler, Judith, *Frames of War: When Is Life Grievable?* (Verso, 2009).

Byrnes, Andrew and Gabrielle Simm, 'People's Tribunals, International Law and the Use of Force' (2013) 36(2) *University of New South Wales Law Journal* 711.

Campbell, Kirsten, 'The Gender of Transitional Justice: Law, Sexual Violence and the International Criminal Tribunal for the Former Yugoslavia' (2007) 1(3) *International Journal of Transitional Justice* 411.

Campbell, Rebecca, *Emotionally Involved: The Impact of Researching Rape* (Routledge, 2001).

Carpenter, Charlie, *Forgetting Children Born of War: Setting the Human Rights Agenda in Bosnia and Beyond* (Columbia University Press, 2010).

Carpenter, Charlie, '"You Talk of Terrible Things so Matter-of-Factly in This Language of Science": Constructing Human Rights in the Academy' (2012) 10(2) *Perspectives on Politics* 363.

Cattien, Jana, 'Feminist Epistemology and the Question of Difference Reconfigured: What Can Wittgenstein Tell Us About "Women"? (2017) 18(3) *Journal of International Women Studies* 5.

Čehajić-Clancy, Sabina, 'Reconciliation in Bosnia and Herzegovina: Perspectives from Social Psychology' (Paper presented at the Humanity in Action, International Conference, Sarajevo, Bosnia and Herzegovina, 2012), https://vimeo.com/72300524.

Center for European Studies, 'Dusan Jovic and Jelena Subotic, Fall 2013 CES Friday Lecture' 16 December 2013, www.youtube.com/watch?v=5fCdqVDfAu0.

Chang, Iris, *The Rape of Nanking: The Forgotten Holocaust of World War II* (Basic Books, 1997).

Chappell, Louise, 'The Role of the ICC in Transitional Gender Justice: Capacity and Limitations' in Susanne Buckely-Zistel and Stanley Ruth (eds), *Gender in Transitional Justice* (Palgrave Macmillan, 2012) 37.

Chappell, Louise, Andrea Durbach and Judge Elizabeth Odio Benito, 'Judge Odio Benito: A View of Gender Justice from the Bench' (2014) 16(4) *International Feminist Journal of Politics* 648.

Charlesworth, Hilary and Christine Chinkin, 'The Gender of Jus Cogens' (1993) 15(1) *Human Rights Quarterly* 63.

Christie, Nils, 'Ideal Victim' in Ezzat A. Fattah (ed.), *From Crime Policy to Victim Policy: Reorienting Justice System* (Palgrave, 1986) 17.

Cismas, Ioana, 'Reflections on the Presence and Absence of Religious Actors in Transitional Justice Processes: On Legitimacy and Accountability' in Roger Duthie and Paul Seils (eds), *Justice Mosaics: How Context Shapes Transitional Justice in Fractured Societies* (International Center for Transitional Justice, 2017) 302.

Clark, Janine Natalya, *International Trials and Reconciliation: Assessing the Impact of the International Criminal Tribunal for the Former Yugoslavia* (Routledge, 2015).

Clark, Janine Natalya, 'Transitional Justice as Recognition: An Analysis of the Women's Court in Sarajevo' (2016) 10(1) *International Journal of Transitional Justice* 67.

Clark, Janine Natalya, 'Working with Survivors of War Rape and Sexual Violence: Fieldwork Reflections from Bosnia-Hercegovina' (2016) (online) *Qualitative Research* 1.

Coalition for RECOM, *Women's Court: Preliminary Decisions and Recommendations* (2015), www.recom.link/womens-court-preliminary-decisions-and-recommendations/.

Cockburn, Cynthia, 'The Continuum of Violence: A Gender Perspective on War and Peace' in Wenona Giles and Jennifer Hyndman (eds), *Sites of Violence: Gender and Conflict Zones* (University of California Press, 2004) 24.

Cohen, Dara Kay, *Rape During Civil War* (Cornell University, 2016).

Cole, Alyson M., *The Cult of True Victimhood: From the War on Welfare to the War on Terror* (Stanford University Press, 2007).

Čolić, Dragan, 'Tukli su me i silovanli' [Trans: 'They Beat and Raped Me'] *Blic* (online), 24 May 2002, www.blic.rs/stara_arhiva/reportaze/27076/Tukli-su-me-i-silovali.

Coomaraswamy, Radhika, 'Sexual Violence During Wartime' in Helen Durham and Tracey Gurd (ed.), *Listening to the Silences: Women and War* (Leiden, 2005) 53.

Copelon, Rhonda, 'Surfacing Gender: Re-Engraving Crimes Against Women in Humanitarian Law' (1994) 5(2) *Hastings Women's Law Journal* 243.

Copelon, Rhonda, 'Gendered War Crimes: Reconceptualizing Rape in Time of War' in Julie Peters and Andrea Wolper (eds), *Women's Rights, Human Rights: International Feminist Perspectives* (Routledge, 1995) 197.

Copelon, Rhonda, 'Surfacing Gender: Reconceptualizing Crimes against Women in Time of War' in Lois Ann Lorentzen and Jennifer Turpin (eds), *The Women and War Reader* (New York University Press, 1998) 63.

Copelon, Rhonda, 'Gender Crimes as War Crimes: Integrating Crimes Against Women into International Criminal Law' (2000) 46 *McGill Law Journal* 217.

Cotterill, Pamela, 'Interviewing Women: Issues of Friendship, Vulnerability, and Power' (1992) 15(5–6) *Women Studies International Forum* 593.

The Council of Europe Parliamentary Assembly, *Rape in Armed Conflicts*, Doc. 8668, Report, Committee on Equal Opportunities for Women and Men, 15 March 2000, http://assembly.coe.int/nw/xml/XRef/X2H-Xref-ViewHTML.asp?FileID=8878&lang=en.

Coulter, Chris, *Bush Wives and Girl Soldiers, Women's Lives through War and Peace in Sierra Leone* (Cornell University Press, 2009).

Court of Bosnia and Herzegovina, 'First Instance Verdict Pronounced in Bosiljko Marković et al.' (News Release, 24 June 2015).

Court of Bosnia and Herzegovina, 'Slavko Savić Sentenced to 8 (eight) Years in Prison' (News Release, 29 June 2015), www.sudbih.gov.ba/index.php?id=4075&jezik=e.

Crary, Alice, 'A Question of Silence: Feminist Theory and Women's Voices' (2001) 76 *Philosophy* 371.

Crimes Against Serbian Civilians (Produced and Directed by Bosnian Serbs' Television, 1993) 00:57:00 (Video).

D'allulakk, Ál-Šajh, Ali D'allulakk, al Ima al akbar, Hukmu at fali n-nisa I al-mugtesibati fi l-Busneti wa l-Harsaki [Trans: 'Regulations Related to the Children of Raped Women in BiH'] (Buhnus wa fatawa islamiyya fi qadaya al-mu asira, 1994) 175.

Daniel-Wrabetz, Joana, 'Children Born of War Rape in Bosnia-Herzegovina and the Convention on the Rights of the Child' in R. Charlie Carpenter (ed.), *Born of War: Protecting Children of Sexual Violence Survivors in Conflict Zones* (Kumarin Press, 2007) 29.

Das, Veena, Arthur Kleinman, Mamphela Ramphele and Pamela Reynolds (eds), *Violence and Subjectivity* (University of California Press, 2000).

Dautbegović-Bošnjaković, Sunita, 'Zaboravljena Dimenzija Ratu u BiH – Vojnikinje' [Trans: 'The Forgotten Dimension of War in BiH – Women Soldiers'] in Damir Arsenijević and Tobias Flessenkamper, *Kojeg Je Roda Sigurnost?* [Trans: *Which Gender Is Security?*] (Sarajevski Otvoreni Centar, Sarajevo 2013).

de Greiff, Pablo, 'Normative Conceptions of Transitional Justice' in Melissa Williams, Rosemary Nagy and Jon Elster (eds) *Nomos LI* (New York University Press, 2012), 22.

de Greiff, Pablo, 'Theorizing Transitional Justice' in Melissa S. Williams, Rosemary Nagy and Jon Elster (ed.), *Transitional Justice: NOMOS LI* (New York University Press, 2012) 31.

deGuzman, Margaret M., 'Giving Priority to Sex Crime Prosecutions at International Courts: The Philosophical Foundations of a Feminist Agenda' (2011) 11 *International Criminal Law Review* 515.

Dembour, Marie-Bénédicte and Haslam Emily, 'Silencing Hearings? Victim-Witnesses at War Crimes Trials' (2004) 15(1) *European Journal of International Law* 151.

Denzin, Norman K. and Michael D. Giardina (eds), *Qualitative Inquiry and the Politics of Advocacy* (Left Coast Press, 2012).

Diken, Bülent and Carsten Bagge Laustsen, '*Becoming* Abject: *Rape* as a *Weapon* of *War*' (2005) 11(1) *Body & Society* 111.

Dimitrijevic, Nenad, *Duty to Respond: Mass Crime, Denial and Collective Responsibility* (CEU Press, 2011).

Director of Representation of Republike Srpske in Belgrade, Serbia Mlađen Cicović, *Naša ispovjest – žene žrtve rata iz Republike Srpske 1992–1995* [Trans: *Our Confessions – Women Victims of War of the Republic of Serbian 1992–1995*], 8 July 2016, http://predstavnistvorsbg.rs/predstavnistvo_rs/index.php/sr/aktuelnosti/prethodni-dogadjaji/1838-nasa-ispovijest-zene-zrtve-rata-iz-republike-srpske-1992-1995.html.

Djokić, Dragomir, 'Memorandum on War Crimes and Crimes of Genocide Committed Against the Serbian People in the Area of the Former Commune of Odžak by Ustashi-Fundamentalist Paramilitary Formations and Members of the National Guard of the Republic of Croatia, Samac, 21 May 1993,' A Letter to the Secretary-General from Dragomir Djokić, the Chargé d'affaires of the Permanent Mission of Yugoslavia to the United Nations (6 August 1993), UN Doc. A/48/299-S/26261.

Djuric-Kuzmanovic, Tanja, Rada Drezgic and Dubravka Zarkov, 'Gendered War, Gendered Peace: Violent Conflicts in the Balkans and Its Consequences' in Donna Pankhurst (ed.), *Gendered Peace: Women's Struggles for Post-War Justice and Reconciliation* (Routledge, 2007) 265.

D. M., 'RS: Zaštita žena – žrtava ratnog nasilja' [Trans: RS: 'Protection of Women – Victims of War Violence'], *Večernje Novosti*, 16 January 2013.

Dolgopol, Tina, 'The Judgment of the Tokyo Women's Tribunal' (2003) 28(5) *Alternative Law Journal* 242.

Douglas, R. M., *Orderly and Humane: the Expulsion of the Germans after the Second World War* (Yale University Press, 2012).

Drumbl, Mark, 'The Future of International Criminal Law and Transitional Justice' in William A. Schabas, Yvonne McDermott and Niamh Hayes (eds), *Ashgate Research Companion to International Criminal Law: Critical Perspectives* (Ashgate, 2013) 531.

Druliolle, Vincent, 'Recovering Historical Memory: A Struggle Against Silence and Forgetting? The Politics of Victimhood in Spain' (2015) 9(2) *International Journal of Transitional Justice* 316.

Đugum, Aida, 'Ukorijenjena stigmatizacija žrtava ratnog silovanja' [Trans: 'Stigmatization of Victims of Rape'], *Radio Slobodna Evropa*, 4 April 2014, www.slobodnaevropa.org/content/ukorijenjena-stigmatizacija-zrtava-ratnog-silovanja/25321741.html.

Duhacek, Dasa Gordana, 'The Women's Court: A Feminist Approach to In/Justice' (2015) 22(2) *European Journal of Women's Studies* 159.

Đukić, Vida, 'Žene žrtve rata zaboravljene u Srpskoj: Dijaspora za jedno veče vise pomogla od Vlade RS za dve godine' [Trans: 'Women Victims of War Forgotten in Srpska; Diaspora Helped for One Evening More than the Government of RS in Two Years'], *Blic Online*, 18 February 2017, www.blic.rs/vesti/republika-srpska/zene-zrtve-rata-zaboravljene-u-srpskoj-dijaspora-za-jedno-vece-vise-pomogla-od-vlade/4h8zpse.

Džidic, Denis, 'Bosnian Transitional Justice Strategy Hits First Bump', *BalkanInsight* (online), 1 November 2012, www.balkaninsight.com/en/article/bosnian-transitional-justice-strategy-hits-first-bump.

Džidic, Denis, 'Bosnia Struggles with War Crimes Investigation Backlog', *BalkanInsight* (online), 14 October 2014, www.balkaninsight.com/en/article/bosnia-failing-to-reduce-number-of-war-crimes-investigations.

Džidic, Denis, 'Bosniak Soldier Convicted of Wartime Rape', *BalkanInsight* (online), 25 May 2015, www.balkaninsight.com/en/article/ex-bosniak-fighter-sentenced-for-war-time-rape.

Džidic, Denis 'Bosnian Serb Fighter Convicted of Wartime Rape', *Balkan Insight* (online), 29 June 2015, www.balkaninsight.com/en/article/ex-bosnian-serb-fighter-sentenced-for-wartime-rape.

Elster, Jon, *Closing the Books: Transitional Justice in Historical Perspectives* (Cambridge, 2004).

Engle, Karen, 'Feminism and Its (Dis)Contents: Criminalizing Wartime Rape in Bosnia and Herzegovina' (1999) 99 *American Journal of International Law* 778.

Engle, Karen. 'Judging Sex in War' (2008) 106(6) *Michigan Journal of Law* 941.

Enloe, Cynthia, *The Curious Feminist: Searching for Women in New in a New Age of Empire* (University of California Press, 2004).

European Bank for Reconstruction and Development, *Commercial Laws of Bosnia and Herzegovina: An Assessment by the EBRD*, Report (2014), www.ebrd.com/downloads/legal/concessions/pppreport.pdf.

European Commission, *Bosnia and Herzegovina Progress Report* (2014), https://ec.europa.eu/neighbourhood-enlargement/sites/near/files/pdf/key_documents/2014/20141008-bosnia-and-herzegovina-progress-report_en.pdf.

Estrich, Susan, *Real Rape* (Harvard University Law Press, 1987).

Fallada, Hans, *Alone in Berlin* (Penguin Books, 2010).

Farr, Vanessa, Wendy Cukier, Zoë Bakoko Bakoru, Jane Sanyu Mpagi, Amani El Jack, Ruth Ojambo Ochieng, Olive C. Kobusingye and Kiflemariam Gebre-Wold, *Gender Perspectives on Small Arms and Light Weapons: Regional and International Concerns*, Bonn International Center for Conversion (2002), www.bicc.de/publications/publicationpage/publication/gender-perspectives-on-small-arms-and-light-weapons-regional-and-international-concerns-128/.

Farwell, Nancy, 'War Rape: New Conceptualizations and Responses' (2004) 49(4) *Affilia* 389.

Ferguson, Kate, 'Masking Genocide in Bosnia' in Cathie Carmichael and Richard Maguire (eds), *The Routledge History of Genocide* (Routledge, 2015) 309.

Finlay, Linda, 'Negotiating the Swamp: The Opportunity and Challenge of Reflexivity in Research Practice' (2002) 2(2) *Qualitative Research* 209.

Foreign and Commonwealth Office, 'Foreign Secretary Announces UK Initiative on Preventing Sexual Violence in Conflict' (Announcement, 29 May 2012), www.gov.uk/government/news/foreign-secretary-announces-uk-initiative-on-preventing-sexual-violence-in-conflict.

Foss, Karen A. and Sonja K. Foss, 'Personal Experience as Evidence in Feminist Scholarship' (1994) 58 *Western Journal of Communication* 39.

Franke, Katherine M., 'Gendered Subjects of Transitional Justice' (2006) 15 *Columbia Journal of Gender and Law* 813.

Fraser, Nancy, 'Rethinking the Public Sphere: A Contribution to the Critique of Actually Existing Democracy' (1990) 25 *Social Text* 56.

Fraser, Nancy, 'Reframing Justice in Globalizing World' in Held David and Ayse Kaya (eds), *Global Inequality: Patterns and Explanations* (Polity Press, 2007) 252.

Fraser, Nancy, 'Rethinking Recognition' in Hans-Christoph Schmidt am Busch and Christopher F. Zurn (eds), *The Philosophy of Recognition: Historical and Contemporary Perspectives* (Lanham, 2010) 211.

Frye, Marilyn, *The Politics of Reality: Essays in Feminist Theory* (Crossing Press, 1983).

Gättens, Marie-Luise, 'Helke Sander's *Liberators Take Liberties* and the Politics of History' in Ingeborg Majer O'Sickey and Ingeborg von Zadow (eds), *Triangulated Visions: Women in Recent German Cinema* (State University of New York Press, 1998) 261.

Gebhardt, Miriam, *Crimes Unspoken: The Rape of German Women at the End of the Second World War* (Polity, 2016).

Geneva Convention Relative to the Protection of Civilian Persons in Time of War (75 U.N.T.S. 287) (entered into force 21 October 1950).

Gender Center, 'Informacija o nalazima i preporukama studije o položaju srpskih žena žrtava ratnog zlocina seksualnog nasilja u Bosni i Hercegovini' [Trans: 'Information on the Findings and Recommendations of the Study on the Situation of Serbian Women Victims of War Crimes of Sexual Violence in Bosnia and Herzgovina'] *Republika Srpska, Vlada, Gender Centar – Centar za jednakost i Ravnorpavnost Polova* (2015), www.vladars.net/sr-SP-Cyrl/Vlada/centri/gendercentarrs/Documents/Informacija%20%20latinica_204855676.pdf.

Global Justice Center, 'Ending Impunity for Widespread and Systematic Use of Sexual Violence in Columbia's Ongoing Armed Conflict' on *Global Justice Center Blog* (9 December 2013), http://globaljusticecenter.net/blog/405-ending-impunity-for-widespread-and-systematic-use-of-sexual-violence-in-colombia-s-ongoing-armed-conflict.

Goldstein, Ivo, *Croatia: A History* (McGill-Queen's Press, 1999).

Gregson, Kendra G., *Veterans' Programs in Bosnia-Herzegovina*, European Stability Initiative (ESI) (2000), www.esiweb.org/pdf/bridges/bosnia/WB-KGregsonVeterans.pdf.

Grossmann, Atina, *Jews, Germans, and Allies: Close Encounters in Occupied Germany* (Princeton University Press, 2007).

Gutman, Roy, 'Foreword' in Alexandra Stiglmayer (ed.), *Mass Rape: The War Against Women in Bosnia-Herzegovina* (University of Nebraska Press, 1994) ix.

Haddad, Heidi Nichols, 'Mobilizing the Will to Prosecute: Crimes of Rape at the Yugoslav and Rwandan Tribunals' (2011) 12 *Human Rights Review* 109.

Hadžiahmić, Lejla, 'Women-Combatants in Defense of Sarajevo: Agents or Victims' (2011) 6(19) WBSO.

Haldemann, Frank, 'Another Kind of Justice: Transitional Justice as Recognition' (2008) 41(3) *Cornell International Law Journal* 675.

Hamber, Brandon and Ingrid Palmary, 'Gender, Memorialization, and Symbolic Reparations' in Ruth Rubio-Marin (ed.), *The Gender of Reparations: Unsettling Sexual Hierarchies While Redressing Human Rights Violations* (Cambridge University Press, 2009) 324.

Hammett, Daniel, Chasca Twyman and Mark Graham, *Research and Fieldwork in Development* (Routledge, 2015).

Hankel, Gerd, 'On Victims and Non-Victims: Observations from Rwanda' in Throsten Bonacker and Christoph Safferling (eds), *Victims of International Crimes: And Interdisciplinary Discourse* (Asser Press, 2013) 29.

Hansen, Lene, 'Gender, Nation, Rape: Bosnia and the Construction of Security' *International Feminist Journal of Politics* 3(1) 2000, 56.

Harbour, Grace, 'International Concern Regarding Conflict-Related Sexual Violence in the Lead-Up to the ICTY's Establishment' in Baron Serge Brammertz and Michelle Jarvis (eds), *Prosecuting Conflict-Related Sexual Violence at the ICTY* (Oxford University Press, 2016) 19.

Harbour, Grace, *Speak and Be Heard: APWLD Guide to Women's Tribunals* (2016), http://apwld.org/apwld-launches-speak-and-be-heard-apwld-guide-to-womens-tribunals/.

Hartman, Geoffrey, 'Memory, Com: Tele-Suffering and Testimony in the Dot Com Era' (2000) 19(3) *Raritan* 1.

Hayner, Priscilla B., 'Introduction: In Pursuit of Justice and Reconciliation: Contributions of Truth Telling' in Priscilla B. Hayner (ed.), *Unspeakable Truths: Facing the Challenge of Truth Commissions* (Routledge, 2010) 1.

Healey, Sharon A., 'Prosecuting Rape Under the Statute of the War Crimes Tribunals for the Former Yugoslavia' (1995) 21(2) *Brook Journal of International Law* 327.

Hedges, Chris, 'Croatian's Confession Describes Torture and Killing on Vast Scale', *New York Times* (online), 5 September 1997, www.nytimes.com/1997/09/05/world/croatian-s-confession-describes-torture-and-killing-on-vast-scale.html.

Helm, Sarah, *Forced Abortions and Medical Experiments: Last Survivors of Nazi Women's Camp Tell Their Horror Stories*, www.dw.com/en/forced-abortions-and-medical-experiments-last-survivors-of-nazi-womens-camp-tell-their-horror-stories/a-18997838.

Helms, Elisa, 'The Gender of Coffee: Women, Refugee Return, and Reconciliation Initiatives after the Bosnian War' (2007) 7(57) *Focaal – European Journal of Anthropology* 17.

Helms, Elissa, *Innocence and Victimhood: Gender, Nation, and Women's Activism in Postwar Bosnia-Herzegovina* (University of Wisconsin Press, 2013).

Henry, Marsha Giselle, '"Where Are You Really From": Representations, Identity and Power in the Fieldwork Experiences of a South Asian Diasporic' (2003) 3(2) *Qualitative Research* 229.

Henry, Nicola, 'Witness to Rape: The Limits and Potential of International War Crimes Trials for Victims of Wartime Sexual Violence' (2009) 3(1) *International Journal of Transitional Justice* 114.

Henry, Nicola, *War and Rape: Law, Memory and Justice* (Routledge, 2011).

Henry, Nicola, 'The Fixation on Wartime Rape: Feminist Critique and International Criminal Law' (2014) 23(1) *Social & Legal Studies* 93.

Henry, Nicola, 'Civil Society and Gender-Based Violence: Expanding the Horizons of Transitional Justice' (2016) 42(1) *Australian Feminist Law Journal* 119.

Henry, Nicola, 'Theorizing Rape: Deconstructing Gender, Sexuality and Violence' (2016) 30(1) *Gender and Society* 44.

Hirsch, Susan, 'The Victim Deserving Global Justice: Power, Caution, and Recovering Individuals' in Kamari Maxine Clarke and Mark Goodale (eds), *Mirrors of Justice: Law and Power in the Post Cold* (Cambridge University Press, 2010) 149.

Holá, Barbora and Joris van Wijk, 'Life After Conviction at International Criminal Tribunals: An Empirical Overview' (2014) 12(1) *Journal of International Criminal Justice* 109.

Hoque, Mofidul (ed.), *Colloquium on Accountability of Sexual Violence Crimes and Experiences of the International Tribunals* (Dhaka Liberation War Museum, 2012).

Houssaye, Henry, *1815: La seconde abdication-la terreur blanche* [Trans: *1815: The Second Abdication – The White Terror*] (Perrin, 1906).

Hovil, Lucy and Chrispus Okello, 'Editorial Note' (2011) 5(3) *International Journal of Transitional Justice* 333.

Hronešová, Jessie, 'Might Makes Right: War-Related Payments in Bosnia and Herzegovina' (2016) 10(3) *Journal of Intervention and Statebuilding* 339.

Hughes, Donna M., Lepa Mladjenovic and Zorica Mrsevic, 'Feminist Resistance in Serbia' (1994) 2(4) *European Journal of Women's Studies* 509.

Human Rights Watch, *The Human Rights Watch Global Report on Women's Human Rights*, Report, Human Rights Watch (1995), www.hrw.org/sites/default/files/reports/general958.pdf.

Hunt, Swanee, *Worlds Apart: Bosnian Lessons for Global Security* (Duke University Press, 2011).

Husić, Sabiha, *'Women Victims of War': Annex to the Shadow Report on the Implementation of the CEDAW Convention and on Women's Human Rights in Bosnia and Herzegovina* (2013), www.ecoi.net/file_upload/1930_1375090959_jointngosubmission-forthe-session-bih-cedaw55.pdf.

Huyse, Luc, 'Victims' in David Bloomfield, Theresa Barnes and Luc Hayes (eds), *Reconciliation After Violent Conflict: A Handbook* (International Institute for Democracy and Electoral Assistance, 2013) 54.

Inicijativa Ženski Mirovni Aktivizam, 'Otvoreno pismo Narodnoj *Skupštini* Republike Srpske povodom rasprave o Informaciji o nalazima i preporukama studije o polozaju srspkih zena zrtava ratnog zlocina seksualnog nasilja u BiH' [Trans: 'Open Letter to the People's Assembly of the Republic of Serbian on the Occasion of the Debate on the Information on the Findings and Recommendations of the Study on the Situation of Srpskih Women Victims of War Crimes of Sexual Violence in Bosnia and Herzegovina'] *Women Organising for Change*, 24 April 2015, http://womenorganizingforchange.org/izjave/otvoreno-pismo-narodnoj-skupstini-republike-srpske-povodom-rasprave-ns-rs-o-informaciji-o-nalazima-i-preporukama-studije-o-polozaju-srpskih-zena-zrtava-ratnog-zlocina-seksualnog-nasilja-u-bih/.

Institute of Development Studies (IDS), *Participation* (n.d.), www.ids.ac.uk/ids/particip.

Instructions on the Procedure for Recognition of the Status of Civilian Victims of War, *Official Gazette of BiH*, No. 62/06.

International Centre for Transitional Justice, Submission to the Universal Periodic Review of the UN Human Rights Council, Seventh Session, ICTJ (2009), www.ictj.org/publication-type/un-universal-periodic-review-submission.

International Covenant on Civil and Political Rights, open for signature 16 December 1966, General Assembly Resolution 220A (XXI) (entered into force 23 March 1976).

International Covenant on Economic, Social and Cultural Rights, opened for signature 16 December 1966, 993 UNTS 3 (entered into force 3 January 1976).

Irwin, Rachel and Velma Šarić, *Poor Protection for Balkan Trial Witnesses (Special Report, Institute for War and Peace Reporting)* (2012), https://iwpr.net/global-voices/poor-protection-balkan-trial-witnesses.

Ivkovich, Sanja Kutnjak, *Reclaiming Justice: The International Tribunal for the Former Yugoslavia and Local Courts* (Oxford University Press, 2011).

Ivkovich, Sanja Kutnjak and John Hagan, *Reclaiming Justice: The International Tribunal for the Former Yugoslavia and Local Courts* (Oxford University Press, 2011).

IWPR ICTY, 'Delic Rape Charge Dropped' *Institute for War & Peace Reporting*, 29 February 2008, https://iwpr.net/global-voices/delic-rape-charge-dropped.

Jacobs, Ingeborg, *Freiwild*: Das Schicksal deutscher Frauen 1945 [Trans: *The Destiny of German Women in 1945*] (Taschenbuch, 2009).

Jahić, Amer, 'Upitna *odštete žrtvama silovanja u BiH*' [Trans: *Questionable Payment for Compensation to Victims of Rape in Bosnia and Herzegovina*], *BalkanInsight* (online), 14 August 2015, www.balkaninsight.com/en/article/upitna-naplata-od%C5%A1tete-%C5%BErtvama-silovanja-u-bih-08-13-2015.

Jakala, Michaelina, *Wartime Rape: War's Worst Experience? A Feminist Grounded Theory Study of Female Non-Raped and Wartime Rape Survivors in Sarajevo, Bosnia and Herzegovina* (Unpublished Doctoral Dissertation, University of Bradford, 2010).

JanMohamed, Abdul, 'Between Speaking and Dying: Some Imperative in Emergence of the Subaltern in the Context of U.S. Slavery' in Rosalind Morris (ed.), *Can the Subaltern Speak? Reflections on the History of an Idea* (Columbia University Press, 2010) 139.

Jansen, Henrica A. F. M., 'Swimming Against the Tide: Lessons from Field Research on Violence Against Women in the Solomon Islands and Kiribati' (United Nations Population Fund Report, 2010).

Jarvis, Michelle and Kate Vigneswaran, 'Challenges to Successful Outcomes in Sexual Violent Cases' in Serge Brammertz and Michelle Jarvis (eds), *Prosecuting Conflict-Related Sexual Violence at the ICTY* (Oxford University Press, 2016) 33.

Jeffery, Laura and Matei Candea, '"Introduction" in "The Politics of Victimhood"' (2006) 17(4) *History and Anthropology* 289.

Jeffreys, Sheila, *The Industrial Vagina: The Political Economy of the Global Sex Trade* (Routledge, 2009).

Johnson, Sheila K., 'Helke Sander's *BeFreier und BeFreite: Krieg, Vergewaltigung, Kinder* and Postmodernism' (1993) 28(1) *Pacific Coast Philology* 81.

Johnstone, Diana, 'Seeing Yugoslavia Through a Dark Glass' (1998) Fall *Covert Action Quarterly* 9.

Jones, Briony, Alex Jeffrey and Michaelina Jakala, 'The "Transitional Citizen": Civil Society, Political Agency and Hopes for Transitional Justice in Bosnia-Herzegovina' in Olivera Simić and Zala Volčič (eds), *Transitional Justice and Civil Society in the Balkans* (Springer, 2013), 87.

Jonjić, Dobrica, Ministry of Social Policy of the Federation of BiH, the Workshop on Reparations for Victims of Conflict Related Sexual Violence (Sarajevo, 9–10 June 2016)

Juncos, Ana E., *EU Foreign and Security Policy in Bosnia: The Politics of Coherence and Effectiveness* (Manchester University Press, 2013).

Justice Report, 'Bosnian War Crimes Strategy 'Failing', *BalkanInsight* (online), 29 January 2016, www.balkaninsight.com/en/article/bosnia-drowning-in-war-crimes-backlog-01-29-2016?utm_source=Balkan+Transitional+Justice+Daily+Newsletter+-+NEW&utm_campaign=cfbd6cb52c-RSS_EMAIL_CAMPAIGN&utm_medium=email&utm_term=0_a1d9e93e97-cfbd6cb52c-319752573.

Justice Report, 'Bosnian War Rape Victims Struggle for Compensation', *Balkan Insight* (online), 9 September 2016, www.balkaninsight.com/en/article/bosnian-war-rape-victims-struggle-for-compensation-09-09-2016.

Kaknjo, Vesna, 'Glavna Tužiteljica' [Trans: 'General Prosecutor'], www.nasarijec.ba/index.php?option=com_content&view=article&id=2162:vesna-kaknjo-glavna-tuiteljica-kantonalnog-tuilatva-zenica&catid=69:interview&Itemid=86.

Kaldor, Mary, *New and Old Wars* (Polity Press, 2012).

Kamusella, Tomasz, *The Politics of Language and Nationalism in Modern Central Europe* (Palgrave Macmillan, 2009).

Kapur, Ratna, '*The Tragedy of Victimization* Rhetoric: Resurrecting the "Native" Subject in International/Postcolonial Feminist Legal Politics' (2002) 15(1) *Harvard Human Rights Law Journal* 1.

Karabegović, Dženana, 'Silovane žene i muškarci žrtve i stigmi u društvu' [Trans: 'Raped Women and Men Victims and Stigma in Society'], *Radio Slobodna Evropa* (online), 19 April 2016, www.slobodnaevropa.org/a/silovane-zene-i-muskarci-zrtve-i-stigmi-u-drustvu/27683892.html.

Kareta Feminist Group, International Initiative of Women of Bosnia-Hercegovina, Bosnia-Hercegovina Refugee Women's Group and Bedem Ljubavi Women's Group, 'Serbia's War Against Bosnia and Croatia' (1993) 23(5) *Off Our Backs* 1–15.

Karstedt, Susanne, 'The Life Course of Collective Memories: Persistency and Change in West Germany Between 1950 and 1970' (2009) 1(165) *Polish Sociological Review* 2009.

Karstedt, Susanne, 'From Absence to Presence, from Silence to Voice: Victims in International and Transitional Justice since the Nuremberg Trials' (2010) 17(1) *International Review of Victimology*.

Katavić, Ivan, 'BiH: Ko koči usvajanje zakona o pravima žrtava torture' [Trans: 'BiH: Who Hinders the Adoption of the Law on the Rights of Victims of Torture'], *Radio Slobodna Evropa* (online), 26 May 2013, www.slobodnaevropa.org/content/bih-ko-koci-usvajanje-zakona-o-pravima-zrtava-torture/24996602.html.

Kelly, Liz, 'Wars Against Women: Sexual Violence, Sexual Politics and the Militarised State', in Susie Jacobs, Ruth Jacobson and Jennifer Marchbank (eds), *States of Conflict: Gender, Violence and Resistance* (Zed Books, 2000) 45.

Kelly, Michael J., 'Definition of Victims' in Thorsten Bonacker and Christoph Safferling (ed.), *Victims of International Crimes: An Interdisciplinary Discourse* (Springer, 2013) 47.

Kelsall, Michelle Staggs and Shanee Stepakoff, '"When We Wanted to Talk About Rape": Silencing Sexual Violence at the Special Court for Sierra Leone' 2007 1(3) *International Journal of Transitional Justice* 355.

Kendall, Sara, 'Archiving Victimhood: Practice of Inscription in International Criminal Law' in Stewart Motha and Honni van Rijswijk (eds), *Law, Memory, Violence: Uncovering the Counter-Archive* (Routledge, 2016).

Kent, Lia, 'Local Memory Practices in East Timor: Disrupting Transitional Justice Narratives' (2011) 5(3) *International Journal of Transitional Justice* 434.

Kent, Lia, 'After the Truth Commission: Gender and Citizenship in Timor Leste' (2016) 17(1) *Human Rights Review* 51.

Kerr, Rachel, 'Peace Through Justice?' The International Criminal Tribunal for Former Yugoslavia' (2007) 7(3) *Southeast European and Black Sea Studies* 373.

Kerr, Rachel, 'Lost in Translation? Perceptions of the ICTY in the Former Yugoslavia' in James Gow, Zoran Pajič and Rachel Kerr (eds), *Prosecuting War Crimes: Lessons and Legacies of the International Criminal Tribunal for the Former Yugoslavia* (Routledge, 2013) 103.

Kesić, Vesna, 'A Response to Catherine MacKinnon's Article "Turning Rape into Pornography: Postmodern Genocide"' (1994) 5 *Hastings Women's Law Journal* 276.

Kesić, Vesna, 'From Reverence to Rape: An Anthropology of Ethnic and Genderized Violence', in Marguerite R. Waller and Jennifer Rycenga (eds), *Frontline Feminisms: Women, War, and Resistance* (Routledge, 2001) 25.

Kesić, Vesna, 'Muslim Women, Croatian Women, Serbian Women, Albanian Women', *Eurozine* (online), 5 September 2003, www.eurozine.com/articles/2003-05-09-kesic-en.html.

Kirchhoff, Johanna and Sabina Čehajić-Clancy, 'Intergroup Apologies: Does It Matter What They Say? Experimental Analysis' (2014) 20(4) *Peace and Conflict: Journal of Peace Psychology* 430.

Kitchin, Rob and Nick J. Tate, *Conducting Research in Human Geography: Theory, Methodology and Practice* (Routledge, 1999).

Knežević, Boris, 'Stravični zločini nad Srbima: devojčica dozivala mamu dok su je silovali muslimanski vojnici' [Trans: 'Terrible Crimes Against Serbs: A Girl Called Her Mother While She Was Raped By Bosniak Soldiers'], *Večernje Novosti*, 15 July 2016, www.blic.rs/vesti/republika-srpska/stravicni-zlocini-nad-srbima-devojcica-dozivala-mamu-dok-su-je-muslimanski-vojnici/sppgmzy.

Kohn, Elizabeth A, 'Rape as a Weapon of War: Women's Human Rights During the Dissolution of Yugoslavia' (1994) 24 *Golden Gate University Law Review* 199

Korac, Maja, 'Representation of Mass Rape in Ethnic Conflicts in What Was Yugoslavia' (1994) 36(4) *Sociologija* 495.

Korjenic, Selma, 'Preventing Sexual Violence in Conflict' on *Prevent Sexual Violence in Conflict* (12 April 2012), http://preventsexualviolenceinconflict.tumblr.com/post/37183224957/bosnia-trial.

Kreso, Meddzida, '(Ne)jednakost pred zakonom' [Trans: '(In)equality Before the Law'] (2006) 5 *Pravda u tranziciji*.

Kristeva, Julia, 'Women's Time' in Toril Moi (ed.), *The Kristeva Reader* (Basil Blackwell, 1986) 187.

Kureljušić, Srđan, 'Visestruka silovanja u Posavskoj Mahali' [Trans: 'Multiple Rape in Posavina Mahala'], *Justice Report* (online), 6 April 2016, www.justice-report.com/bh/sadr%C5%BEaj-%C4%8Dlanci/prije-optu%C5%BEenog-je-silovala-jo%C5%A1-%C4%8Detvorica.

Law on Basic Social Protection, Protection of Civilian Victims of War and Protection of Families with Children, *Official Gazette of the Federation Bosnia and Herzegovina*, Nos 36/99, 54/04, 39/06 and 14/09.

Law on Changes and Amendments to the Law on Basis of Welfare, Care for Civilian War Victims, Care for Families with Children, *Official Gazette of Federation of Bosnia and Herzegovina*, No. 39/06.

Law on the Prosecutor's Office of Bosnia and Herzegovina, *Official Gazette of Bosnia and Herzegovina*, Nos 24/02, 3/03, 37/03, 42/03, 9/04, 35/04, 61/04, https://advokat-prnjavorac.com/legislation/Law-on-The-Prosecutors-Office-of-BH.pdf.

Law on the Protection of Civilian War Victims, *Official Gazette of the Republika Srpska*, Nos 25/93, 1/94, 32/94, 37/07 and 60/07).

Law on Rights of Veterans, Disabled Veterans and Families of Killed Veterans of the Defence and Homeland War of Republika Srpska, *Official Gazette of the Republika Srpska*, Nos 46/04 and 53/04.

Lawry-White, Merryl, 'The Reparative Effect of Truth Seeking in Transitional Justice' (2015) 64(1) *International and Comparative Law Quarterly* 141.

Lee, Raymond M. and Claire M. Renzetti, 'The Problems of Researching Sensitive Topics: An Overview and Introduction' (1990) 33(5) *American Behavioral Scientist* 510.

The Lieber Code of April 24, 1863.

Lindgren, Magnus and Vesna Nikolić-Ristanović, 'Crime Victims: International and Serbian Perspective', *OSCE Report*, 2011, www.osce.org/serbia/85268?download=true.

Lloyd, Betty-Ann, Frances Ennis and Tannis Atkinson, *The Power of Woman-Positive Literacy Work: Program-Based Action Research* (Fernwood, 1994).

Luban, David, 'A Theory of Crimes Against Humanity' (2004) 29 *Yale Journal of International Law* 85.

Lucas, Marieme Helie, 'Bosna-Sarajevo: Ženski sud u bivšoj Jugoslaviji' [Trans: 'Bosnia-Sarajevo: Women's Court in the Former Yugoslavia'] (2015), www.zenskisud.org/pdf/Marieme_Helie_Lucas_bhs.pdf.

Lugones, Maria C. and Elizabeth V. Spelman, 'Have We Got a Theory for You! Feminist theory, Cultural Imperialism and the Demand For "The Women's Voice"' in Susan Archer Mann and Ashly Suzanne Patterson (eds), *Reading Feminist Theory: From Modernity to Postmodernity* (Oxford University Press, 2016) 23.

Luka, Banja, 'Forminaran sekcija zena zrtava torture isilovanja' [Trans: 'Formed Section of Women Victims of Torture and Rape'], *SRNA*, 16 January 2013, www.srna.rs/novosti1/70486/formirana-sekcija-zena-zrtava-torture-i-silovanja-.htm.

Lundy, Patricia and Mark McGovern, 'Whose Justice? Rethinking Transitional Justice from the Bottom Up' (2008) 35(2) *Journal of Law and Society* 265.

Lunn, Jenny (ed.), *Fieldwork in the Global South: Ethical Challenges and Dilemmas* (Routledge, 2014).

Lykes, Brinton and Alison Crosby, 'Creative Methodologies as a Resource for Mayan Women's Protagonism' in Brendon Hamber and Gallagher Elizabeth (eds), *Psychosocial Perspectives on Peacebuilding* (Springer, 2014) 147.

McAuliffe, Padraig, *Transformative Transitional Justice and the Malleability of Post-Conflict States* (Edward Elgar, 2017).

McCormick, Richard W., 'Rape and War, Gender and Nation, Victims and Victimizers: Helke Sander's *BeFreier und Befreite*' (2001) 16(1) *Camera Obscura* 99.

McEvoy, Kieran and Kirsten McConnachie, 'Victimology in Transitional Justice: Victimhood, Innocence and Hierarchy' (2012) 9(5), *European Journal of Criminology* 527.

McEvoy, Kieran and Kirsten McConnachie, 'Victims and Transitional Justice: Voice, Agency and Blame' (2013) 22(4) *Social & Legal Studies* 489.

McKay, Susan, 'Gender Justice and Reconciliation' (2000) 23(5) *Women's Studies International Forum* 561.

Mackenzie, Megan, 'Securitizing Sex? Towards a Theory of the Utility of Wartime Sexual Violence' 12 (2010) *International Feminist Journal of Politics* 202–220.

MacKinnon, Catharine 'Turning Rape into Pornography: Postmodern Genocide' (1993) IV(1) *Ms Magazine* 24.

MacKinnon, Catharine 'Rape, Genocide and Women's Human Rights' in Alexandra Stiglmayer (ed.), *Mass Rapes Against Women in Bosnia-Herzegovina* (University of Nebraska Press, 1994) 183.

MacKinnon, Catharine A., 'War, Genocide and Women's Human Rights' (1994) 17 *Harvard Women's Law Journal* 5.

MacKinnon, Catharine A., *Are Women Human?: And Other International Dialogues* (Belknap Press, 2007).

McMahon, Patrice and Jennifer Miller, 'On a Wing and a Prayer: The Effect of the ICTY on the Balkans' (Paper presented at the Annual Meeting of the Midwest Political Association 67th Annual National Conference, The Palmer House Hilton, Chicago, IL, 2 April 2009).

Marcus, Sharon, 'Fighting Bodies, Fighting Words: A Theory and Politics of Rape Prevention' in Judith Butler (ed.), *Feminists Theorize the Political* (Routledge, 1992) 385.

Markham, David, *The Road to St Helena: Napoleon after Waterloo* (Pen & Sword, 2008).

Matić, Milovan, '"Bolji" dio BiH pred bankrotom: Godina u RS počinje slavlje, a završava ekonomskim krahom?' [Trans: '"Better" Part of BiH from Bankruptcy: Year of the RS Begins Celebration and Ending the Economic Collapse?'], *BUKA* (online), 8 January 2016, www.6yka.com/novost/96978/bolji-dio-bih-pred-bankrotom-godina-u-rs-pocinje-slavljem-a-zavrsava-ekonomskim-krahom.

Maunaga, Goran, 'Edib Buljubašić: Repak mi dao 1.000 maraka za ubistvo' [Trans: 'Edib Buljubašić: Repak Gave Me 1,000 Marks for Murder'], *Vijesti Dana*, 14 September 2008, www.glassrpske.com/novosti/vijesti_dana/Edib-Buljubasic-Repak-mi-dao-1000-maraka-za-ubistvo/lat/11352.html.

Medica Zenica and Medica Mondiale, '*We Are Still Alive': Research on the Long-Term Consequences of War Rape and Copying Strategies of Survivors in Bosnia and Herzegovina*, Report (2014), www.medicamondiale.org/fileadmin/redaktion/5_Service/Mediathek/Dokumente/English/Documentations_studies/141128_Research_We-Are-Still-Alive_CR-Medica-Zenica_medica-mondiale.pdf.

Melrose, Margaret, 'Labor Pains: Some Considerations on the Difficulties Researching Juvenile Prostitution' (2002) 5(4) *International Journal of Social Research and Methodology, Theory and Practice* 331.

Meznaric, Silva, 'Gender as Ethno-Marker: Rape, War and Identity in the Former Yugoslavia' in Valentine M Moghadam (ed.), *Identity Politics and Women: Cultural Reassertion and Feminisms in International Perspectives* (Westview Press, 1994) 76

Mibenge, Chiseche Salome, *Sex and International Tribunals: The Erasure of Gender from the War Narrative* (University of Pennsylvania Press, 2013).

Milanović, Marko, 'The Impact of the ICTY on the Former Yugoslavia: An Anticipatory Post-Mortem' (2016) 110(2) *American Journal of International Law* 233.

Miller, Nick, *The Nonconformists: Culture, Politics, and Nationalism in a Serbian Intellectual Circle, 1994–1991* (Central European University Press, 2007).

Ministry of Justice, *Strategija tranzicijske pravde u Bosni i Hercegovini 2012–2016* [Trans: *Draft Strategy of Transitional Justice in Bosnia and Herzegovina 2012–2016*], www.mpr.gov.ba/aktuelnosti/propisi/konsultacije/Strategija%20TP%20-%20bosanski%20jezik%20fin%20doc.pdf.

Ministry of Justice, *The BiH Law on Free Legal Aid was Adopted in November 2016*, Official Gazette, 4 November 2016, www.mpr.gov.ba/biblioteka/zakoni/default.aspx?id=5655&langTag=en-.

Minow, Martha, 'The Hope for Healing: What the Truth Commissions Can Do?' in Robert I. Rotberg and Dennis Thompson (eds), *Truth v. Justice the Morality of Truth Commissions* (Princeton University Press, 2010) 235.

Mirjana dokumentarni film [Trans: *Mirjana Documentary Film*] 7 December 2011, www.youtube.com/watch?v=A4sirVibWkI.

Mischowski, Gabriela and Gorana Mlinarevic, '. . . *And That It Does Not Happen to Anyone Anywhere In The World': The Trouble with Rape Trials – Views of Witnesses, Prosecutors and Judges on Prosecuting Sexualised Violence During the War in the former Yugoslavia*, Report, Medica Mondiale (2009), www.medicamondiale.org/fileadmin/redaktion/5_Service/Mediathek/Dokumente/English/Documentations_studies/medica_mondiale_and_that_it_does_not_happen_to_anyone_anywhere_in_the_world_english_complete_version_dec_2009.pdf.

Miškovska Kajevska, Ana, *Taking a Stand in Times of Violent Societal Changes: Belgrade and Zagreb Feminists' Positionings on the (Post-)Yugoslav Wars and Each Other (1991–2000)* (PhD Thesis, University of Amsterdam, 2014).

Miškovska Kajevska, Ana, *Feminist Activism at War: Belgrade and Zagreb Feminists in the 1990s* (Routledge, 2017).

Misztal, Barbara, *Theories of Social Remembering* (McGraw-Hill Education, 2003).

Mitchell, David S., 'The Prohibition of Rape in International Humanitarian Law as a Norm of Jus Cogens: Clarifying the Doctrine' (2005) 15 *Duke Journal of Comparative & International Law* 219.

Mladjenovic, Lepa, *Anti-ratni bilten SOS-a* [Trans: *Anti-War SOS Bulletin*] (SOS telefon za žene i decu žrtve nasilja, 1993).

Mladjenovic, Lepa, 'Nacrt za projekta za centar za zene silovane u ratu' [Trans: 'The Draft of Project for the Centre for Women Raped During the War'] *Zene za Zene* (1993) 111.

Mladjenovic, Lepa, 'Beyond War Hierarchies: Belgrade Feminists' Experience Working with Female Survivors of War' in Sara Sharratt and Ellyn Kaschak (eds), *Assault on the Soul: Women in the Former Yugoslavia* (Haworth Press, 1999) 83.

Mlinarević, Gorana, Jakov Čaušević and Jasmina Čaušević, *Prosecution of Wartime Sexualized Violence at the Court of Bosnia and Herzegovina: What Happened to the Interest of Justice? An Analysis and Recommendations of Gender Sensitive Trial Monitoring for Wartime Sexualized Violence Cases in Bosnia and Herzegovina for the Period 23/05/2011–25/05/2012* (Report, Association Alumni of the Centre for Interdisciplinary Postgraduate Studies, 2012), www.civilsocietylibrary.org/CSL/529/Prosecution-of-Wartime-Sexualized-Violence-at-the-Court-of-Bosnia-and-Herzegovina-What-Happened-to-The-Interest-of-Justice.

Mobekk, Eirin, 'Conference Report' in Anja E. Ebnöther and Philipp H. Fluri (eds), *After Intervention: Public Security Management in Post-Conflict Societies: From Intervention to Sustainable Local Ownership* (2005) 377, www.dcaf.ch/content/download/35127/525471/file/complet.pdf.

Moffett, Luke, 'Reparations for "Guilty Victims": Navigating Complex Identities of Victim-Perpetrators in Reparation Mechanisms' (2016) 10(1) *International Journal of Transitional Justice* 146.

Mojzes, Paul, *Balkan Genocides: Holocaust and Ethnic Cleansing in the Twentieth Century* (Rowman & Littlefield, 2011).

Movement of Mothers of Srebrenica and Žepa Encalves (n.d.), http://enklave-srebrenica-zepa.org/english.onama.php.

Mujkić, Asim, *Mi Građani Etnopolisa* [Trans: *We, The Citizens of Ethnopolis*] (Šahinpašić, 2007).

Murphy, Colleen, *The Conceptual Foundations of Transitional Justice* (Cambridge University Press, 2017).

Mutić, Nedin, 'Self and Other in Balkan (Post-) War Cinema' in Pål Kolstø (ed.), *Media Discourse and the Yugoslav Conflicts: Representations of Self and Other* (Routledge, 2016) 215.

Myrttinen, Henri and Megan Daigle, *When Merely Existing Is a Risk; Sexual and Gender Minorities in Conflict, Displacement and Peacebuilding*, Report, International Alert (2017), http://international-alert.org/publications/when-merely-existing-is-a-risk.

Myrttinen, Henri, Lana Khattab and Charbel Maydaa, '"Trust No One: Be Aware of Everyone": Vulnerabilities of LGBTI Refugees in Lebanon' in Jane Freedman, Zeynep Kivilcim, Nurcan Özgür Baklacıoğlu (eds), *A Gendered Approach to the Syrian Refugee Crisis* (Routledge, 2017) 61.

N1 BiH, 'Majke Srebrenice i porodice ubijenih Srba ispred Suda BiH' [Trans: 'Mothers of Srebrenica and the Families of Killed Serbs in Front of the Court'], *Vijesti* (online), 26 January 2016, http://ba.n1info.com/a78994/Vijesti/Vijesti/Majke-Srebrenice-i-porodice-ubijenih-Srba-ispred-Suda-BiH.html.

Nadj, Daniela, *ICTY Wartimes Sexual Violence Jurisprudence and the Surrounding Debate: A Critical Feminist Analysis* (PhD Thesis, University of Westminster, 2011).

Nagy, Rosemary, 'Transitional Justice as Global Project: Critical Reflections' (2008) 29(2) *Third World Quarterly* 275.

Naimark, Norman M., 'The Russians and the Germans: Rape during the War and Post-Soviet Memories' in Raphaelle Branche and Fabrice Virgili (eds), *Rape in Wartime* (Palgrave Macmillan, 2012) 201.

Nakičević, Omer, *Fetva o djeci silovanih žena u Bosni I Herzegovini* [Trans: *Fatwa on Children Born by Raped Women in BiH*] (Glasnik Rijaseta IZ u BiH, 1996).

Naples, Nancy, 'The Outsider Phenomenon' in Carolyn D. Smith and William Kornblum (eds), *In the Field: Reading of the Field Research Experience* (Praeger, 1996) 139.

Naples, Nancy, *Feminism and Method: Ethnography, Discourse Analysis, and Activist Research* (Routledge, 2003).

Naša ispovjest – žene žrtve rata iz Republike Srpske 1992–1995 [Trans: *Our Story – Women Victims of War of the Republic of Serbian 1992–1995*] (Udruženje žena žrtava rata Republike Srpske, Republički Centra za istraživanje rata, ratnih zločina i traženje nestalih lica Republike Srpske i Predstavništva Republike Serbije u Srbiji, 2016).

Ní Aoláin, Fionnuala, 'Advancing Feminist Positioning in the Field of Transitional Justice' (2012) 6(2) *International Journal of Transitional Justice* 205.

Ni Aoláin, Fionnuala, 'Advancing Feminist Analysis of Transitional Justice' in Martha Albertson Fineman and Estelle Zinnstag (eds), *Feminist Perspectives on Transitional Justice: From International and Criminal to Alternative Forms of Justice* (Intersentia, 2013) 43.

Ní Aoláin, Fionnuala, 'Gendered Harms and their Interface with International Criminal Law: Norms, Challenges and Domestication' (2014) 16(4) *International Feminist Journal of Politics* 622.

Niarchos, Catherine N., 'Women, War, and Rape: Challenges Facing The International Tribunal for the Former Yugoslavia' (1995) 17 *Human Rights Quarterly* 649.

Nikolić-Ristanović, Vesna, 'Living Without Democracy and Peace: Violence Against Women in the Former Yugoslavia' (1999) 5(1) *Violence Against Women* 63.

Nikolić-Ristanović, Vesna, 'Sexual Violence' in Vesna Nikolić-Ristanović (ed.), *Women, Violence and War: Wartime Victimization of Refugees in the Balkans* (Central European University Press, 1999) 41.

Nikolić-Ristanović, Vesna, *Women, Violence and War: Wartime Victimization of Refugees in the Balkans* (Central European University Press, 2000).

Ninemsn, 'Jolie Moved to Tears after Meeting Rape Victims', *Nine News* (online), 29 March 2014, www.9news.com.au/entertainment/2014/03/29/09/27/jolie-moved-to-tears-after-meeting-rape-victims.

Nizich, Ivana, 'Violations of the Rules of War by Bosnian Croat and Muslim Forces in Bosnia and Herzegovina' (1994) 5(1) *Hastings Women Law Journal* 25.

Noor, Masi, Nurit Shnabel, Samer Halabi and Arie Nadler, 'When Suffering Begets Suffering the Psychology of Competitive Victimhood Between Adversarial Groups in Violent Conflicts' (2012) 16(4) *Personality and Social Psychology Review* 351.

Norma, Caroline, *Japanese Comfort Women and Sexual Slavery During the China and Pacific Wars* (Bloomsbury, 2016).

Nowen, Sarah M. H., '"As You Set Out for Ithaka": Practical, Epistemological, Ethical, and Existential Questions about Socio-Legal Empirical Research in Conflict' (2014) 27(1) *Leiden Journal of International Law* 227.

Nowrojee, Binaifer and Regan Ralph, 'Justice for Women Victims of Violence: Rwanda After the 1994 Genocide' in Ifi Amadiume and Abdullahi An-Na'im (eds), *The Politics of Memory: Truth, Healing and Social Justice* (Zed Books, 2000) 162.

Obradović-Wochnik, Jelena, 'Revisionism, Denial and Anti-ICTY Discourse in Serbia's Public Sphere: Beyond the "Divided Society" Debate' in James Gow, Rachel Kerr and Zoran Pajic (eds), *Prosecuting War Crimes: Lessons and Legacies of the International Criminal Tribunal for the former Yugoslavia* (Routledge, 2014) 182.

O'Brien, Melanie, '"Don't Kill Them, Let's Choose Them as Wives": The Development of the Crimes of Forced Marriage, Sexual Slavery and Enforced Prostitution in International Criminal Law' (2015) 20(3) *The International Journal of Human Rights* 386.

Official Gazette of the Republika Srpska, Nos 25/93. 32/94, 37/07, 60/07, 111/09 and 118/09.

Omerdić, Muharem 'The Position of the Islamic Community on the Care for Children of Raped Mothers' in Mirsad Tokača (ed.), *Plucked Buds* (Commission on Gathering the Facts on War Crimes in Bosnia and Herzegovina, 2002) 428.

Orentlicher, Diane F., *Shrinking the Space for Denial: The Impact of the ICTY in Serbia*, Report (Open Society Justice Initiative, 2008), www.opensocietyfoundations.org/sites/default/files/serbia_20080501.pdf.

Orford, Anne, 'Commissioning the Truth' (2006) 15(3) *Columbia Journal of Gender and Law* 851.

OSCE, *Accountability for War Crimes* (2012), www.osce.org/bih/108141?download=true.

OSCE, *War Crimes Trials Before the Domestic Courts of Bosnia and Herzegovina: Progress and Obstacles*, Human Rights Department (2005), www.nuhanovicfoundation.org/user/file/2005_osce_report_war_crimes_trials_before_domestic_courts_in_bih.pdf_-_to_be_added%21.pdf.

OSCE, *Combating Impunity for Conflict-Related Sexual Violence in BiH: Progress and Challenges: An Analysis of Criminal Proceedings Before the Court of Bosnia and Herzegovina between 2005 and 2013*, OSCE Mission to Bosnia and Herzegovina (2014), www.files.ethz.ch/isn/179069/English.pdf.

O'Reilly, Maria, 'Peace and Justice through a Feminist Lens: Gender Justice and the Women's Court for the Former Yugoslavia' (2016) 10(3) *Journal of Intervention and State Building* 419.

O'Rourke, Catherine, 'International Law and Domestic Gender Justice, or Why Case Studies Matter' in Martha Albertson Fineman and Estelle Zinnstag (eds), *Feminist Perspectives on Transitional Justice: From International and Criminal to Alternative Forms of Justice* (Intersentia, 2013) 11.

Otto, Dianne, 'Critically Performing Legal Justice People's Tribunals and the Politics of Listening: A Personal Reflection' (2017) 5(2) *London Review of International Law* 225.

Parameswaran, Radhika, 'Feminist Media Ethnography in India: Exploring Power, Gender, and Culture in the Field' (2001) 7(1) *Qualitative Inquiry* 69.

Pavlović, Tatjana, 'Women in Croatia: Feminists, Nationalists and Homosexuals' in Sabrina P. Ramet (ed.), *Gender Politics in Western Balkans: Women and Society in Yugoslavia and the Yugoslav Successor States* (Pennsylvania State University Press, 1999) 131.

The Permanent Peoples' Tribunal, *Crimes Against Humanity in the Former Yugoslavia*, held in Berne, Switzerland, 17–20 February 1995 (Judgment only available in Italian), http://permanentpeoplestribunal.org/23-crimes-against-humanity-in-the-former-yugoslavia-i-bern-17-20-february-1995/?lang=en.

The Permanent Peoples' Tribunal, *Crimes Against Humanity in the Former Yugoslavia II*, held in Barcelona, Spain, 7–11 December 1995 (Judgment only available in Italian), http://permanentpeoplestribunal.org/25-crimes-against-humanity-in-the-former-yugoslavia-ii-barcelona-7-11-december-1995/?lang=en.

Peskin, Victor, 'Beyond Victor's Justice? The Challenge of Prosecuting the Winners at the International Criminal Tribunals for the Former Yugoslavia and Rwanda' (2005) 4 *Journal of Human Rights* 216.

Peskin, Victor, *International Justice in Rwanda and the Balkans: Virtual Trials and the Struggle for State Cooperation* (Cambridge University Press, 2008).

Peskin, Victor, 'Victor's Justice Revisited: Rwandan Patriotic Front Crimes and the Prosecutorial Endgame at the ICTR' in Scott Straus and Lars Waldorf (eds), *Remaking Rwanda: State Building and Human Rights after Mass Violence* (University of Wisconsin Press, 2011) 173.

Pitter, Laura and Alexandra Stiglmayer, 'Will the World Remember? Can the Women Forget?' (1993) 3(5) *Ms. Magazine* 19.

'Pope Urges Bosnian Rape Victims Not to Have Abortions', *Los Angeles Times*, 28 February 1993, http://articles.latimes.com/1993-02-28/news/mn-234_1_bosnian-serbs.

Popić, Linda and Belma Panjeta, *Compensation, Transitional Justice and Conditional International Credit in Bosnia and Herzegovina: Attempts to Reform Governments Payments to Victims and Veterans of the 1992–1995 War*, Royal Norwegian Embassy in Bosnia and Herzegovina and Embassy of Switzerland in Bosnia and Herzegovina (2010), www.norveska.ba/PageFiles/417487/Study_Linda_Popic_english.pdf.

Porter, Elisabeth, 'Women's Truth Narratives: The Power of Compassionate Listening' (2007) 5(2) *Critical Half: Bi-Annual Journal of Women for Women International* 20

Pottier, Johan, 'Escape from Genocide: The Politics of Identity in Rwanda's 1994 Massacres' in Vigdis Broch-Due (ed.) *Violence and Belonging: The Quest for Identity in Post-Colonial Africa* (Routledge, 2005) 195.

Priddy, Alice, 'Tackling Impunity for Sexual Violence' in Annyssa Bellal (ed.), *The War Report: Armed Conflict in 2014* (Oxford University Press, 2015) 678.

Protocol Additional to the Geneva Conventions of 12 August 1949, and Relating to the Protection of Victims of International Armed Conflicts (API), 8 June 1977.

Protocol Additional to the Geneva Conventions of 12 August 1949, and Relating to the Protection of Victims of Non-International Armed Conflicts (APII), 8 June 1977.

Pucanj u dušu [Trans: *Shot in the Soul*] (Directed by Enes Hotic, Exit Media Film, 2015).

Radio Široki Brijeg, 'Furundžija na slobodi' [Trans: 'Furundžija at Large'], *Radio Široki Brijeg* (online), 17 August 2004, www.radiosirokibrijeg.com/arhiv/1394-furundzija-na-slobodi-1394.

Railić, Božica Živković, '*Promocija monografije Naša ispovijest – žene žrtve rata iz Republike Srpske 1992–1995* [Trans: *Promotion of Monograph Our Confession – Women Victims of War from Republika Srpska 1992–1995*], Media center Belgrade, 12. September 2016, www.webtv.rs/play/86914/promocija-monografije-nasa-ispovijest--zene-zrtve-rata-iz-republike-srpske-1992--1995.

Rames, Victoria S, *Healing the Spirit: Reparations for Survivors of Sexual Violence Related to the Armed Conflict in Kosovo*, UN Human Rights Office of the High Commissioner (2013), www.ohchr.org/Documents/Issues/Women/WRGS/PeaceAndSecurity/StudyHealingTheSpirit.pdf.

Ramet, Sabrina, *The Dissolution of Yugoslavia: Competing Narratives of Resentment and Blame* (De Gruyter Oldenbourg, 2007).

Rangelov, Iavor, 'Civil Society and Transitional Justice in the Balkans: Three Models of Interactions' (2015) *Security in Transition*, www.securityintransition.org/publications/civil-society-and-transitional-justice-in-the-balkans-three-models-of-interaction/.

Rauđi Krossinn Islandi, 'ICRC Lecture: Sexual Violence in Armed Conflict and Other Situations of Violence' 10 December 2013, www.youtube.com/watch?v=X4Iv9oMd-FQ.

Raping Serbian Women (Produced and Directed by Tanja Peternek-Aleksić, 1993) 00:55:00 (Video).

Reinharz, Shulamit and Lynn Davidman, *Feminist Methods in Social Research* (Oxford University Press, 1992).

Reis, Chein, 'Ethical, Safety and Methodological Issues Related to the Collection and Use of Data on Sexual Violence in Conflict' in Anne Marie de Brouwe, Charlote Ku, Renee Romkens and Larissa van der Herik (eds), *Sexual Violence as an International Crime: Interdisciplinary Approaches* (Intersentia, 2013) 187.

Rejali, Darius M., 'After Feminist Analyses of Bosnian Violence' (1996) 8 *Peace Review* 365.

Renzetti, Claire M. and Raymond M. Lee (eds), *Researching Sensitive Topics* (Sage, 1993).

Robins, Simon, 'Towards Victim-Centred Transitional Justice: Understanding the Needs of Families of the Disappeared in Postconflict Nepal' (2011) 5(1) *International Journal of Transitional Justice* 75.

Roht-Arriaza, Naomi, 'Foreword' in Hugo van der Merwe, Victoria Baxter and Audrey R. Chapman (eds), *Assessing the Impact of Transitional Justice: Challenges for Empirical Research* (US Institute of Peace, 2009) vii.

Rome Statute of the International Criminal Court (opened for signature 17 July 1998) (2187 UNTS 90) (entered into force 1 July 2002).

Ronen, Yaël, *Prosecutions and Sentencing in the Western Balkans* (with the assistance of Sharon Avital and Oren Tamir), DOMAC (2010), http://en.ru.is/domac/domac-reports/.

Rooney, Eilish, 'Intersentionality: A Feminist Theory for Transitional Justice' in Martha Albertson Fineman and Estelle Zinnstag (eds), *Feminist Perspectives on Transitional Justice: From International and Criminal to Alternative Forms of Justice* (Intersentia, 2013) 89.

Rosland, Sissel, 'Victimhood, Identity, and Agency in the Early Phase of the Troubles in Northern Ireland' (2009) 16(3) *Identities: Global Studies in Culture and Power* 294

Ross, Andrew A. G., *Mixed Emotions: Beyond Fear and Hatred in International Conflict* (University of Chicago Press, 2014).

Roy, Arundhati, 'Brutality Smeared in a Peanut Butter: Why America Must Stop War Now', *Guardian* (online), 23 October 2001, www.theguardian.com/world/2001/oct/23/afghanistan.terrorism8.

RTV Oko, 'Sjećaš li se mene u ropstvu' [Trans: 'Do You Remember Me in Slavery?'], 7 February 2017, www.youtube.com/watch?v=w98DAtuTUYw.

RTV SLON and AdRev, 'Skoro 50.000 žena u BiH silovano u ratu' [Trans: 'Nearly 50,000 Women Raped in Bosnia During the War'], 25 November 2014, www.youtube.com/watch?v=Z1j6fwy8l2c.

Ruff-O'Herne, Jan, 'Fifty Years of Silence: Cry of Raped' in Helen Durham and Tracey Gurd (eds), *Listening to the Silences: Women and War* (Brill Academic Press, 2005) 3.

Russell, Diana E. H. and Nicole Van de Ven, *Crimes Against Women: Proceedings of the International Tribunal* (Femmes Publications, 1976).

Russell-Brown, Sherrie L, 'Rape as an Act of Genocide' (2003) 21 *Berkeley Journal of International Law* 350.

Saidel, Rochelle G., *The Jewish Women of Ravenbrück Concentration Camp* (University of Wisconsin Press, 2006).

Salecl, Renata, 'War Trauma Twenty Years After: From Bosnia to St. Louis' (2016) 28 *Journal of the Centre for Freudian Analysis and Research* 8, 1.

Sander, Helke, 'Prologue' in Alexandra Stiglmayer (ed.), *Mass Rapes Against Bosnian women* (University of Nebraska Press, 1994) xvii.

Sander, Helke and Barbara Johr (eds), *BeFreier und BeFreite: Krieg, Vergewaltigung, Kinder* [Trans: *Liberator and Liberated: War, Rape, Children*] (Taschenbuch, 1995).

Schmidt-Harzbach, Ingrid, 'Eine Woche im April' [Trans: 'One Week In April'] in Helke Sander and Barbara Johr (eds), *BeFreier und BeFreite: Krieg, Vergewaltigung, Kinder* [Trans: *Liberator and Liberated: War, Rape, Children*] (Taschenbuch, 1995) 21.

Seifert, Ruth, 'The Second Front: The Logic of Sexual Violence in War' (1996) 19(1–2) *Women Studies International Forum* 35.

Senjak, Marijana, 'Kontekst: Žene žrtve silovanja u ratu' [Trans: 'Context: Women Victims of Rape in War'], *Al Jazeera Balkans TV*, 25 June 2012, http://balkans.aljazeera.net/video/kontekst-zene-zrtve-silovanja-u-ratu?page=1.

Sense Tribunal, 'Defense Wants Delic Acquitted of Rape Charges', *Sense Tribunal*, 14 February 2008, www.sense-agency.com/icty/defense-wants-delic-acquitted-of-rape-charges.29.html?cat_id=1&news_id=10750.

Seto, Donna, *No Place for a War Baby: The Global Politics of Children Born of Wartime Sexual Violence* (Routledge, 2013).

Shandilya, Krupa, 'Writing/Reading the Subaltern Woman: Narrative Voice and Subaltern Agency in Upamanyu Chatterjee's *English, August*' (2014) 9(3) *Postcolonial Text* 1.

Sharratt, Sara, 'Interview with Elizabeth Odio Benito, Justice of the International Criminal Tribunal for the Former Yugoslavia' in Sara Sharratt and Ellyn Kaschak (eds), *Assault on the Soul: Women in the Former Yugoslavia* (Haworth Press, 1999) 39.

Sharratt, Sara, *Gender, Shame and Sexual Violence: The Voices of Witnesses and Court Members at War Crimes Tribunals* (Routledge, 2011).

Sieber, Joan E. and Barbara Stanley, 'Ethical and Professional Dimensions of Socially Sensitive Research' (1988) 43(1) *American Psychologists* 49.

Sigsworth, Romi and Nahla Valji, 'Continuities of Violence Against Women in South Africa: The Limitations of Transitional Justice' in Susanne Buckley-Zistel and Ruth Stanley (eds), *Gender in Transitional Justice* (Palgrave Macmillan, 2011) 115.

Šimić, Goran, *Suđenja za ratne zločine u Bosni i Hercegovini* [Trans: *War Crimes Trials in Bosnia and Herzegovina*] (Dobra knjiga, 2013).

Šimić, Goran, 'Transitional Justice Strategy for Bosnia and Herzegovina: An Overview', *Peace Direct*, 7 May 2013, www.insightonconflict.org/2013/05/transitional-justice-strategy-bosnia-herzegovina/.

Simić, Olivera, 'Challenging Bosnian Women Identity as Rape Victims, as Unending Victims: The "Other" Sex in Times of War' (2012) 13(4) *Journal of International Women's Studies* 129.

Simić, Olivera, 'But I Want to Speak Out: Making Art From Women's Testimonies' (2014) 40(1) *Australian Feminist Law Journal* 51.

Simić, Olivera, *Surviving Peace* (Spinifex Press, 2014).

Simić, Olivera, 'Wartime Rape and its Shunned Victims' in Amy E. Randall (ed.), *Genocide and Gender in the Twentieth Century: A Comparative Survey* (Bloomsbury, 2015) 237.

Simić, Olivera, '"Doing the Research I Do Has Left Scars": Challenges of Researching in the Transitional Justice Field' (2018 forthcoming) 1(5) *Transitional Justice Review.*

Simić, Olivera, 'Drinking Coffee in Bosnia: Listening to Stories of Wartime Violence and Rape' (2017) 18(4) *Journal of International Women Studies* 321.

Simm, Gabrielle, 'Peoples' Tribunals, Women's Courts and International Crimes of Sexual Violence' in Andrew Byrnes and Gabrielle Simm (eds), *Peoples' Tribunals and International Law* (Cambridge University Press, forthcoming).

Simm, Gabrielle and Andrew Byrnes, 'International Peoples' Tribunals in Asia: Political Theatre, Juridical Farce, or Meaningful Intervention' (2014) 4(1) *Asia Journal of International Law* 103.

Simons, Marlise, 'An Ex-Bosnian Serb Commander Admits rape of Muslims in War', *New York Times* (online), 10 March 1998, www.nytimes.com/1998/03/10/world/an-ex-bosnian-serb-commander-admits-rape-of-muslims-in-war.html.

Simpson, Gerry, *Law, War and Crime: War Crimes Trials and the Reinvention of International Law* (Polity Press, 2007).

Simpson, Kirk, 'Voices Silenced, Voices Rediscovered: Victims of Violence and the Reclamation of Language in Transitional Societies' (2007) 3(2) *International Journal of Law in Context* 89.

Sinnreich, Helene, '"And It Was Something We Didn't Talk About": Rape of Jewish Women During the Holocaust' (2008) 14(2) *Holocaust Studies: A Journal of Culture and History* 1.

Skjelsbæk, Inger, 'Victim and Survivor: Narrated Social Identities of Women Who Experienced Rape During the War in Bosnia-Hezegovina' (2006) 16(4) *Feminism and Psychology* 373.

Skjelsbæk, Inger, *The Political Psychology of War Rape: Studies from Bosnia and Herzegovina* (Routledge, 2012).

Slavnić, Alexander, 'Zaboravljene žrtve silovanja u BiH' [Trans: 'Forgotten Victims of Rape in Bosnia and Herzegovina'], *DW*, 7 March 2015, www.dw.com/bs/zaboravljene-%C5%BErtve-silovanja-u-bih/a-18560219.

Slišković, Marija, *Sunčica* (Hrvatsko društvo logoraša srpskih koncentracijskih logora, 2011).

Smart, Carol, *Feminism and the Power of the Law* (Routledge, 1989).

Soh, C. Sarah, *The Comfort Women: Sexual Violence and Postcolonial Memory in Korea and Japan* (The University of Chicago Press, 2008).

Sooka, Yasmin, 'Foreword to the Book' in S. Peté and M. du Plessis (eds), *Repairing the Past: International Perspectives on Reparations for Gross Human Rights Abuses* (Intersentia, 2007) vii.

Sorguc, Albina, 'Domestic Violence Revives Bosnian Women Nightmares', *BIRN*, 19 February 2015, www.balkaninsight.com/en/article/domestic-violence-revives-ex-prisoners-wartime-nightmares/1440/3.

SOS Magazine, 'Žene za Žene' [Trans: 'Women for Women'] (Beograd, November 1993).

Spahić, Mustafa Mujki, 'Gore od silovanja: zlo mjesovitih brakova' [Trans: 'Worse than Rape: The Evil of Mixed Marriages'], *Ljiljan*, 10 August 1994, 22.

Spaic, Igor, 'Bosnian Clerks Unite to Condemn Wartime Sexual Violence', *Balkan Insight* (online), 30 June 2017, www.balkaninsight.com/en/article/bosnian-clerics-unite-to-condemn-wartime-sexual-violence-06-30-2017.

Spivak, Gayatri Chakravorty, 'Can the Subaltern Speak?' in Cary Nelson and Lawrence Grossberg (eds) *Marxism and the Interpretation of Culture* (University of Illinois Press, 1998) 271.

Stanley, Penny, 'Reporting of Mass Rape in the Balkans: *Plus Ca Change, Plus C'est Même Chose*? From Bosnia to Kosovo' (1996) 2(2) *Civil Wars*.

Stauffer, Jill, *Ethical Loneliness: The Injustice of Not Being Heard* (Columbia University Press, 2016).

Stephenson, Max and Laura Zanotti, 'Implementing Liberal Peace in Post-conflict Scenarios: The Case of Women in Black Serbia' (2012) 3(1) *Global Policy Volume* 46.

Stiglmayer, Alexandra (ed.), *Mass Rape: The War Against Women in Bosnia-Herzegovina* (University of Nebraska Press, 1994).

Stiglmayer, Alexandra, 'The Rapes in Bosnia-Herzegovina' in Alexandra Stiglmayer (ed.), *Mass Rape: The War Against Women in Bosnia-Herzegovina* (University of Nebraska Press, 1994) 82.

Strobl, Rainer, 'Constructing the Victim: Theoretical Reflections and Empirical Examples' (2004) 11 *International Review of Victimology* 295.

Strobl, Rainer, 'Becoming a Victim' in Shiomo Giora Shoham, Paul Knepper and Martin Kett (eds) *International Handbook on Victimology* (CRC Press, 2010) 3.

Subotic, Jelena, *Hijacked Justice: Dealing with the Past in the Balkans* (Cornell University Press, 2009).

Subotic, Jelena, 'No Escape From Ethnicity? Confessions of an Accidental CNN Pundit' (2010) 43(1) *PS: Political Science & Politics* 115.

Sud Bosne i Hercegovine, *10 godina rada Odjela za ratne zločine Suda Bosne i Hercegovine: 2005–2015*, Sarajevo (2015) [Trans: *The Court of Bosnia and Herzegovina: 10 Years of Work of the War Crimes Chamber: 2005–2015*], www.sudbih.gov.ba/files/docs/brosura/10_anniversary_of_Section_I.pdf.

Tanesini, Alessandra, *An Introduction to Feminist Epistemologies* (Blackwell, 1999).

Tanjug, 'War Crimes Trial of Naser Oric Begins in Bosnia', *Tanjug* (online), 26 January 2016, www.b92.net/eng/news/region.php?yyyy=2016&mm=01&dd=26&nav_id=96816.

Tausan, Marija, 'Huge War Crimes Case Backlog Overwhelms Bosnia', *Justice Report* (online), 23 October 2015, www.justice-report.com/en/articles/huge-war-crimes-case-backlog-overwhelms-bosnia.

Teitel, Ruti G. *Transitional Justice* (Oxford University Press 2000).

Teitel, Ruti G., 'Transitional Justice Genealogy' (2003) 16 *Harvard Human Rights Journal* 69.

Thomas, Dorothy Q. and Ralph E. Regan, 'Rape in War: Challenging the Tradition of Impunity' (1994) 14(1) *SAIS Review* 81.

Thompson, Janna, 'Apology, Justice and Respect: A Critical Defence of Political Apology' in Mark Gibney, Rhoda E. Howard-Hassman, Jean Marc Coicaud and Niklaus Steiner (eds), *The Age of Apology: Facing Up to the Past* (University of Philadelphia Press, 2008) 31.

Tisdall, Kay, John M. Davis, and Michael Gallagher, *Researching with Children and Young People: Research Design, Methods and Analysis* (Sage, 2008).

TRIAL, *Written Information for the Consideration of Bosnia and Herzegovina's Combined Fourth and Fifth Periodic Reports by the Committee on the Elimination of Discrimination Against Women*, Track Impunity Always (2013), tbinternet.ohchr.org/Treaties/CEDAW/.../INT_CEDAW_NGO_BIH_13143_E.pdf.

TRIAL, *General Allegation on the Situation in Bosnia and Herzegovina to the Special Rapporteur on Truth, Justice, Reparations and Guarantees of Non-Recurrence*,

Track Impunity Always (2014), https://trialinternational.org/wp-content/uploads/2016/05/TRIAL_BiH_GA_SRTJ_Feb2014.pdf.

TRIAL, *Violence Against Women, Its Causes and Consequences After Her Mission to Bosnia and Herzegovina*, Report, Track Impunity Always (2014), www.fld.ba/upload/documents/Follow-up%20BiH%20_%20Violence%20against%20Woman%20-%20copie%202%201.pdf.

TRIAL, 'BiH: Groundbreaking Court Decision Paves the Way for Wartime Victims to Get Compensation' *Trial International* (2015), https://trialinternational.org/latest-post/bih-groundbreaking-court-decision-paves-the-way-for-wartime-victims-to-get-compensation/.

TRIAL, *Follow-Up Report on the Implementation by Bosnia and Herzegovina's of the Recommendations Issued by the Committee on the Elimination of Discrimination Against Women in July 2013*, CEDAW/C/BIH/CO/4-5 (2015), http://tbinternet.ohchr.org/Treaties/CEDAW/Shared%20Documents/BIH/INT_CEDAW_NGS_BIH_21073_E.pdf.

TRIAL, '*Ostvarivanje zahtjeva* za *naknadu štete žrtava ratnih zločina* u *okviru krivičnih postupaka* u Bosni i Hercegovini – stanje, problem, perspective' [Trans: 'Enforcement of Damage Compensation Claims of Victims of War in Criminal Proceedings in Bosnia and Herzegovina: Situations, Challenges and Perspectives'] (2015), http://trial.ba/wp-content/uploads/2015/10/ENG_Ostvarivanje-zahtjeva-za-naknadu-%C5%A1tete-%C5%BErtava-ratnih-zlo%C4%8Dina-u-okviru-krivi%C4%8Dnih-postupaka-u-Bosni-i-Hercegovini-%E2%80%93-stanje-problemi-i-perspektive-.pdf.

TRIAL, *Mirsad Repak*, TRIAL (2016), https://trialinternational.org/latest-post/mirsad-repak/.

Tromp, Nevenka, *Prosecuting Slobodan Milošević: The Unfinished Trial* (Routledge, 2016)

Tsai, Lily, 'Quantitative Research and Issue of Political Sensitivity in Rural China' in Allen Carlson, Mary E. Gallagher, Kenneth Lieberthal, and Melanie Manion (eds), *Contemporary Chinese Politics: New Sources, Methods, and Field Strategies* (Cambridge University Press, 2010) 246.

Tucker, Avizier, 'Paranoids May Be Prosecuted: Post-Totalitarian Transitional Justice' in Jon Elster (ed.) *Retribution and Reparation* (Cambridge, 2006) 181.

Turpin, Jennifer, 'Many Faces: Women Confronting War' in Lois Ann Lorentzen and Jennifer Turpin (eds), *The Women and War Reader* (New York University Press, 1999) 32.

Turshen, Meredeth, 'The Political Economy of Violence against Women During Armed Conflict in Uganda' (2000) 67(3) *Social Research* 803.

Umutesi, Marie Béatrice, 'Is Reconciliation Between Hutus and Tutsis Possible?' (2006) 60(1) *Journal of International Affairs* 157.

United Nations in Bosnia and Herzegovina, 'Declaration on Denouncing Stigmatization of Survivors of Conflict-Related Sexual Violence Adopted By BiH Inter-Religious Council', http://ba.one.un.org/content/unct/bosnia_and_herzegovina/en/home/presscenter/declaration-on-denouncing-stigmatization-of-survivors-of-conflic.html.

UN, *Concluding Comments of the Committee on the Elimination of Discrimination Against Women: Bosnia and Herzegovina*, Committee on the Elimination of All Forms of Discrimination against Women (CEDAW), CEDAW/C/BiH/CO/3 (2 June 2006).

UN, *Concluding Observations on the Combined Fourth and Fifth Periodic Reports of Bosnia and Herzegovina*, Committee on the Elimination of All Forms of Discrimination against Women (CEDAW), CEDAW/C/BIH/CO/, 4–5 (26 July 2013).

UN, *Guidance Note of the Secretary General, Reparations for Conflict-Related Sexual Violence* (2014), www.ohchr.org/Documents/Press/GuidanceNoteReparationsJune-2014.pdf.

UN Commission on Human Rights, *Report on the Situation of Human Rights in the Territory of the Former Yugoslavia Submitted by Mr Tadeusz Mazowiecki*, UN Doc. E/CN.4/1993/50 (10 February 1993).

UNDP, *Priručnik za nevladine organizacije u Bosni i Hercegovini* [Trans: *Handbook for Non-Governmental Organizations in Bosnia and Herzegovina*], Report, UNDP (2006), www.omladina-bih.net/download/Prirucnik.pdf.

UNDP, *Sexual Violence in Conflict, in Team of Experts, Rule of Law/Sexual Violence in Conflict, Annual Report* 2012 (2013), www.undp.org/content/undp/en/home/librarypage/crisis-prevention-and-recovery/un-team-of-experts–rule-of-law-and-sexual-violence-in-conflict-.html.

UNFPA, 'Dealing with a Legacy of Rape and Torture in Bosnia and Herzegovina, Bosnia: Rape a Legacy of War', UNFPA, 20 October 2010, www.unfpa.org/news/dealing-legacy-rape-and-torture-bosnia-and-herzegovina.

UNFPA, *Stigma Against Survivors of Conflict-Related Sexual Violence in Bosnia and Herzegovina: Research Summary* (2016), http://unfpa.ba/upload/documents/UNFPA%20Stigma%20Short%20ENG%20FIN1.pdf.

UNGA, 'World Conference on Human Rights: Report of the Secretary-General' (World Conference on Human Rights Vienna, 14–25 June, 1993) A/CONF.157/23 (13 October 1993).

UNGA, *Rape and Abuse of the Women in the Areas of Armed Conflict in the Former Yugoslavia*, A/RES/48/143 (5 January 1994).

UNGA, *Basic Principles and Guidelines on the Right to Remedy and Reparation for Victims of Gross Violations of International Human Rights Law and Serious Violations of International Humanitarian Law*, Res. 60/147, 60th sess., 64th plen. mtg, Agenda Item 71(a), A/RES/60/147 (16 December 2005).

UNGA, *Report of the Special Rapporteur on Violence Against Women, Its Causes and Consequences, Rashida Manjoo*, A/HRC/23/49/Add.3 (4 June 2013), www.ohchr.org/Documents/HRBodies/HRCouncil/RegularSession/Session23/A-HRC-23-49-Add3_en.pdf.

UNGA, *Report of the Special Rapporteur on the Promotion of Truth, Justice, Reparation and Guarantees of Non-Recurrence, Pablo de Greiff*, 27th sess., Human Rights Session A/HRC/27/56/Add.1 (22 July 2014).

UNGA, *Report of the Working Group on the Universal Periodic Review: Bosnia and Herzegovina*, Human Rights Council, A/HRC/28/17 (4 December 2014).

UNHCR, *Report of the Commission on Human Rights on its First Special Session*, UN Doc. E/CN.4/1992/2-1/8 (14 August 1992).

UN Human Rights Office of the High Commissioner, *Special Rapporteur on Violence Against Women, Including Its Causes and Consequences, Preliminary Report on Violence Against Women, Its Causes and Consequences*, 263, UN Doc. E/CN.4/1995/42 (22 November 1994), www.ohchr.org/EN/Issues/Women/SRWomen/Pages/SRWomenIndex.aspx.

UN Human Rights Office of the High Commissioner, *Consideration of Reports Submitted by State Parties Under Article 19 of the Convention: Concluding observation of the Committee against Torture*, Committee against Torture, Forty-fifth Session

(1–19 November, 2010), www2.ohchr.org/english/bodies/cat/docs/CAT.C.BIH.CO.2-5.pdf.
UN ICTY, *About the ICTY*, www.icty.org/en/about.
UN ICTY, *In Numbers*, www.icty.org/sid/10586.
UNSC, *Final Report of the Commission of Experts Established Pursuant to Security Council Resolution* 780 (1992), Annex 241 n. 65, UN Doc. S/1994/674 (1994).
UNSC, *Letter Dated 24 May 1994 from the Secretary-General to the President of the Security Council*, UN Doc S/1994/674 (27 May 1994).
UNSC, *Report of the Secretary-General's Investigative Team Charged with Investigating Serious Violations of Human Rights and International Humanitarian Law in the Democratic Republic of the Congo*, UN Doc. S/1998/581 (26 June 1998), https://daccess-ods.un.org/TMP/364274.494349957.html.
UNSC Report, S/2015/716, Report of the Secretary-General on Women and Peace and Security (16 September 2015).
UNSC, *Report of the Secretary-General on Conflict-Related Sexual Violence* (S/2016/361) (20 April 2016).
UNSC Res. 808, 48th sess., 3175th mtg, UN Doc. S/25240 (3 February 1993).
UNSC Res. 827, 3217th mtg, UN Doc. S/RES/ 827 (25 May 1993).
UNSC Res. 1325, 4213th mtg, UN Doc. S/RES/1325 (31 October 2000).
UNSC Res. 1820, 5916th mtg, UN Doc. S/RES/1820 (19 June 2008).
UNSC Res. 1888, 6195th mtg, UN Doc. S/RES/1888 (30 September 2009).
UN Secretary-General, *Women, Peace and Security: Study Submitted by the Secretary-General Pursuant to Security Council Resolution 1325*, Report, United Nations (2002), www.un.org/ruleoflaw/files/womenpeaceandsecurity.pdf.
US Senate Committee on the Judiciary, *The Morgenthau Diaries (Germany)*, US Government Printing Office (1967).
Unprotected (Directed by Post-Conflict Research Centre, Sarajevo, PCRC and Pinch Media, 2011).
Van der Auweraert, Peter and Igor Cvetkovski, *Reparations for Wartime Victims in the Former Yugoslavia: In Search of the Way Forward*, Report, International Organization for Migration (2013), www.iom.int/files/live/sites/iom/files/What-We-Do/docs/Reparations-for-Wartime-Victimes-in-the-Former-Yugoslavia-In-Search-of-the-Way-Forward.pdf.
Vasović, Perica, 'Molila sam da me zakolju' [Trans: 'I Beg Them to Kill Me'], *Večernje Novosti*, 27 March 2006, www.novosti.rs/vesti/naslovna/reportaze/aktuelno.293.html:181409-Molila-sam-Boga-da-me-zakolju.
Verrall, Saeeda, 'The Picture of Sexual Violence in the Former Yugoslavia Conflicts as Reflected in ICTY Judgments' in Serge Brammertz and Michelle Jarvis (eds), *Prosecuting Conflict-Related Sexual Violence at the ICTY* (Oxford University Press, 2016) 299.
Victims of War, *Official Gazette of Brcko District No.* 33, 15 September 2012.
Vijesti.ba 'Promovisana "Monografija o ratnom silovanju i seksualnom zlostavljanju u BiH"' [Trans: 'Promotion of the "Monograph of War Rape and Sexual Abuse in BiH"'], *Vijesti.ba* (online), 28 September 2015, http://vijesti.ba/clanak/279890/promovisana-monografija-o-ratnom-silovanju-i-seksualnom-zlostavljanju-u-bih.
Viseur *Sellers*, Patricia 'Sexual Violence and Peremptory Norms: The Legal Value of *Rape*' (2002) 34 *Case Western Reserve Journal of International Law 287.*
Viseur Sellers, Patricia, 'Gender Strategy Is Not a Luxury for International Courts' (2009) 17(2) *American University Journal of Gender, Social Policy & the Law* 327.

Vive Žene, Tuzla, *Osiguranje pristupa pravdi za svjedoke/žrtve kroz jačanje postojećih i uspostavljanje novih mreža podrške svjedocima diljem Bosne i Hercegovine* [Trans: *Securing Access to Justice for Witnesses/Victims Through Strengthening Existing and Establishing New Networks of Support for Witnesses in Bosnia and Herzegovina*] (2016), www.vivezene.ba/download/Finalna%20verzija%20Rezime%20projekta%20bos.pdf.

von Münch, Ingo, *Frau, komm!: Die Massenvergewaltigungen deutscher Frauen und Mädchen 1944/45* [Trans: *Women, Come!: The Mass Rape of German Women and Girls 1944/45*] (ARES Verlag, 3rd ed., 2009).

Wald, Patricia M., 'Dealing with Witnesses in War Crime Trials: Lessons from the Yugoslav Tribunal' (2002) 5 *Yale Human Rights and Development Journal* 217.

Waldorf, Lars, *Mass Justice for Mass Atrocity: Transitional Justice and Illiberal Peace Building in Rwanda* (PhD Thesis, National University of Ireland, Galway, 2013).

Watts, Charlotte, Mary Ellsberg, Lori Heise and Claudia Garcia Moreno, *Putting Women First: Ethical and Safety Recommendations for Research on Domestic Violence Against Women* (World Health Organization Report, 2007).

Weinsten, Harvey M., 'Victims, Transitional Justice and Social Reconstruction: Who Is Setting the agenda?' in Inge Vanfraecham, Antony Pemberton and Felix Mukwiza Ndahinda (eds), *Justice for Victims: Perspectives on Rights, Transition and Reconciliation* (Routledge, 2014) 161.

Weitsman, Patricia, 'The Discourse of Rape in Wartime; Sexual Violence, War Babies and Identity' (Paper presented at the Annual Meeting of the International Studies Association Portland, OR, 26 February–1 March 2003).

White, Sarah C., 'Depoliticising Development: The Uses and Abuses of Participation' (1996) 6(1) *Development in Practice* 6.

Williams, Carol J., 'Bosnia's Orphans of Rape: Innocent Legacy of Hatred', *Los Angeles Times* (online), 24 July 1993, http://articles.latimes.com/1993-07-24/news/mn-16356_1_bosnian.

Women Aid International, *Warburton Mission II Report: EC Investigative Mission into the Treatment of Muslim Women in the Former Yugoslavia: Report to EC Foreign Ministers*, Ministry of Foreign Affairs Copenhagen (1993), www.womenaid.org/press/info/humanrights/warburtonfull.htm.

Women's Court – Feminist Approach to Justice, *Methodology of Work* (2012), www.zenskisud.org/en/Metodologija.html.

Women's Court – Feminist Approach to Justice, *Women's Court – Feminist Approach to Justice, Rules of the Women's Court* (n.d.), www.zenskisud.org/en/pdf/RULES_Womens_Court.pdf.

Women in Black, Belgrade, *Ženski Sud Feministički Pristup Pravdi: Izveštaj januar 2014–decembar 2014* [Trans: *Women's Court Feminist Approach to Justice: Report January 2014–December 2014*] (2015), www.zenskisud.org/pdf/Izvestaj_ZS_jan_2014_dec_2014.pdf.

Women in Black, Belgrade, *Ženski sud – feministički pristup pravdi, Izvestaj januar–august 2016* [Trans: *Women's Court – Feminist Approach to Justice: Report January–August 2016*], http://zenskisud.org/pdf/2016/Zenski_sud_janaur_avgust_2016_izvestaj_sh.pdf.

Women Living Under Muslim Laws, 'India Court of Women on Dowry and Related Forms of Violence Against Women: Daughters of Fire' (Bangalore, India, 27–29 July 2009), www.wluml.org/fr/node/5387.

Woodward, Susan L., 'Violence-Prone Area or International Transition? Adding the Role of Outsiders in Balkan Violence' in Veena Das, Arthur Kleinman, Mamphela Ramphele and Pamela Reynolds (eds) *Violence and Subjectivity* (University of California Press, 2000) 19.

Yoshiaki, Yoshimi, *Comfort Women: Sexual Slavery in the Japanese Military During World War II* (Columbia University Press, 1995).

Zajović, Staša (ed.), *Women's Court: About the Process* (2015) Women in Black, www.helsinki.org.rs/doc/Womens%20Court%20About%20the%20Process.pdf.

Zajović, Staša, 'The Women's Court: A Feminist Approach to Justice: Review of the Process of Organizing the Women's Court' in Staša Zajović (ed.), *Women's Court: About the Process* (Women in Black, 2015) 6, www.helsinki.org.rs/doc/Womens%20Court%20About%20the%20Process.pdf.

Zajović, Staša, *Women in Black: War, Feminism and Antimilitarism* (n.d.) Women's Feminist – Antimilitarist Peace Organization, http://zeneucrnom.org/index.php?option=com_content&task=view&id=78&Itemid=21.

Zarkov Dubravka, 'Gender, Orientalism and the History of Ethnic Hatred in the Former Yugoslavia' in Helma Lutz, Ann Phoenix and Nira Yuval-Davis (eds), *Crossfires: Nationalism, Racism and Gender in Europe* (Pluto Press for the European Forum of Left Feminists, 1995) 105.

Zarkov, Dubravka, 'War Rapes in Bosnia: On Masculinity, Femininity and Power of the Rape Victim Identity' (1997) 39(2) *Tijdschrift voor Criminologie* 140.

Zarkov, Dubravka, 'The Body of the Other Man: Sexual Violence and the Construction of Masculinity, Sexuality and Ethnicity in Croatian Media' in Caroline Moser and Fiona Clark (eds), *Victims, Perpetrators or Actors? Gender, Armed Conflict and Political Violence* (Zed Books, 2001) 69.

Zarkov, Dubravka, 'Feminism and the Disintegration of Yugoslavia: On the Politics of Gender and Ethnicity' (2002) 24(3) *Social Development Issues* 59.

Zarkov, Dubravka, 'Sexual Violence and War in Former Yugoslavia' (Paper presented at the Three Queens Debate: Gender-Based War Crimes, Cordaid, The Hague, January 2005), www.iccwomen.org/news/docs/CORDAID_Debate_Jan05_Zarkov.doc.

Žarkov, Dubravka, *The Body of War: Media, Ethnicity, and Gender in the Break-Up of Yugoslavia* (Duke University Press, 2007).

Zawati, Hilmi M., *Fair Labeling and Dilemma of Prosecuting Gender-Based Crimes at the International Criminal Tribunals* (Oxford, 2014).

Zuvela, Maja, 'Bosnian War Rape Victims Suffer in Silence, Wait for Justice', *Reuters*, 19 December 2012, www.reuters.com/article/us-bosnia-rape-idUSBRE8BI0SD20121219.

Zyberi, Gentian and Jernej Letnar Černič, 'Transitional Justice Processes and Reconciliation in the Former Yugoslavia: Challenges and Prospects' (2015) 33(2) *Nordic Journal of Human Rights* 132.

Index

For Product Safety Concerns and Information please contact our EU representative GPSR@taylorandfrancis.com
Taylor & Francis Verlag GmbH, Kaufingerstraße 24, 80331 München, Germany

www.ingramcontent.com/pod-product-compliance
Ingram Content Group UK Ltd.
Pitfield, Milton Keynes, MK11 3LW, UK
UKHW011010180926
475701UK00004B/662
9780367893675